A RANSOMED YANKEE

Frank Scott Mitton (?)

Words under the *Milo* painting on the book cover are too small to read, but are shown below as follows:

Bottom left:

WHALESHIP MILO

E. C. Jones Agent   New Bedford, Massachusetts

Built in Newburyport – 1811

397 Tons – 107' 3" Length - 39" Breadth - 14" 6" Depth

Bottom center:

The Whaleship Milo sailed on one of the longest voyages on record. She left the port of New Bedford on November 26, 1863, and did not return until May 7, 1869. Jonathan C. Hawes was the captain.

It was in 1865, between June 21 and 25, that the Confederate raider, "Shenandoah" captured and set fire to six whalers off Cape Thaddeus, Arctic Ocean. Their crews were put aboard the "Milo" which was then bonded and sailed to San Francisco.

Bottom right:

DESTRUCTION of WHALESHIPS off CAPE THADDEUS, ARCTIC OCEAN, by the CONFEDERATE STEAMER SHENANDOAH

June 23, 1865

(Russell Painting Insert)

After the painting by Benjamin Russell – 1874   CAPTAIN J. C. HAWES

A RANSOMED YANKEE

EPIC VOYAGE OF THE WHALESHIP *MILO*

Civil War Naval History

FRANK ELLIOTT SISSON II

RED ANVIL PRESS

RED ANVIL PRESS
1393 Old Homestead Drive, Second floor
Oakland, Oregon 97462—9506.
E-MAIL: editor@elderberrypress.com
TEL/FAX: 541.459.6043
http://elderberrypress.com
All Red Anvil books are available from your favorite bookstore, amazon.com,
or from our 24 hour order line: 1.800.431.1579
Library of Congress Control Number: 2008933883
Publisher's Catalog—in—Publication Data
A Ransomed Yankee/Frank Elliott Sisson II
ISBN-13: 978-1-934956-02-1
ISBN-10: 1-934956-02-3
1. American Civil War.
2. Whaling Vessels.
3. American History.
4. U.S. Maritime History
5. USS Milo.
6. CSS Shenandoah.
I. Title
This book was written, printed and bound in the United States of America.
Cover Painting *Whaleship Milo* by Arthur Moniz. Courtesy of Peter Hawes and the Arthur Moniz Gallery. New Bedford, Massachusetts[1].

.

Contents

Illustrations

Maps of Interest

Whaleship *Milo* Departs, 1863

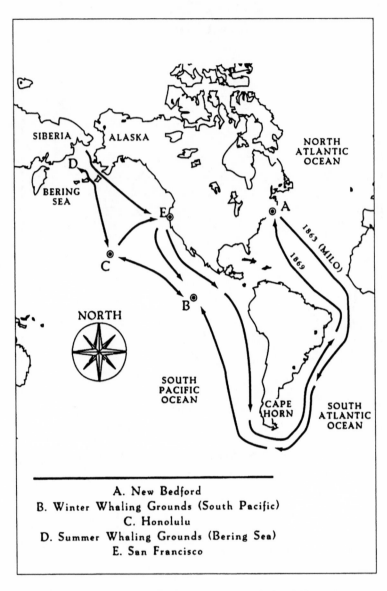

SIBERIA ALASKA

NORTH ATLANTIC OCEAN

D

BERING SEA

E

A

1863 (MILO)

1869

C

NORTH

B

SOUTH PACIFIC OCEAN

CAPE HORN

SOUTH ATLANTIC OCEAN

A. New Bedford
B. Winter Whaling Grounds (South Pacific)
C. Honolulu
D. Summer Whaling Grounds (Bering Sea)
E. San Francisco

Whaleship *Milo* Epic Voyage, 1863–1869

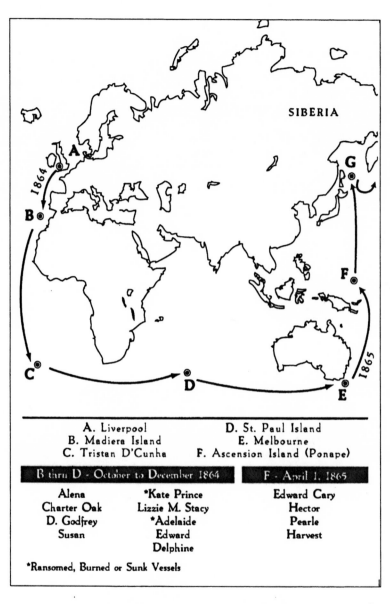

A. Liverpool   D. St. Paul Island
B. Madiera Island   E. Melbourne
C. Tristan D'Cunha   F. Ascension Island (Ponape)

B thru D - October to December 1864   F - April 1, 1865

Alena   *Kate Prince   Edward Cary
Charter Oak   Lizzie M. Stacy   Hector
D. Godfrey   *Adelaide   Pearle
Susan   Edward   Harvest
          Delphine

*Ransomed, Burned or Sunk Vessels

CSS *Shenandoah* Cruise, 1864–1865

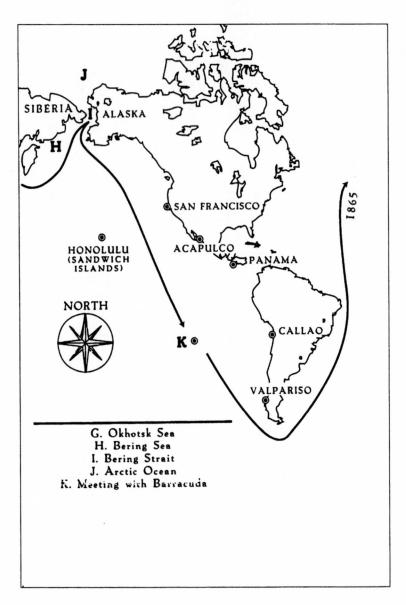

CSS *Shenandoah* Cruise, 1864–1865

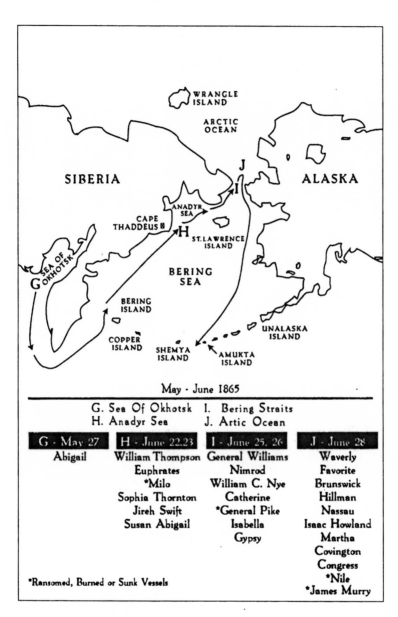

May · June 1865

| G. Sea Of Okhotsk | I. Bering Straits |
| H. Anadyr Sea | J. Artic Ocean |

G · May 27	H · June 22,23	I · June 25, 26	J · June 28
Abigail	William Thompson	General Williams	Waverly
	Euphrates	Nimrod	Favorite
	*Milo	William C. Nye	Brunswick
	Sophia Thornton	Catherine	Hillman
	Jireh Swift	*General Pike	Nassau
	Susan Abigail	Isabella	Isaac Howland
		Gypsy	Martha
			Covington
			Congress
*Ransomed, Burned or Sunk Vessels			*Nile
			*James Murry

CSS *Shenandoah* Arctic Cruise, 1865

Dedication

To my parents

Elliott Hawes and Lila Hazel Sisson

And

My wife

Anne

Forward

A Watercolor Painting

Destruction in the Bering Sea 1865[2]

Almost by accident, I was able to obtain a full-size custom color reproduction of the above watercolor painting. It was originally painted in 1874 by New Bedford artist Benjamin Russell. Russell was not only a gifted artist but also had spent a few years at sea as a seaman on a whaleship. I have owned the reproduction, which is roughly thirty-five inches wide and twenty-two inches high, for over twenty-five years now, and have viewed it every day where it hangs on the wall of my den in a very conspicuous spot. The painting depicts the ransomed whaleship *Milo* off the coast of Russian Siberia in the Bering Sea, with full sails on the right, and the three-masted steamer Confederate raider CSS *Shenandoah* with sails down on the left. In the background are five whaleships that have been set on fire and are shown burning, having been destroyed by the Confederate. The title of the watercolor scene is *Destruction of Whale Ships off Cape Thaddeus Arctic Ocean June 23, 1865 by the Conf Stm* Shenandoah. Captain Jonathan C. Hawes was master of the *Milo* and Lieutenant James I. Waddell, Confederate States Navy, commanded the CSS *Shenandoah*. Although I have had this reproduction for many years, I remember seeing the painting for the first time as a child at the New Bedford Whaling Museum in Massachusetts. New Bedford is still known as the "Whaling Capital of the World."

Actually, Russell's painting is familiar to many and can be found on the Internet when seeking information on the American Civil War. Further, the original watercolor was remade into a lithograph which is owned by the President Franklyn Roosevelt Collection. However the original watercolor was bequeathed to the New Bedford Whaling Museum by Frederic B. Hawes in 1968. More importantly,

16

it was Captain Hawes who took the initiative to commission Benjamin Russell to produce the painting in the first place. He did not want the event to be forgotten as it had such a great impact on the whaling fleet and on the history of America. The event was considered a significant event in the official United States Civil War Naval Chronology and a facsimile reproduction of the same watercolor painting is shown in part VI, Special Studies and Cumulative Index, the final part of the Chronology.[3] Parts I through V of the Chronology each cover a year of the war, 1861 through 1865. Much to my surprise, I discovered a copy of this hard-to-find part VI in my office at the Washington Navy Yard in 1978, while doing consulting work for the United States Navy after having retired from the United States Air Force.

Having viewed the painting almost every day for many years, I have come to wonder what really happened in the Bering Sea during that time, why it happened, what other events were going on around the world at that time, who were the two principal captains involved, and what happened to them and others before and after the event took place. My curiosity led me to spend many, many hours on research into the lives of the two sea captains, Jonathan Capen Hawes, the master of the whaleship, and James

Iredell Waddell, the Confederate. These two sea captains met for a few brief moments on that one occasion in the Bering Sea.

The painting, however, is reflective of the more than three hundred merchant and whaling vessels that were destroyed, and the few that were ransomed, along with the captains of these vessels, by Confederate cruisers during the Civil War. Today, the descendents of these shipmasters translate into thousands of people who are scattered around the country and even to other parts of the world. In this sense, Captain Jonathan Hawes is symbolic of all the shipmasters whose ships were confronted by the rebel cruisers. Although this story is about him, there are other stories for each of the victims of the Confederate actions at sea. Include the crewmembers and women of all those destroyed and ransomed ships who were impacted by loss of money, property and livelihood, and the numbers of all of those affected in one way or another by the rebel actions, multiply greatly into very large numbers of descendents today.

I used family notes and history records, the Internet, public libraries, New Bedford Whaling Museum Library, and a number of reference books to find out more about the facts behind the event and other influences that allowed it to happen. Along with this research, I decided to write as complete and true story as possible about the events leading up to the scene that is shown in the painting as well as events following the scene. It is an exciting story and one that needs to be told in full for its place in the history of America.

My interest in military history and related matters can be attributed to four years at the United States Military Academy at West Point, graduating as Second Lieutenant in the United States Air Force in 1951, and becoming a military pilot. I spent twenty years in the military service and traveled to many parts of the world before retiring. On one mission, I flew a four-engine transport aircraft from an aircraft overhaul depot in Florida to Okinawa for continuing service during the Vietnam War. Because the winds were not favorable for the normally direct flight from California to Hawaii, our flight plan took us up to Elmendorf Air Force Base in Alaska, and from there over the Aleutian Islands for an overnight stopover at Shemya Island near the western end of the island chain where there is now a large military airfield. The Aleutian Islands separate the North Pacific Ocean from the Bering Sea. During that flight, I was able to recall the scene painted by

Russell showing ice floats and wintry conditions of the Bering Sea. My flight was in December 1966, and took me relatively close to the scene where the Confederate pirate destroyed the whalers in 1865. I was able to briefly experience in some way the weather and environment that the whalers experienced during their summers in the Bering Sea and Arctic Ocean during the 1860s. During that flight, I made up my mind to learn more about whaling history and the Bering Sea when I had more time.

I did not actually acquire the Russell reproduction until after I retired from the United States Air Force. But, it would be many years later after retiring from all other business activities that I was able to take the time to do the research on this book and begin writing the story. It has been a challenging task, but certainly a rewarding and great learning experience. Some of the events that took place apply to current conditions in terms of the relationship of the United States with other countries and with military strategy and operations. The story also points out what it was like living in the Civil War period when communications were sent by messenger, news traveled very slowly, and military intelligence was almost impossible to gather. I have another reason for writing this story and you will find out more about this as you read through the story.

1. Whaleship *Milo*

The Whaleship *Milo*[4]

At nine o'clock on the morning of November 26, 1863, the whaleship *Milo* quietly sailed out of New Bedford harbor on a voyage that would make an everlasting impact on the lives of the people of this seaport as well as the lives of other people across the country. It would be a long, profitable and enjoyable voyage, but also, frightening, humanitarian and even sad. However, it would be an epic experience for its part as a principal whaling ship that happened to be involved in a significant and historical naval event shortly after the end of the American Civil

War. The weather was clear in southeastern Massachusetts as the ship headed out of the harbor. At ten thirty, the harbor pilot was discharged, having done his duty to guide the ship safely out of the harbor. Following this, the *Milo* headed southwest to clear the nearby Elizabeth Islands and at eleven thirty, came in contact with the whaler, *Tropic Bird*, heading for New Bedford after twenty-five months at sea and loaded with four hundred barrels of sperm oil. At twelve noon, the captain ordered the anchors stowed and at three o'clock, the watch was set and the crew was busy doing various duties aboard ship.[5]

All of this occurred one week after the famous Gettysburg address by President Abraham Lincoln, at which time the country was deeply immersed in the dreadful and costly Civil War. President Lincoln was there to make an important statement about the Gettysburg battlefield and the soldiers who had given their lives during the three-day battle from July 1 to July 3, 1863. After a very thorough recollection of what had happened at Gettysburg, along with events leading up to this Civil War battle, and with his own notes aimed at putting the pieces into perspective, he gave the short but historic address to those attending the ceremony on November 19, 1963.

Over fifty-thousand soldiers from both sides were killed, wounded, or missing during this battle. The Gettysburg battlefield was the costliest battle of the Civil War with more lives lost there than on any other battlefield, and it was also the turning point of the war for the North. However, there were many battles yet to take place and many months to go before the war was finally over. On the other hand, the outlook after the battle was brighter for the Union than it had been before, and President Lincoln was elated to be giving this speech.

The *Milo* was built in 1811 at Newburyport, Massachusetts. It was a three-mast brig with full square sails and was built to withstand the harsh icebound environment of the Arctic Sea. It was a four-hundred-ton vessel, 108 feet long and 29 feet wide at mid-deck, and it had a depth of 14 feet, 6 inches deep. It had recently returned from a whaling venture in the Pacific Ocean and was now under new ownership. Captain Jonathan C. Hawes was the master and was also part owner of the *Milo*. This was a particularly dangerous time for any American ship to sail out onto the seas, as the Civil War was raging and the Confederate Navy had acquired a fleet of armed cruisers and gunboats with which to harass and destroy Yankee whaling and merchant ships across the oceans of the world. This was the seventh departure for Captain Hawes over a period of twenty years from New Bedford, and third time as master. It was the first time he had ventured out to sea during the Civil War. He was well qualified to lead this voyage into the Pacific and up to the Bering Sea in spite of possible threats from Confederate gunships. This was the third time for him to command a ship on a whaling journey to the Bering Sea.

By 1863, New Bedford was the whaling capital of the world and was by far the most successful of all ports in the whaling business. It had grown from six small schooners in 1763, owned by Joseph Russell III, whose family was instrumental in purchasing land from the Wampanoag Indian Nation many years before in 1652. That purchase encompassed land from Rhode Island to Cape Cod and was originally called Dartmouth. Bedford Village was a small town in Dartmouth and became officially incorporated as the town of New Bedford in 1787. Russell used the schooners to hunt whales in the local waters and tow the captured whales to shore where they were boiled and then the workers processed whale blubber in large kettles under fire, which they called "trying out," and transformed the blubber into whale oil which was stored in barrels to be sold for making candles and fuel for oil lamps. New

Bedford harbor was ideal for the whaling industry as it was protected from the Atlantic Ocean by Nantucket Island, Martha's Vineyard Island, Cape Cod, and the Elizabeth Islands, and it was a large and natural harbor. However, credit for developing the techniques for lengthy whaling voyages belongs to the Nantucket Island whalers during the early 1700s. In particular, the Joseph Rotch family developed the methods of processing whale oil on board the ships in "try-pots" and also developed the business enterprise to market whale oil and other whale by-products to the world. However, since Nantucket Island was so small and was isolated by the surrounding ocean, it was impossible to support the growing whaling industry with indigenous island labor and limited industry there. Consequently in 1765, the Rotch family moved to the mainland and set up business in the New Bedford harbor area where there was a sufficient labor force and a sizable industrial base. After that, New Bedford began its growth to world leadership in whaling. The world demand for whale oil to light up the cities of the world became greater than the supply, and by 1863, New Bedford had close to 375 whaling ships registered in its fleet, and it was one of the wealthiest cities in the country. This led to the motivation for young men to go to sea to seek their fortunes, and that was why Captain Hawes was willing to take the *Milo* out of the harbor on this day in 1863, during the bloody Civil War, and set sail for the whaling grounds in the Bering Sea.

Provisions for whaling voyages were substantial in order to provide food and water for a crew of thirty-some people for up to three or fours years' duration. The *Milo* was no exception, and there were the initial stores of meat, dried vegetables, water, flour, medical drugs, rope, harpoons, maps, navigational equipment, canvas, boats and other supplies needed for the long journey. In addition, there were about twelve hundred barrels in the ship's hold that the Captain Hawes hoped to fill with whale oil. If more barrels were needed, they would be constructed at sea. Supplemental provisions were purchased during the voyage at ports along the way to provide for fresh meat, vegetables, milk, and other items with short shelf lives. Financial support for the journey was provided by the ship owners who put up the money and took the risks associated with this venture. Edward C. Jones was the principal owner, having an 11/16 share. Other owners were Ann H. Dunbar, 1/16; Caleb Anthony, 1/16; Jonathan C. Hawes, 1/16; all of New Bedford and George H. Dunbar, 2/16, of New York. The ship was registered in the New Bedford Port Society Seaman's Register under the new ownership on November

27

25, 1863. The *Milo* listed thirty-one crew members along with Captain Hawes, as follows:

Ship *Milo* New Bedford Jona C. Hawes N. Pacific Nov 25, 1863	
Andrew J. Avery	Foreign
John Joseph	New Bedford
Augustus O. Jenny	Foreign
Joseph L. Smith	New Bedford
Samuel Caduce	Foreign
William Holline	Foreign
George Baker	Foreign
John F. Hawes	New Bedford
Joseph F. Francis Jr.	Azores
James Thompson	Philadelphia
Claudie Mobre	Foreign
John W. Pierce	Fairhaven
James C. Henrys	Dartmouth
Charles H. Andrew	New Bedford
George Riley	New York
Washington Ney	Foreign
Joseph King	Foreign
Joseph Corllis	New York
Thomas Whitney	New Haven
Joseph Francis	Foreign
Jarvis Merritt	Greenwich
Charles Thompson	New York
Albert Braun	Foreign
Wendele Salisbury	New Bedford
Edwin Brown	New York
Peter Peters Jr.	New Bedford
Frederick Luce	Foreign
P. J. Brown	New York

The register did not list Jerusha Hawes, wife of the captain, but Jerusha, better known as "Jessie," was on board with two small children, Addie and infant Frederic, called Fred. This was not uncommon, as many whaling masters took their wives and families along for companionship and comfort during the long journey at sea. This was the second time on a whaling voyage for Jessie and Addie, and the first for baby Fred who was born after Jessie's first whaling voyage, and a little over seven months prior to this day.

On the very same day in November that the *Milo* weighed anchor and headed out to sea, the Mine Run Campaign commenced in Virginia, putting Major General George G. Meade's Army of the Potomac against General Robert E. Lee's Army of Northern Virginia. General Meade had scheduled the campaign to begin on November 24, but the weather was stormy and the rains came down heavily causing the roads to turn into mud. General Meade elected to delay the march until the twenty-sixth, when the weather was forecast to improve. His strategy was to move his eighty-thousand-man army against Lee's right and to attack from Lee's rear, where Lee was entrenched south of the Rapidan River with an army of fifty thousand Southerners. Lee's intelligence discovered Meade's intentions and Lee prepared for the attack. After a number of attacks and counterattacks the battle was inconclusive. After dark, Lee withdrew to prepare field fortifications along Mine Run. The next day, the Union army closed on the Confederate position. Skirmishing was heavy, but a major attack did not materialize. On December 2, Meade concluded that the Confederate forces were too strong to attack further and he ordered his forces to pull back during the night. This ended the winter campaign. There were about nineteen hundred casualties, thirteen hundred for the North and six hundred for the South.

The Civil War was now in its thirtieth month, and there was no plan for victory and no end in sight. This had been a problem for President Lincoln from the outset of the war, which began only a month and a few days after his inauguration. From the beginning, he worked long and hard to put together a cabinet of capable men to manage the various departments of government, but he ran into obstacles from the first day in office. His choice of secretary of the navy, Gideon Welles, was criticized openly by his secretary of state, William Seward, and at the same time, Seward tried unsuccessfully to position his own appointees into the naval chain of command. Welles discovered these attempts, confronted Lincoln with Seward's plan, won Lincoln's confidence, and Welles quickly took charge of the navy.

From the beginning, Lincoln spent much of his time running the war with frequent visits to army and navy high commands. Up until this time, he could not find a general who could take command of the Union Army and execute a successful military campaign. The Union Navy offered a different kind of problem for the North. It did a good, but certainly not a thorough, job of blockading the South from the Northeast coast all the way around the Gulf coast to the borders of Mexico, and in protecting American interests on the California coast and into the Pacific Ocean, covering Alaska, Hawaii, and Central and South America. But more significantly, the navy was unsuccessful in protecting Yankee shipping on the high seas. The South had figured out a way to disrupt and put fear into Yankee shipping, and this had a serious impact on the shipping industry of the North.

Almost immediately after the beginning of the Civil War, the Confederate government established a relationship with English private parties to provide warships and military supplies to the Confederates in exchange for cotton from the South. Cotton would keep the English textile mills in business. This was done in spite of the fact that England chose to be a neutral nation and consequently was forbidden from supplying arms to the Confederate government. However, the laws pertaining to neutrality were somewhat ambiguous and the British government took the position that the United States would have to show proof of the violations before any action would be taken by the British courts. This did not make it easy for the United States diplomats stationed in England. Charles Francis Adams, son of President John Quincy Adams, had been appointed by President Lincoln as United States minister to Great Britain, the top diplomat in England. Although Benjamin Moran, Adam's secretary, considered Adams a "cold Codfish," Adams became one of the most efficient diplomats in the history of the State Department.

The South had secretly sent agents to England to establish the means to purchase ships that could be converted into ships of war. These ships were called Confederate cruisers. They were sailing ships with supplemental steam power, which made them very fast and hard to catch. They were also armed with heavy cannon and guns with which to subdue any Yankee merchant or whaling vessel intercepted at sea. On the other hand, they were no match for a federal man-of-war, and they made a point of avoiding any such contact.

Up until the beginning of the Civil War, the South was the main source of cotton to supply the English textile factories, and this was a matter of business survival. At the same time, the South had no capability to build warships on their own as the North had sufficient control of all the ports and shipping lanes in the Southern waters to neutralize any attempts to build ships of war. Therefore, the arms business between the South and private interests in England made the relationship a powerful alliance and one that actually influenced the duration of the Civil War. The South shipped cotton through the leaky blockade to England and the English private parties secretly supplied the South with ships of war, ammunition, and other military supplies.

Captain James Dunwoody Bulloch was the chief naval agent in England for the Confederate States of America. Bulloch was a member of a Georgian family that played a distinguished role in American politics and nautical affairs.

His father, James Stephens Bulloch, was one of a group who backed the steamship *Savannah* in the first Atlantic crossing by a ship powered by steam. James Dunwoody was the only child of his father's first marriage to Esther Elliot in 1817, and his middle name, Dunwoody, was Esther's mother's maiden name. He was born near Savannah in 1823 and from his early years had wanted to follow the sea. His father remarried in 1832, to Martha Stewart who had three children, Anna, Martha, and Irvine. Later on, Martha married Theodore Roosevelt, Senior, father of President Teddy Roosevelt. Moreover, during the Civil War, his half brother, Irvine, sailed on the Confederate raiders *Nashville*, *Alabama*, and *Shenandoah*.

Just prior to the war, he had been skipper of the mail steamer, *Bienville*, following a fourteen-year career in the U.S. Navy and later as the skipper of a number of vessels in the Merchant Marine. On January 11, 1861, Georgia seceded from the Union. Upon learning this, Bulloch immediately returned the *Bienville* to its New York owners and terminated his relationship with them. Before heading south, he made a visit to his relatives in New York, the Roosevelts. There, a small child solemnly listened to the conversation about the growing crisis confronting the country. Bulloch had many friends in the northern shipping industry and was hoping that the North and South would heal their differences. Years later in the White House, President Theodore Roosevelt would recall the visit of his "uncle James."

Early in the morning on April 13, 1861, Confederate General Pierre Gustave Toutant de Beauregard, also known as General P.G.T. Beauregard, ordered the firing on Fort Sumter, and the war began. On that same day, Bulloch offered his services to the South. Three weeks later, Confederate secretary of the navy, Stephen P. Mallory, ordered Bulloch to go abroad to secure ships and military supplies and to build a Confederate navy that could prey on Union shipping. On the evening of May 9, 1861, Bulloch left Montgomery, Alabama, to sail for Europe. At that time, the Confederacy had only one fighting ship, the *Sumter*, which was the first of the cruiser class ships of war to be converted from a merchant ship. Mallory wanted Bulloch to first purchase ships already built and then concentrate on the construction of cruisers. This was a very difficult challenge for a thirty-eight-year-old naval officer, particularly since there was very little cash and only cotton to work with along with very poor relations between the Confederate States of America and the British government. To show how bad the relations were, President Jefferson

Davis of the Confederacy had sent Commissioners William Yancey, Pierre Rost, and Dudley Mann to England, but the British government refused to receive them. The obstacles were formidable. To make matters worse for Bulloch, he was constantly thwarted by the efforts of the very effective team of Ambassador Adams and Secretary Moran, both of whom were aware of the activities going on with the Confederates, and both were relentless in their efforts to upset the Confederate applecart.

The same was true in France. John Slidell who, prior to the Civil War was a senator from the state of Louisiana, joined the Confederacy and was appointed the commissioner to France. Although he played cards with the French Minister and was received by Napoleon III, he could never get the emperor to grant his wishes for ships and ammunition for the South. Napoleon had published a proclamation of neutrality in the spring of 1861, and he would not go against his word. Furthermore, like Bulloch, Slidell was opposed by a shrewd and clever United States consul, John Bigelow. Bigelow outguessed, outsmarted, and outmaneuvered both Slidell and Bulloch, and their subagents. Bigelow was also credited with preventing Napoleon III from recognizing the Confederacy.

Consequently, in France, Slidell had a difficult task and was unable to help the South's cause to any great degree.

After arriving in England on June 4, 1861, Bulloch called upon the Confederate Commissioners, Yancey, Rost, and Mann, and then began his rather lengthy assignment as a secret Confederate agent. The Commissioners were in no position to provide much help to Bulloch. He shed his uniform for the duration of the war to avoid attracting attention from the British government or from the United States diplomats stationed in England and France. As soon as he could arrange a meeting, he met with the Fraser, Trenholm and Company, a British company that acted as a financial point-of-contact for the Confederacy in England. They made the arrangements for converting cotton into cash for the purchase of ships and other war supplies. Bulloch met with Charles K. Prioleau, who was a partner and resident manager of the company, and worked closely with him until the end of the war. After the first meeting with Prioleau, Bulloch set up his office in that company's headquarters and began his clandestine operation of purchasing supplies for the Confederacy from England and France.

The plan to buy already completed ships immediately hit a snag as Bulloch found out that there were simply no ships for sale. His next move was to contract for a new ship to be built from scratch. With Prioleau underwriting the purchase order, he then contracted with the shipbuilding firm of Fawcett, Preston and Company of Liverpool, England, to build a ship of 185 feet in length, and constructed along the lines of a British gunboat. The ship was to be equipped with heavy firepower at a cost of around £46,000 and to be completed by December 1861. She was originally named the *Oreto*, and was actually launched in Liverpool on March 22, 1862, and immediately departed for Nassau Island for a trial run.

Earlier, while the *Oreto* was being readied for launch in Liverpool, Bulloch went to another shipyard across the Mersey River from Liverpool, to Laird's shipyards in Birkenhead to build his next cruiser. When the keel was laid, the vessel was given the number *290*. At this point, Bulloch realized he had some time on his hands while waiting for ship number *290* to be completed. He took advantage of this time to coordinate with two Confederate agents for the Rebel Army who purchased large supplies of guns, powder, food and medicine, but then Bulloch had the problem of getting the items across the ocean, past the blockade and into the Confederacy. To resolve the problem of shipping the supplies to the Confederacy, Bulloch secretly purchased a steamer called the *Fingal* for £17,500, and loaded it with all the supplies he could get on board. He took command of the ship himself and sailed it to Savannah, establishing a record that was never again equaled during the war, and furthermore demonstrated that the blockade was not effective and could be breached. He stayed in the South for five months and again slipped through the blockade on a dark night on a fast ship back to Liverpool.

Meanwhile, after arriving in Nassau, the *Oreto* ran into difficulties with the local government and was forced to transfer stores and arms at an isolated location called Green Cay. There, she was commissioned as CSS *Florida*, with veteran Lt. John Newland Maffitt, CSN, in command. During this time, yellow fever raged among her crew, and she was gradually reduced to an effective force of one fireman and four deckhands. In desperation, Maffitt sailed to Cuba and there, he, too, was stricken with the dread disease. In spite of the difficulties, the incredible Maffitt sailed her from Cuba to Mobile Bay, Alabama. There, Maffitt braved a massive array of projectiles from the Union blockaders, and raced through to a hero's welcome at Fort Morgan to the delight of the citizens of Mobile. Having taken on board additional stores, ammunition, and new crew members, CSS *Florida* escaped to sea on January 13, 1863, and thereby began her mission of seeking and destroying Yankee shipping whenever and wherever they showed on the horizon.

When ship number *290* was launched on July 29, 1862, the ship was given the name, *Enrica*, and sailed immediately for Porta Praya in the Azores, supposedly on a trial run at sea. As soon as she arrived in the Azores, Captain Raphael Semmes, CSN, took command. He and other officers boarded her and fitted her out with adequate arms and ammunition as a Confederate cruiser. She was commissioned at sea off Terceira, Azores, on August 24, 1862, as the CSS *Alabama*.

Captain Semmes had been in command of the CSS *Sumter* during its several months as a Confederate cruiser between June 1861 and January 1862, at which time she was neutralized and disarmed by Spain. Later on she was sold at auction coincidently to the previously referenced British firm of Fraser, Trenholm and Company, and recommissioned the *Gibraltar*. She served as a blockade runner for the Confederacy under British colors for the duration of the Civil War. During her time as the Confederate cruiser, *Sumter*, she had taken eighteen prizes, of which eight were burned, nine were released or bonded, and only one was recaptured. Furthermore, the diversion of Union blockade ships to hunt her down was no insignificant service to the Confederate cause. More importantly for the South, during this time Captain Semmes developed the skills needed to successfully command a Confederate cruiser.

By November of 1863, the South had put together a substantial fleet of gunships from a variety of sources, among them, the individual Confederate states, purchases from private parties, captured ships, and ships built in England and France. By far, the two most notorious cruisers were the English-built *Florida* and *Alabama*. These two steamers, both with a full set of sails, would ultimately take over a hundred prizes; most of which were burned at sea and all hands were taken as prisoners. All ship owners and sailors were well aware of these fast and deadly Confederate cruisers and the damage they had caused. Any Yankee merchant or whaling ship venturing on the high seas was fearful and on guard, but if confronted by one of these cruisers, there was little that could be done to avoid capture and destruction. It was dangerous on the high seas.

41

The *Alabama* and the *Florida*, along with the many other Confederate gunboats were known to be out there somewhere. The United States Navy had been unable to find them or contain them up until this time.

After leaving New Bedford harbor on a southwestward course, the *Milo* made a turn to the southeast after clearing the Elizabeth Islands and headed out into the Atlantic Ocean. By the second of December, the *Milo* was almost directly south of Newfoundland and over a thousand miles east of Washington, DC,[7] and she was holding a compass heading of southeast by east. The past several days, however, had seen intermittent rain squalls and rougher seas. As Captain Hawes looked out on the sea ahead when the sun was setting in the west, he wondered if a Confederate cruiser was on the horizon. Jessie stood by his side and wondered and worried as well! After all, the entire family was on board.

2. Jonathan Capen Hawes—Early Years

New Bedford circa 1815⁸

Jonathan Capen Hawes was born on May 8, 1826 to Levi and Azubah (Capen) Hawes in New Bedford, where his parents had moved in the year 1818. Levi was a direct descendant of Edward Hawes who was the first Hawes to arrive from England in 1635, making him one of the early immigrants to arrive in America. In 1648, Edward married Eliony Lumber, and they settled outside of Boston and began to raise a large family. Throughout the following 190 years, the Hawes family, like most families in the early days of America, had been through many ups and downs, including the King Phillips War and the Revolutionary War. Levi had served as a minuteman during the War of

43

1812 and afterward in 1818, purchased land in the Tarkiln Hill area of New Bedford and became a successful farmer. He also amassed considerable property through successful land speculation. The Levi Hawes family was a large family with eight children, and Jonathan, who was called "Jon" by his family and friends, was the only one who would grow up to become a successful sea captain, and later, substantial property owner.

Jon spent his entire childhood in New Bedford. This community was a very colorful place to grow up as it had all the interests one could imagine at that time. The family farm was close to town, and consequently, Jon became very aware of all the interests available in New Bedford with its land and sea connections. The sea connections were the most fascinating, and it became quite obvious to Jon that the men who were involved in whaling and ships were the most important men in New Bedford. Even as a young boy, he could tell that the wealthy men were whaling men, and they had the power and influence over most other people in town. The large estates belonged to ship owners and ship captains and he was always impressed with the way they dressed and they way they talked. Jon, at a very early age, wanted to become a whaling man and a sea captain.

Fairhaven, a town across the harbor from New Bedford, was connected to New Bedford by a toll bridge in 1796. In 1812, Fairhaven set off from New Bedford, incorporating Acushnet in her corporate limit. Tarkiln Hill, where the Hawes family relocated in 1818, was located in Acushnet. By 1835, the New Bedford area had many mansions and many interests. There were plenty of things for a young boy to do and lots of fun to be had. Jon grew up as a very happy young man. When Jon was eleven years old, the famous runaway slave, Frederick Douglass, arrived in New Bedford. His trip from Providence was facilitated by a chance encounter with two of New Bedford's leading citizens, William Taber and Joseph Ricketson. Douglass later became an outspoken advocate of abolition of slavery in America, and his name became famous throughout the country.

Jon Hawes acquired an education in the local New Bedford schools which had incorporated the New Bedford High School into its school system in 1827, a year after Jon's birth. Jon graduated from high school at age thirteen, and then began learning the trade of sailmaker under the direction of William Cook, an expert in the field. At thirteen, Jon was nearly six feet tall, taller than most of his contemporaries. This was the beginning of Jon's venture into the world of sailing ships and sea venture. Jon spent three years as an apprentice and learned a great deal about sails and sailing ships.

The Hawes family was a churchgoing family, dedicated to the Congregational Church and lived by the Christian faith. They did not deviate from the teachings of the church and Bible. Jon had many friends and got along well with everyone. He did have one special young friend in mind, and her name was Jerusha Blake, who lived in Stoughton, . Massachusetts, close to the Hawes' relatives living there. Jerusha was about the same age as Jon, and both were too young to have more than a fancy to each other at that time. Regardless, Jon thought highly of Jerusha Blake and considered her a special young lady.

Upon finishing his apprenticeship as a sailmaker, Jon, at age sixteen, decided to take the next step and become a sailor. By this time, Jon was over six feet tall, and was well above average height for young men of his age in 1842. The interest in going to sea was not at all unusual in the New Bedford community where many of the young men wanted to find careers in the whaling business and an opportunity for fame and wealth. After many discussions with his parents and friends in the whaling business, Jon shipped on the bark *Roman* as a greenhand under the command of Captain Alexander Barker, departing New Bedford on June 25, 1842. This was about a year after Herman Melville left New Bedford on his first whaling voyage, also as a greenhand, which ultimately lead to his writing the novel *Moby Dick*.

Jon's first voyage lasted two years and three days. The *Roman* returned with twenty-two hundred barrels of whale oil and several thousand pounds of whalebone stowed on board when the ship dropped anchor at the end of its voyage in New Bedford harbor. The voyage took them around the Cape of Good Hope in South Africa to the Indian Ocean and into the Pacific South Seas, with a number of stopovers at many of the islands there for provisions as well as rest for the crews. Jon learned a great deal more about sailing and whaling during these two years at sea from the point of view of a greenhand observer. This is another way of saying that Jon started at the very bottom of the crew order, but, at the same time, that gave him the opportunity to view whaling from every angle and every level of the ship. In the two years and few days at sea, Jon learned the ropes and was ready for the next step. Captain Barker was a kind and excellent skipper, and he liked the attitude and motivation that Jon displayed throughout the voyage. He helped Jon get through the learning experience and encouraged Jon to aspire to bigger and greater challenges in whaling.

Jon started learning the first day aboard ship. This was not his first time aboard a whaler, but it was the first time that he was aboard for the long haul as a member of a crew, and this would be his world for the next couple of years. In retrospect, his point of view was very much different than ever before. Now he was confronted with everyone else aboard ship from the captain down to the lowest deckhand, which was Jon, the greenhand.

One of the first things Jon learned was that whales supplied two important resources, whale oil and baleen. Whale oil was used as a lamp fuel and for making candles, as there was no electricity, natural gas, or kerosene for lighting in those days. It was also used as an ingredient of margarine, shoe polish, and soap. Sperm whales offer the greatest amount of whale oil, and are the largest whales to have teeth. Sperm whales do not contain baleen. Baleen is a tough and flexible substance that comes from the mouths of "right" whales, or baleen whales. Baleen plates, also known as bone, can grow up to four yards in length, and they are used to trap krill, a right whale's main source of food. They were used to make corset stays in those days, as well as umbrella ribs, skirt hoops for the ladies, and carriage springs. These resources came from the giant species of whales, right whales and sperm whales, and the only way to catch them was to hunt them at sea. That was what the whalers went after, and that was what made whaling a profitable venture. As Jon would learn, getting these resources was a dangerous and bloody business involving lengthy voyages at sea. But, whaling was also a path to fame and fortune.

When Jon signed on as a greenhand, he joined with some of his young friends as greenhand sailors. These were the sailors that had never been to sea on a whaler before. As a crewmember, you were not paid wages, but you had to negotiate for a share, or "lay'" of the future profits of the voyage. Jon's lay for this voyage was 1/190 of the ship's profits. A greenhand's lay was about $150 for two years' work! Today in the early twenty-first century, that would amount to about four thousand dollars, but it was the smallest share provided to a crewmember.

The Bark *Roman* was a three-masted ship, about ninety feet long, had twelve sails, and carried several smaller whaleboats that were launched whenever a whale was

49

sighted. The entire crew of twenty-one men was a mixed group of experienced sailors and greenhands. In charge was Captain Barker. There were also two mates, three boatsteerers, a steward, thirteen sailors, and a cabin boy. The sailors included seven African-Americans. Jon took along a supply of his own clothing as he knew that if he needed clothing from the captain, it would cost him money from his lay, or share of the ship's profit.

Jon quickly learned that below the deck were the living quarters along with a blubber room for storing ropes, spare sails, provisions, and other items. The captain and the mates had cabins in the rear. Jon and the white members of the crew lived in the steerage section, forward of the rear quarters. The African-American sailors occupied the forecastle at the front of the ship. The blubber room was between the steerage section and the forecastle, and directly below the try-pots on the upper deck. Below the deck for the living quarters was the hold, where barrels, clean drinking water, and other provisions were stored.

As one of the young crew members, Jon performed all the odd jobs and learned what it took to sail and maintain the *Roman*. These odd jobs included swabbing the decks to keep them clean, particularly after landing a whale as the whale's blood can be very slippery. Jon also tidied ropes as no one wanted the captain to trip over one. Another job was to serve meals. The captain liked his food hot and served on time. In his spare time, Jon spent hours learning how to carve intricate art onto the teeth of sperm whales. This was called the art of scrimshaw. He learned how to do this from the old sailors, and they had plenty of whale teeth to work on as the *Roman* went after sperm whales. In doing this, designs are carved into the surface of a whale's tooth with a knife or sail needle, and then filled with lampblack, made from soot or ink. Most scrimshaw designs were of whaling scenes, but sailors also drew their family or sweethearts.

Jon took his turns at the lookout duty. The lookout was positioned high on a platform near the top of the main mast. The lookout's duty was to report any activity seen on the horizon, particularly another sail or more importantly, a whale. This duty was somewhat scary at first, until the lookout became used to the height of the platform and the rather large movements of the mast above the deck. The lookout was manned most of the time, day and night. Only when the weather was severe was the lookout position abandoned. Jon adapted to this duty right away and actually looked forward to the possibility of discovering something of value out there on the horizon.

The *Roman* had been at sea for over three months and was off the coast of Argentina, when a lookout cried out, "There she blows!" The lookout meant that he had spotted a whale's spout, which is the spray of moist, warm air released from the whale's blowhole when it surfaces to breathe. The captain hoped it was a sperm whale which offers the greatest amount of whale oil. Experienced whalers can tell different whale species by the size and shape of their spout. The crew failed to catch the whale at this first sighting, but it got them prepared to move even quicker at the next sighting. The captain's logbook records the different whale species and how many barrels of oil they produce. Vertical sketches show escaped whales and horizontal ones show those that are killed. On this first sighting, a vertical sketch was recorded in the ship's logbook.

In the meantime, Jon was getting accustomed to the constant roll and shifting movement of the ship as it sailed on the sea. During the first three months, the weather had changed constantly; some days were delightful with cool breezes and pleasant temperatures, while other days brought rain and stormy weather. On the way, the *Roman* had made stops in the Azores and Cape Verde Islands for fresh provisions of food and other supplies. The scene from the deck of the *Roman* was constantly changing, and the changes became the norm. By September, the *Roman* was heading into the southern hemisphere summertime, and this was the best time of year to sail around the Cape of Good Hope at the southern tip of South Africa.

A few days after the first whale was spotted, Jon heard another loud shout by the lookout, "There she blows!" The captain ordered a whaleboat to be lowered for the chase. Jon got on board with five older experienced sailors and the boatsteerer. With the boatsteerer at the bow of the boat, the sailors rowed steadily toward the whale. They realized it was a sperm whale, and there would be lots of whale oil from this one. As soon as the whaleboat was close enough, the boatsteerer harpooned the whale, and following that, Jon took his first "Nantucket sleigh ride." This is what they called the event when a whale boat was dragged behind the whale at speeds up to twenty-five miles per hour by the rope attached to the harpoon. This weakened the whale until it lay exhausted on the surface. At that time, the officer on board speared it with his killing lance. The dying whales spout turned red with blood, and the crew cried out, "Chimney's afire!" Jon helped to kill his first whale. It was bloody and dangerous work. Jon had been taught to stay well clear of the harpoon rope line when the sleigh ride begins, as he could get rope burns and be dragged overboard by the whale.

Of course, killing the whale was just the beginning. Next, the whale was towed back to the *Roman*, where the crew tied it to the ship. After this, a platform was hung over the whale. The platform was called the "cutting stage." The captain and a mate stripped the blubber from the whale's body. The blubber is the fatty, outer layer of the whale's skin. This is called "flensing." Then, a large hook was inserted behind the whale's front fin. The rope and chains were attached to the hook, and then to a system of pulleys. A strip of blubber about five feet wide was cut around the whale's body, and the crew pulled at the rope until the hook pulled away a long section of the strip, known as a "blanket piece." A blanket piece weighed about a ton and would be cut into smaller sections later. This continued until the entire carcass was stripped of the blubber from head to tail, just like pealing an orange in one continuous strip, one strip at a time. There were a variety of tools, knives, and hooks used to strip the blubber. These were called head spades, boarding knives, blubber pikes, and gaffs. The knives were used to remove the blubber from the whale and to cut it into smaller sections. The hooks and gaffs were then used to lift or drag the pieces of blubber into the try-pots for rendering into whale oil.

During this operation, it was necessary to keep the decks clean as the whale's blood made them very slippery. Jon and some of his fellow greenhands had the job of keeping the decks clean. They did not want the captain to slip on the deck! After the blubber was completely removed, the sperm whale's head was cut from its body and raised onto the deck. A liquid wax called spermaceti was removed from the whale's head where it was later made into odorless candles. As much as 528 gallons of spermaceti wax could be drained from a large whale's head. Also, the sperm whale's teeth were removed by ropes and pulleys from its jawbone and used for scrimshaw and many other purposes. Like beeswax, the spermaceti wax did not elicit a repugnant odor when burned. Furthermore, spermaceti wax was harder than both tallow and beeswax. It did not soften or bend in the summer heat. Historians note that the first "standard candles" were made from spermaceti wax.

Now it was time to convert the whale's blubber into useable oil, the process whalers called trying out. Fires were lit in the try works brick ovens on deck, and sections of blubber were lowered into the try-pots. During this process, the blubber boiled and was converted into oil, which was then poured into wooden barrels and stored in the ship's hold. In order to work with manageable-sized blubber, the larger sections of blubber were carved into smaller sections called "horse pieces." Next, thin slices were cut into the horse pieces, and these were called "bible leaves" because they opened like pages of a book. These cuts were made with a special sharp knife tool that made the procedure easy to do. The bible leaves were then put into the try-pots and heated by the fires of the brick oven try works. The blubber melted into oil where it was skimmed off the surface, cooled, and drained into the wooden barrels. The captain insisted on one final caution during this process, and that was to have wet cloths readily available to smother sparks which could set the oil-soaked ship afire! This was a task for Jon and his greenhand friends during his first whaling voyage. The chain of events described above was the essence of the whaling business.

During the course of the remaining months on this first whaling voyage, this process was to be repeated many, many times, and consequently, Jon became very experienced in the killing of whales and the processing of the blubber. The score was kept on a daily basis in the *Roman*'s log showing vertical or horizontal whale sketches, depending on the outcome. During this voyage, there were many vertical sketches, and needless to say with twenty-two hundred barrels of oil on the *Roman*'s return to New Bedford, there were many horizontal sketches as well.

This voyage took the *Roman* from the Cape of Good Hope to the Indian Ocean for South Sea whaling. During the voyage, the *Roman* stopped at a number of major ports and smaller islands as a matter of routine. These stopovers provided the means for the captain to procure additional provisions for the lengthy voyage. They also provided time for the entire crew to enjoy a social life, even for a short time, with the locals. After so much time at sea, the men were naturally looking for some time together with the fair sex. The young native ladies at the small island stopovers were most willing to accommodate the wishes of the men on board the whaleships, and in fact, would actually row out or even swim to the arriving ships and arrange to board the ship. There were few rules for the natives except those provided by the many missionaries who had found their calling at most of the inhabited islands. These rules had little impact on the culture of the natives which, of course, had evolved over history. After being at sea for long periods of time, it was no wonder that the men lost control of themselves, and at the same time, the ladies were enjoying the social life to the utmost.[9] So was the life of a whaleman. Jon had his eyes open during these times and soon began to understand more about getting along with the ladies. The young women of the islands were nothing like the young ladies back home. Their attitudes were totally different, and they had few inhibitions about their relationship with the men of the whaleships. Needless to say, this was a difficult situation for a young man to face for the first time after growing up in a rather puritan culture. Jon was in fact growing up quickly at this point, but he was also always in control of himself and aware of his personal responsibilities. He avoided what was wrong, and he did what was right. He decided to set the example for others on board and not be tempted by what was going on.

The *Roman* returned to New Bedford on July 28, 1844, after two years and one month at sea. This was a successful voyage in terms of profit and also in terms of Jon's learning the whaling business and growing up a bit. This first whaling voyage was the stepping stone for Jon to become a master mariner and illustrious skipper. Jon had learned a lot on this first voyage and was now ready to move up the whaling ladder and return to sea again.

A short time later, Jon did return to sea with Captain Barker as skipper on the same ship, *Roman*, departing New Bedford on November 2, 1844, but this time as a boatsteerer. His lay this time was 1/180 of the *Roman*'s profit, a little more than the first voyage as a greenhorn, but it was an increase in pay. The *Roman* took essentially the same course this time as it did the previous voyage, to the Indian Ocean by way of the Cape of Good Hope. The two years at sea on his first voyage provided an opportunity to learn the business from the bottom to the top. He performed the lowly tasks of a seaman, yet he observed the work of those above him in the crew chain of command. Boatsteerer was the best position for Jon for this next stage. The boatsteerer was a petty officer and was a key member of the whaling crew. His performance was critical to the outcome of the voyage. The boatsteerer was the person who put the first harpoon into a chased whale. Once whales were sighted and the captain gave the order, whaleboats, each manned by six men, would be lowered away to give chase. When a boat was almost touching the unsuspecting whale, the officer on board would call to the boatsteerer at the bow oar position to stand, turn, and strike. Once a harpoon or two was securely fastened in the whale's back, the boatsteerer would change places with the officer on board and assume the steering oar. Oftentimes, the next event would be a high-speed Nantucket sleigh ride, provided by the stricken whale. A boatsteerer had to be flawless in his job of steering the whaleboat during such a ride, as the lives of the other crew members were at risk.

Once the ride was spent, the officer on board would then wield the lance that would deal the deathblow to the wounded whale. It was a dangerous business, with the lives of all six men aboard hanging upon the skill and timing of these two officers in charge. Like everything else, practice makes perfect, and Jon had plenty of practice. He became an expert in his position as boatsteerer.

During the second voyage on the *Roman*, stops for provisions were made at some of the same islands visited on the previous voyage. Jon was puzzled by these visits, but he began to understand how best to deal with the natives who made themselves available for pleasure for a stick of tobacco or other inexpensive gifts. It was not easy for Jon to fend off the natives as he was quite attractive and more imposing than the rest of his shipmates. On the other hand, Jon never backed off from his principals. More importantly, Jon was determined to be a role model for the others and consequently remained aloof from the temptations.

The second voyage on the *Roman* took over two years, just like the first voyage. Furthermore, this voyage also produced about twenty-two hundred barrels of oil and other products, so Jon had plenty of individual chases with which to practice and learn the job of boatsteerer. Now Jon was ready for his next move up the ladder.

On October 2, 1847, Jon signed on as third mate on the whaleship, *Liverpool*, of New Bedford. This was his first assignment as an officer on board a whaleship, and his lay was negotiated at 1/50 of the profit. This was a substantial increase in compensation, and Jon was quite satisfied with the numbers. Jon was now twenty-one years old, and a seasoned veteran of the seas. He would now be an officer in charge of a whale boat during a whale chase. He would be the officer to kill the whale with the final blow after the chase was completed. By now, Jon had spent nearly five years at sea, and he was well prepared for the job of third mate. He would also begin to learn the details of navigation, something he would need as captain on a future voyage. The *Liverpool* ventured into the North Pacific Ocean and Bering Sea, sailing around Cape Horn in South America. While at sea in the winter months, whaling was done in the southern Pacific. Then, during the summer months, whaling was located up north in the Bering Sea and up into the Arctic Ocean.

On this voyage, the *Liverpool* made several stops in the Sandwich Islands and anchored in the Port of Honolulu during stopovers while cruising between the southern Pacific in winter months and the Bering Sea in the summer months. This was the very best port available to the whaling fleet in the Pacific Ocean. Honolulu was the major city in Sandwich Islands and was a major trade center for the whaling business, in terms of both supplying products and services to the whalers and also for buying whale products from the whalers. The city provided almost any item anyone would want from provisions for the whaler ships to retail stores and entertainment. At this time, the city of Honolulu was a modern city with laws similar to those of England and the United States and a culture that was influenced by the large number of missionaries serving there. It had a very large business base that encompassed international trade as well as retail and service businesses for the local community. Trading with the United States was a major part of its foreign business base.

The Sandwich Islands was the name given to Hawaii by Captain James Cook on his discovery of the islands in January, 1778. The name was made in honor of one of his sponsors, John Montagu, Fourth Earl of Sandwich, who was at the time the First Lord of the Admiralty and Cook's superior officer. During the late nineteenth century, the name fell into disuse and was replaced by Hawaii.

One of the special features available in Honolulu was the Hawaiian luau, the most complete spread of the finest food and beverage found anywhere. As with the other islands in the Pacific Ocean, it was quite common for the young Hawaiian ladies to meet seamen from the whaleships soon after the ship entered and dropped anchor in the harbor. Whaleships were the norm at that time, and there were literally hundreds that dropped anchor during each season. Jon found that Honolulu, like all the other ports, offered temptations to the men on the whaleships that dropped anchor there which had to be addressed. The natives simply had a culture that was very different than the New England puritanical culture. The natives were perfectly comfortable with how they conducted their lives. To the islanders, marriage was something that could last for hours, or days, or even a lifetime, but it was not the same as back home. Jon knew now that someday he would marry and settle down, but it would be with someone who had the same values as he did. He vowed that he would find his bride back in the New Bedford area, and it would probably be with Jerusha Blake, but it would take time to make this happen. Soon the stopovers in Honolulu were a thing of the past on this voyage as the *Liverpool* was heading home.

During this voyage, the *Liverpool* spent nearly three years at sea before returning to New Bedford in April, 1851, with a full load of oil and whale products. Jon now had over seven years at sea and had passed the test of third mate. He had made a good profit on this voyage and was now ready for the big move up the ladder.

3. James Iredell Waddell—Early Years

The same year that Jonathan Hawes signed on as third mate on the *Liverpool*, another noteworthy event occurred in 1847: Ensign James Iredell Waddell graduated from the United States Naval Academy, which at that time was called the United States Naval School Annapolis. His class was the second class to graduate from this distinguished institution which would become the prime source of regular officers for the United States Navy up to the present day. The first class to graduate from the Naval Academy was in 1846. The Naval School Annapolis was officially renamed the United States Naval Academy on July 1, 1850.

James Waddell was born on July 13, 1824, in Pittsboro, North Carolina. He was named after James Iredell, famous in political circles in North Carolina in the late 1700s and early 1800s. Iredell had immigrated to America from England when he was seventeen years of age. He moved to North Carolina where his relatives lived. He studied law and became a hardworking attorney and political influence in North Carolina. On November 10, 1790, after the Revolution, George Washington appointed James Iredell as associate justice of the Supreme Court. Iredell became one of the first justices to be appointed to the nation's highest court, and North Carolina honored him by naming a county in his name, Iredell County. This was a tough beginning for James Iredell Waddell who had a namesake that would be difficult to live up to.

Young Waddell grew up as an orphan during his early years in Pittsboro, North Carolina, where he was the terror of the town. Whenever something happened in the neighborhood that caused alarm in the community, "James Iredell" was the first to be blamed. He just had that kind of reputation, and the townspeople loved to refer to him unfavorably as "James Iredell." He was adopted and brought up by his paternal grandmother, who was simply not up to handle such a young terror. In fact, his grandmother's health became an issue, and she was not able to continue with the upbringing of James. To alleviate this condition, Alfred Moore, Waddell's maternal grandfather, picked up the responsibility for James and had the young man, who at that time was thirteen years of age, move to his residence in Orange Country, North Carolina, in 1837. It was there that James was sent to Bingham's School in Hillsboro, North Carolina, for his education. By then, he had become a more reserved young man, and seemed to have lost his sense of mischief that he was so well known for in Pittsboro. In his memoirs, he credits this to "the breezes of a loftier region sweeping over the red hills of old Orange (County) that purified my heart."[10]

Another event occurred in the world during that time that would later on touch Waddell's life. This was the loss to the Mexican dictator, General Antonio Lopez de Santa Anna, of the *Alamo* in San Antonio, Texas, on March 6, 1836, following the Texas Declaration of Independence from Mexico. This loss was reversed a few weeks later on April 21, 1836, when Sam Houston's army attacked Santa Anna's Mexican Army near Houston while it was sleeping. Houston routed the Mexican Army in a short eighteen minutes and captured General Santa Anna as well. Following this, Texas became an independent country, and in 1845, it was annexed as a State of the United States by vote in the United States Congress. James Waddell would be involved in later events related to the United States and Mexican disputes, but that would be a few years down the road.

In the meantime, back in North Carolina, Grandfather Moore was well known in political as well as business circles. One of his friends was George Edmund Badger who was a native North Carolinian, born in New Bern in

1795 and a former student at Yale University. He was admitted to the bar in North Carolina in 1814. He was active in state politics and helped the Whigs win the election in 1840, when President William Henry Harrison became the winner. After his inauguration, Harrison appointed George Badger as secretary of the navy. During the short term of Badger's appointment, Badger conferred upon young Waddell an acting midshipmen's appointment to the navy and ordered him to report to the only three-decker in the U.S. Navy, the USS *Pennsylvania*, which was docked on the Elizabeth River near Norfolk, Virginia. At this time, Waddell was seventeen years old. He reported to the *Pennsylvania* in December 1841 and began his naval career. By this time, Badger had resigned his appointment as secretary of the navy upon the death of President Harrison. He later became U.S. senator from the state of North Carolina and served from 1846 until 1855. James Waddell was blessed with an influential grandfather, friends in high places, and good timing for the events that took place in his life.

Midshipman Waddell spent his first night on the *Pennsylvania* on duty for the 12 AM to 4 AM night watch. This was the first time he was ever on a ship of war, much less a ship of any kind, and he was completely ignorant of anything about such a vessel. His duty was to walk the deck. When he stopped to take a look at something that caught his attention, the officer of the watch called out, "Mr. Waddell, WALK THE DECK, SIR!"[11] Young Waddell had never heard his name accented like this before and was somewhat taken back. He doubted the gentility of Lieutenant Keith with his gruff manner and stern tone, but he weathered the storm and carried on. He was one of many young midshipmen who were there with him on the *Pennsylvania*. Some were older, and some were merely boys around his age, but all of them were independent and restless. In May of 1842, James was severely injured and this caused him to loose eleven months of professional service.

As he later put it, "The material of which boys are made is always tested as midshipmen by a more experienced and expert manhood."[12] He returned home on medical leave to recuperate. As soon as his health returned, he was ordered to duty on the sloop of war, *Vandalia* operating in the Gulf of Mexico. He served on that vessel for three years under the leadership of two commanders, operating in the Gulf of Mexico and the Windward Islands. During that cruise the vessel was afflicted with yellow fever and lost valuable officers and more than half of her crew. After this cruise, he was ordered to serve on the steamer *Colonel Hasmy* which had been dispatched for the Brazos River in Texas to support General Zachery Taylor's campaign against the Mexicans in an ongoing border dispute. However the ship's boilers were in such bad condition, she never made it beyond New Orleans.

Following this short assignment, Midshipman Waddell was then ordered from the worn-out *Colonel Hasmy* to the brig-of-war, *Somers*, commanded by Lieutenant Duncan N. Ingraham. Waddell joined her in Pensacola, Florida, and as he later put it, he entered into his old occupation of cruising in the Gulf of Mexico. In August 1846, it became certain that General Zachary Taylor would engage Mexican General Ampudia and his Mexican Army in the ongoing border dispute with the Mexicans. To support General Taylor, Commodore Conner, commander of the Gulf fleet, directed his ships to proceed with dispatch from Veracruz, on the east coast of Mexico, to Point Isabel, at Brownsville, Texas, to provide support for the military supply base there for Taylor's forces.

The *Somers* was the first ship to arrive at Point Isabel. Upon arrival, Commander Ingraham detailed from his command a force, to be held in readiness to land in order to aid in the protection of the supply base, and to perform other tasks as needed. Executive Officer Lieutenant Clairborne informed the three midshipmen on board the *Somers* to draw lots to determine which two would accompany the force ashore. Waddell drew a blank. The vessel was close enough, however, to hear the roar of artillery and the rattle of muskets to know that a battle was going on. The hearts of those aboard the vessel went out to their countrymen ashore. Soon the Mexicans were thrown back in defeat at the northern Mexican city of Monterrey, and they withdrew. Commodore Conner returned his fleet to Veracruz where it would be called for more military action later on. That would occur after General Santa Anna returned to Mexico from exile and took over the government again. He then organized an army of over twenty thousand men and planned to march north and reestablish the Mexican American border at the Nueces River in Texas, rather that the more southern Rio Grande River. President Polk decided enough was enough, and he ordered the capture and surrender of Mexico City to bring an end to all the disputes. What followed was the first major amphibious assault on a foreign territory by the United States.

General Winfield Scott executed the assault at Veracruz on March 9, 1847. He marched from Veracruz to Mexico City fighting many battles along the way. Scott was successful and defeated Santa Anna. Mexico surrendered and Santa Anna resigned the presidency and retired from public life shortly thereafter. The Treaty of Guadeloupe Hidalgo was signed by both the United States and Mexico on February 2, 1848, giving what is now California, Nevada, Utah, New Mexico, and Arizona to the United States, all for the sum of fifteen million dollars. This was done in accordance with the philosophy of Manifest Destiny, a phrase used first by the Jackson Democrats in the 1840s to promote the annexation of what is now the Western United States. It perceived the United States as a free and democratic land from "sea to shining sea."

From the *Somers*, now back at Veracruz, Midshipman Waddell was ordered to report to Commander Franklyn Buchanan, superintendent of the Naval School at Annapolis, Maryland. He took the store ship *Relief* to Pensacola, where he went ashore and traveled overland to Annapolis, arriving in January 1847. The Class of 1847 originally numbered 250. However, in consequence to the small accommodations of the school and the existence of war, the secretary of the navy decided to divide the class into three groups. Waddell was in the second group. All midshipmen had seen substantial sea service, and all had become, at this point, experienced young seaman. Waddell was proud of what they had been through and wrote later that this was the best way to train future leaders of the U.S. Navy. Needless to say, he passed his examination with flying colors and graduated with the Class of 1847. Waddell preferred to say that he passed the exams at this point, rather than say he graduated. He felt he should accomplish more before he could claim to be graduated.

Following graduation, Waddell was first assigned to the Naval Observatory in Washington DC, and worked with the wind and current charts division. Duty at the Naval Observatory was of rather short duration and was with the Wind and Current Charts Office. The observatory was one of the oldest institutions of the U.S. Navy, having been founded in 1830. It is currently one of the popular sites in Washington, DC and is a tour attraction there. From the Naval Observatory, Waddell was ordered back to the Naval School in the Executive Department. He does not write much about this assignment but writes that from the Naval School, he was ordered to the frigate *Independence*, the flagship of the Mediterranean Squadron, under the command of Commodore Morgan, commander-in-chief.

He remained on the *Independence* for about a year and was then transferred to the store ship *Relief.* While on the *Relief*, he returned to the United States in 1850. His health failed on the return trip, and he was placed on sick leave upon reaching shore.

After a few months, he regained his health and was ordered back to the newly named United States Naval Academy Executive Department. For the next two years, he remained in that assignment and worked on the Naval Academy curriculum and, also during this time, made summer training cruises with the cadet midshipmen. Waddell wrote later that he was always happy with his work at the Naval Academy. In 1852, after two years at the academy, he was ordered again to sea duty, but this time on the sloop of war, *Germantown*, for duty in the Brazil region of South America for the next forty-three months.

During this assignment, he became very proficient in seamanship and was one of the youngest navigators in the U.S. Navy. Waddell believes he was at the time the only second lieutenant to serve as navigator of an American man-of-war on board the *Germantown*. He began that assignment as a "passed midshipman"[13] from the Naval Academy and returned as a second lieutenant. This voyage occurred during the years 1852 to 1856. At this point, Waddell felt he had now graduated from the United States Naval Academy, and he was proud of what he had accomplished.

Although both Jonathan Hawes and James Waddell went into different types of maritime careers, both received practical training from the bottom up in their respective fields. They learned their profession by doing all the different kinds of work required in each profession. Waddell would later write that this is the best way to become a professional, and that in fact, the midshipmen that would come later to the Naval Academy would not be as well trained as those that went before. This was because the newer midshipmen classes would not perform all of the lower tasks during their education in the years that followed. In other words, they would spend most of the time in class, and not learning all of the sea tasks by doing them.[14]

Regardless, both Hawes and Waddell had been trained thoroughly in their respective professions, and both were ready for greater challenges down the road. Major challenges for each did come about later on.

4. Moving Up the Ladder

Becoming a leader in one's chosen field takes a substantial amount of training and dedicated practice in the fundamentals of one's profession. Both Jonathan Hawes and James Waddell had the opportunity to train and practice and were at the point of becoming leaders in their fields by the early 1850s.

After the return of the *Liverpool* to New Bedford in 1851, with a full load of whale oil and related whale products, Jonathan Hawes was ready for his next assignment. This time, he signed on as first mate, again on the *Liverpool*, departing on November 18, 1851, for another two year plus voyage. Moreover, his lay was 1/19 of the ship's profit, a substantial increase in compensation. Jonathan was now twenty-five years of age, six feet three inches tall, and still a highly disciplined young man. He was respected for his character by the captain and all of the crew. Now he was second in command to the captain. In this capacity, if the captain became disabled, Jonathan was to take command of the ship. He also performed additional duties to relieve the captain of some of his responsibilities. One of these was to take more of a part in navigation as well as the command of the ship's crew. Also as first mate, Jonathan continued as officer in charge of one of the whale boats lowered during the many chases.

The duties from his previous voyages did not seem to change that much, although his scope of attention increased significantly in his new role as first mate. However, the primary focus every day was on chasing whales and storing oil in the ship's hold. The more oil, the more profit for the ship's owners and the more share dollars for the crew. The first mate had the largest number of shares after the captain, so it was incumbent upon the first mate to focus on filling the hold with oil in the most efficient manner and to be the captain's most helpful crew member.

This voyage took the *Liverpool* to the Pacific, again by way of Cape Horn on the tip of South America. The next winter months were spent in the southern Pacific, off the coast of Mexico, where whaling was best at that time of year, and then up into the Bering Sea during the summer months. Again, port calls were made in Honolulu for provisions and shore leave on the way to and from the Bering Sea. Now that Jon was second in command, he felt more responsibility than at any time before, and he wanted to set the example for the men on his ship. Port calls at Honolulu were strictly for business, and that meant ship maintenance and provisioning for the next leg of the voyage. Jon made the effort to avoid social contact with the islanders outside of business. The journey to the Pacific Ocean and the Bering Sea was successful, and the *Liverpool* returned to New Bedford in 1853 with a full load of whale oil and related material. Jonathan had proved himself and was now ready to take command on the next voyage. That would take place soon.

In the meantime, after arriving home from the second voyage on the *Liverpool*, Jonathan had some free time on his hands and took this opportunity to visit family and friends in Stoughton, Massachusetts. He liked to visit Stoughton because he wanted to spend more time with his longtime friend, Jerusha Blake. Jerusha lived in Stoughton, and also was a neighbor and good friend of the branch of the Hawes family that lived there. Jerusha had grown into a beautiful young lady and was well educated for young women at that time. Jonathan thought he might even be interested in a marriage sometime later on. However, at this time these thoughts had to be put on hold, as Jonathan had an exciting offer for his next whaling voyage.

On October 17, 1854, Jonathan C. Hawes sailed out of New Bedford on the *Eliza Adams*, as captain of the ship. This was his first command, and he was ready for the task. His lay was now 1/14 of the ship's profit, and he was beginning to gain wealth and status in the community. He was now twenty-eight years old and a seasoned veteran of the seas. His job now was to make sure everyone on board did his job to the best of his ability. He was a large man, tall and commanding. He was a disciplined skipper and was compassionate as well. He now had the experiences which would let him know what to do whenever the time came. Captain Hawes was a born leader, and his crew respected him without question. Port calls were made to Honolulu several times during this voyage on the way to and from the Bering Sea.

Jonathan tried to distance himself away from the island ladies who were always in hot pursuit of the whale men when they arrived at port. Now that he was captain of the ship, he was even more determined to set the example for others to follow. On one occasion, however, he was introduced to a young lady while doing business with a whaling business broker in Honolulu. She was beautiful and the daughter of a Hawaiian tribal chief and was thereby considered a princess. She was smitten with Jon who not only was a whaling captain and considered an aristocrat, but also was tall and handsome. During this and following port calls to Honolulu during this voyage, she did everything a woman could do to attract Jonathan into some kind of relationship, but this did not happen. Jonathan withstood the temptation and held his ground. It was not easy for Jonathan to withstand the advances, but because he was all business, he never let anything interfere with his business goals. Furthermore, Jonathan knew that his life would be shared with Jerusha Blake if he had anything to do with it, and he wanted to set the stage for that to happen.

The voyage was successful and the ship returned to New Bedford in April 1857, after sailing to the North Pacific, Bering Sea, and Arctic Ocean. Captain Hawes had been on a two-year plus several months' journey that produced a full load and profits for all parties. He was now assured that he had the toughness to take charge and be successful in future whaling voyages, and he planned to do just that. His next major objective was to be captain again and also have ownership in a venture. This would be a goal that would take some more time and had to be planned with care.

Following this voyage, Jonathan began to think even more seriously about the future and, specifically, a future with a family. He was now over thirty years old. Although he had been at sea for a majority of the past several years, he did have enough time on shore to be aware of the possibilities of marriage and to feel the need for that kind of companionship. Being a native of New Bedford, he knew many of the young ladies there who were at the age to consider matrimony, but he also knew that the life of a wife, while a husband was at sea, could be difficult and lonely. Furthermore, he still had his sights set on Jerusha Blake and began his strategy to set the stage for a more serious relationship with her. He was also aware of the fact that many of the whaling captains took their wives with them on the whaling voyages where the wives offered not only companionship, but also took on important duties aboard ship, including navigation. He had met such wives during the many "gams" that occurred at sea when ships met each other on the high seas and exchanged visits for gossip, meals, and other news. It was especially social when the ships that gammed had wives on board. He thought it would make sense to marry a lady who would like to go to sea with him. That would be the best of all worlds.

With these thoughts in mind, he began his move to court Jerusha Blake who was the real girl of his dreams and had been for a long time. After his last voyage as captain of the *Eliza Adams*, Jonathan now had time to plan visits to Stoughton as he had no commitments planned for the immediate future. Jonathan thought it would be smart to spend a little time with Jerusha and find out where this would lead. If he waited until he completed another whaling voyage for marriage, Jerusha might not wait for him. Jerusha also had a strong feeling toward Jonathan and had often thought of marriage. It made sense to both of them to take the step now.

They were married in June of 1857, and this was the beginning of a great adventure for both. The families were ecstatic, and the couple was given a memorable send-off. Jerusha soon would become "Jessie" to Jonathan and all of their friends. They set up quarters at Lunds Corner in Acushnet and became an up-and-coming young couple, ready to tackle the world. Their first child, Addie Robbins, was born on February 22, 1858. Jonathan was now in a position to plan his next venture with Jessie at his side and with the responsibility of a small family to support.

While Jonathan Hawes was getting his life in order, James Waddell was also getting his life in order. After completing his assignment on the *Germantown* in 1855, Second

Lieutenant James Waddell was assigned duty on the store ship *Release*, and the ship was dispatched to Colon, Panama, in support of the U.S. Navy Pacific Squadron. Colon, also known as Aspinwall, was founded in 1850, in honor of Christopher Columbus. Colon is the preferred name for this port city in Panama. Aspinwall was a name used by the sizable community comprised of United States citizens who were there during the building of the Panama railroad and later, the related canal. It was called Aspinwall in honor of one of the original backers of the railroad project and influential shipping business leader. William H. Aspinwall secured a contract authorized by the Congress for the establishment of a shipping line of mail steamships to carry mail from the west coast of Panama to California and Oregon. This was in conjunction with another shipping line to carry mail from the eastern side of Panama to the eastern United States. The "gold rush" had caused an enormous increase in shipping between the east and west coasts of the country. For Mr. Aspinwall, the result of owning the shipping contract made the concept of a railroad across the Isthmus most advantageous, and consequently it was his plan in the beginning to build a railroad.

After arriving in Colon, Waddell became acquainted with Engineer Fulton, whom Waddell claimed was the builder of the Panama railroad. Actually, Colonel George M. Totten was the man in charge of the railroad and the force behind its construction and completion. Fulton told Waddell that ten thousand men had died and been buried along the line of that railroad. Ultimately men had come from all over the world to help build the railroad. They had overcome the many, many obstacles and had succeeded in spite of setbacks. There was a frightful toll of death evidenced by the hundreds of wooden crosses that marked the graves of those who succumbed and gave rise to the epigrammatic and gruesome statement that "every tie in the Panama Railroad represents the life of some man who paid the price of its construction with his life."[15] The railroad was started in May of 1850, and was completed on January 27, 1855. The railroad was forty-seven and a half miles in length. It required 170 bridges and culverts of fifteen feet or more, 134 of less than fifteen feet, and was successfully completed at a total expenditure of just over seven million dollars. It was a great success and greatly improved the flow of people, mail, and commerce from east to west and vice versa, and this was badly needed at that time.

Before leaving Colon, Waddell was stricken with fever and the *Release* was coincidently ordered to proceed immediately to the Boston Navy Yard, a rather long voyage, particularly considering the condition of the crew. From day to day, someone was stricken with fever and soon the ship's complement was reduced to one seaman and one boy. The ship's captain was stricken and could not carry on, so Waddell became the acting commander and took charge in the absence of the captain, Lieutenant Brazier. At one point, the captain became delirious with fever and came on deck with only his shirttail. Waddell feared he might go overboard, but Brazier looked astern and went back to his quarters. As the ship proceeded up the Atlantic toward the northeast, the captain took a poll of the officers to ask their opinion as to taking the ship to New York, rather than Boston, due to the sickness on board. Waddell was the only officer who advised the captain to obey his orders and continue to Boston. The result was that the *Release* was taken to Boston, laid up, and everyone was detached from her. On this cruise, Waddell had proved himself as an officer who could be counted on to complete the assigned task.

Following this, after a short assignment as Executive Officer in Baltimore under Commander Robert F. Pinkney,

Waddell found himself again ordered to the Naval Academy in 1857, assigned to the Executive Department where he served under Commander Thomas T. Craven, commandant of midshipmen. Waddell was very happy and comfortable serving at the Naval Academy again and remained there until July 1859.

5. Jessie Hawes Goes to Sea

In the summer of 1858, Jonathan Hawes was offered the command of the bark, *Emma C. Jones*, a New Bedford whaleship. This caused much excitement in the Hawes family as there were many considerations to be taken, not the least was what to do with Jessie. This could be the best time to take Jessie with him on a long voyage, as she was still young enough to withstand the ordeals of the sea. Even better, she would get used to life on the ship, and may even come to like the excitement and drama of an active whaleship. Furthermore, she was aware that this voyage would increase the wealth of the Hawes family and lead to a future with more exciting options. Moreover, she thought, if she were part of the voyage, she would be more entitled to participate in the rewards the voyage would bring. Accordingly, after much discussion of the subject between the two of them, they both came to the conclusion that she would go on the voyage. This was a very exciting time for the Hawes family. Now they had many plans to make to get ready for the journey. It was summertime, and the *E.C. Jones* was slated to begin the voyage in August. The Hawes family had much to accomplish before the journey began.

Captain Hawes had many tasks to complete prior to the departure, and this would take much of his time. He had to put together a crew with capable officers and experienced crewmen as well as recruit young greenhands that were always part of a new ship's roster. He had to begin provisioning for the trip, and this required making arrangements for food, boats, hardware, medical supplies, sailing supplies, rope, lumber, and a range of additional supplies that he was familiar with from previous sailing ventures. He had to plan the route that the voyage should take, and this required knowledge of where the whales would be and at what time of year. The voyage would last for at least two years and would take them to faraway places, from New Bedford to the North Pacific via Cape Horn at the tip of South America, and back. Planning for and executing the plans was challenging and exciting and made the time go by very quickly. Captain Hawes enjoyed this part of the whaling business.

Jessie also had many tasks to accomplish in order to get ready for the journey. She had to decide on what clothing to take, clothing that would last the rough journey, and keep her warm and dry, particularly on cold and windy days at sea. More importantly, she had a young daughter now,

Addie, and she had to make certain that all of Addie's needs would be met during the voyage. Addie was, after all, slated to go along on the voyage. This was not an easy task for Jessie as she was a novice at going to sea and was very new at being a mother. On the other hand, this was an exciting time for Jessie as she was planning to go into an unknown environment, and she wondered what it would be like.

After many good-byes and visits with friends and family, the *Emma C. Jones* departed New Bedford on August 10, 1858. It was a routine departure with help from a harbor pilot getting the ship out of the harbor under full sails on a very nice day, weather wise. It all respects, it was like any other departure with one exception, and that was that Jessie was on board. This would be a voyage that would feel the influence of Jessie, and it would also be a voyage that would be recorded for history through Jessie's eyes and writings. Jessie began her diary on the first of September, just over twenty days from the departure date. She called her diary, *Lady's Journal of a Whaling Voyage in the South Atlantic*, by Mrs. Jessie C. Hawes. Jessie made the events that took place seem normal and personal and quite different from what most "landlubbers" know about what goes on at sea during a whaling voyage. In another respect, the fact that Jessie was on board made no difference as to what went on from day to day. It was, after all, a whaling venture and a business. Everything that happened would have happened if Jessie were not on board. But, Jessie wrote about things that would have otherwise never have been told, as no one else would have thought to bother about such things. The results were a view of whaling from the perspective of a woman who was actually there to witness the events that took place and then write about them. What a pleasant result. The rest of August was spent sailing east south east on the *E.C. Jones* in the Atlantic Ocean and covering several hundred miles.

Fayal Island, Azores, circa 1858[16]

On September 4, Jessie wrote that they arrived at Fayal Island in the Azores, and she and Jon went ashore along with a Captain Allen, skipper of the whaleship *Onward*, who had also arrived there with his wife to visit the island. This was a long way from home for Jessie, who had hardly been out of Massachusetts in her entire life. However she took it in stride, and they all stayed at the Silvia home in Fayal for a couple of days, leaving on the seventh of September. While in Fayal, she and Jon made visits with friends on the island and even visited the Prussian consul's house and gardens. After dinner on September 7, boats from the whaleships came ashore and took the passengers back to their respective vessels, and shortly after, they left Fayal Island. Jessie began to learn that whaling was not always being lonely at sea, but it involved a lot of getting together and socializing with friends at sea and on land, while visiting at ports of call. However, after returning to the ship, Jessie took on a slight fever and became a little seasick. She recovered in short order and was feeling fine the next day.

On the tenth of September, only a few days out of Fayal, the *E.C. Jones* and *Onward* met again at sea and the Captains arranged for a "gam." A gam is a gathering of two or more ships at sea. Often there is an exchange of visits between ships to make a social affair out of the event. Captain Allen's wife came on board and helped Jessie with ironing. Jessie wrote that on the visit to the *Onward* on the fourteenth, she and Captain Hawes took Addie along. On the nineteenth, Capt. Allen and his wife again came on board the *E. C. Jones*, and by this time, Jessie felt that their visits with Captain Allen and his wife were going to be of a long duration. This did not turn out to be the case. Again, however, on the twenty-sixth, Jonathan, Jessie, and Addie went on board the *Onward* and stayed until nightfall. While on the *Onward*, a heavy squall arrived, and the Hawes family had to wait until the skies cleared and the rain stopped before returning to their ship. While returning on their whaleboat, Jessie wrote that one of the men fell overboard. However, they were able to get him back into the boat safely. By this time, Jessie was sure that whaling at sea was not a boring and lonely way of life. It seemed as though something was always coming along as a surprise. On the twenty-ninth, they saw whales in the morning, and by noon, they had two alongside which were cut, tried, processed, and stowed away by the next noon. These events briefly summed up what happened during the first few weeks of the voyage.

The next few days during early October 1858 were routine for Jessie. She washed and ironed and took care of Addie on board the *E.C. Jones*, just like any wife and young mother would be doing back home in New Bedford. The weather was stormy during the first few days of October, but then cleared and became warm as the *E.C. Jones* headed south. On the twelfth of October, just two days after being at sea for two months, they crossed the equator and headed into the southern hemisphere.

The next few months saw warm weather with both sunny days and stormy days. There were a number of gams with other whaling ships, and these seemed to make the sea voyage more bearable, and they always came by surprise. The visits with other ships made the time go by quickly and provided an opportunity to exchange news, food, mail, and small talk. At other times, the crew was busy chasing whales, and the log showed that they captured a fair number. Some fishing was done from the ship, and fresh fish were caught and eaten. Captain Hawes enjoyed this pleasantry and was quite successful with his fishing pole. Other crew members enjoyed the same pleasure.

Of course, the main targets were the whales, and the *E.C. Jones* was able to catch a good number of them. After five months at sea, they had already stored five hundred barrels of oil in the hold. Jessie and Addie would usually stay in the captain's quarters when whales were caught as they did not want to get in the way of the busy and hardworking crew. On occasion, however, particularly when the weather was good, they did go up on deck to observe the whole process. On Christmas Day in 1858, they spent a quiet day on board ship in the southern Atlantic, and Jessie wondered how the folks back home were enjoying the day. Jessie was sure all her family and friends back home were having a great time celebrating with church services, presents, and a Christmas turkey dinner. Jessie felt a little lonely. On the other hand, she was there with Jonathan and Addie, and that made things all right.

In February, the *E.C. Jones* was off the coast of South America and very close to Montevideo, Uruguay. They were also close to the ships, *Charles W. Morgan*, *Statir*, and *Huntress*, all from the New Bedford area, and with whom they had a social "gam" for a few days. The *Morgan* was heading back to New Bedford and took on mail from the other ships to be delivered upon arrival. The *Huntress* had been involved in a collision and was somewhat damaged, but not critically. Both the *E.C. Jones* and *Statira* loaded whalebone aboard the *Morgan* for delivery in New Bedford. The *Morgan* had room for the cargo, and the transfer provided more space for the *E.C. Jones* and *Statira* as they planned to be at sea for several more months. Captain Luce of the *Statira* and Captain Hawes got together and decided to venture into Montevideo to spend a few days. Both ships sailed into the river leading to Montevideo following a large and majestic British man-of-war, and anchored when the city was in sight. There was a lot of activity in the harbor at Montevideo that day and night, and Jessie heard music coming from one of the ships in the harbor. It was an exciting evening, but everyone, including Jessie, was tired from the previous few days' activity and the journey up the river to Montevideo.

After resting for a day aboard ship, Jonathan, Jessie, and Addie, along with Captain Luce, went ashore to Montevideo and checked into a local hotel. It was Sunday, the twentieth of February, and the whole town appeared to be vacant to Jessie who wrote that all the people go out to the country on Sunday in Montevideo, but in the evening they all go to the theater. A few days later, it was Addie's first birthday, and the Hawes family, along with Captain Luce, took a carriage ride to the country and visited a fine garden that had some of the nicest fruit that Jessie had ever seen. They all seemed to enjoy the change of being on shore for a few days. The next Sunday, they went for a carriage ride again, but went to the same garden. Jessie figured that this was the only garden around, but they enjoyed it once again. The stop at Montevideo was enjoyable, and certainly a welcome change from being on ship. On the sixth of March, Captain Hawes settled all the tasks necessary to get the ship ready for sea again, and the Hawes family returned to the *E.C. Jones* to continue the voyage. Jessie wrote that returning to the ship was like home again after living ashore. She had been with the local people most of that time, but could not understand a word they were saying.

The next few months brought stormy weather, few gams, and few whales. They had actually captured only one whale during March, April, and May. This was somewhat typical of whaling in that some days were very busy catching whales and processing them, and other days were quiet and unproductive. The weather would change like anywhere else in the world, but it seemed more abrupt at sea. On the other hand, Jessie was busy taking care of Addie and other wifely and motherly duties. She did not have time to dwell on the negatives of whaling. Jessie adored Jonathan and would do anything to make him happy. Jonathan was glad to have Jessie with him on board. Addie, of course, accepted everything as a natural occurrence, and at one year old, did not question why things were the way they were, and was basically a happy baby girl.

The next sight of shore would be the African coastline on the first of June. The *E.C. Jones* cruised along the west coast of Africa for the entire month and saw whales only one time and caught none. It was a frustrating time for Jessie, but not unusual to have long periods of time without whale sightings for a typical whaling voyage. Captain Hawes was being very patient as he had been through this many times before. Addie, of course, was too young to think about any of this and was content with life the way they was. During the same time, they came in contact with only two other whalers, the *Richmond* and the *Cornelia Swift*, both Yankee whalers. Things were pretty quiet. Jessie was anxious to go on shore again. Jessie wrote about spending her birthday, July 4, on board the ship and never being so lonesome. In the meantime, during July, Jessie spent some time drawing sketches of the African coastline which proved that she was a talented artist.[17]

The next few months were spent sailing the south Atlantic and stopping at a number of familiar whaling ports for food, supplies, entertainment, and a change of scenery for the folks on board. It was not normal to spend all of the time at sea. It was necessary for everyone on board to get on land at times to balance out their lives. It was also necessary to periodically refresh supplies and have some social activities during a long cruise. This was simply part of the whaling scene.

By Jessie Hawes on Board *E.C. Jones.*

During the last six months of 1859, the *E.C. Jones* had numerous gams with other whalers. They usually entertained guests with food and drink, although Jessie never did feel comfortable with serving alcohol. She did, however, as it seemed to be the custom. They also made a number of stops at ports of call near the African coast. Jessie wrote about such stops at Elephant Bay, Little Fish Bay and St. Catherine's. They even made a stop at St. Helena in the southern Atlantic and spent a few days there. On one of the days, they took a memorable carriage ride with friends out to the tomb of Napoleon. She wrote about a dance at one of the ports and being with a governor at another. Some of the gams were with the same ships on many occasions. After a while, Jessie wrote that she was beginning to enjoy this roaming life.

The whales began to show up, and the *E.C. Jones* was able to add more barrels of oil to the hold. On one occasion in October, Captain Hawes was swept overboard and hurt his back while chasing a whale. He returned to the ship, only to fall down the cabin stairs and hurt his arm. Jonathan was in bad shape for a few days, but Jessie took good care of him, and he did recover in short order. Visits aboard other ships continued through November and early December. Usually it was Jonathan who went to the other ships, and this upset Jessie a great deal. Her final entry into the diary was a statement to the affect that she did not understand why Jonathan would not take her along. She wrote, however, the Jonathan had never had a wife at sea before, and he simply did not understand her feelings. She would not complain, however, and when he returned, she was all smiles and happy. Jessie stopped writing her diary after this last occurrence.[18]

By writing her journal, Jessie was able to convey what life at sea was like from a woman's point of view, and this was a great contribution for her to make, even if it only covered a part of the overall voyage. She let us know the things that we would not otherwise know without her words, particularly in terms of the things that went on at sea, the good and the bad. The fact that going to sea involved stops at ports of call, seeing friends and meeting people, going to far-off places one only dreamed about, and that there were many pleasant experiences. It was not all about being at sea for several years at a time and never seeing another sole or another place. It was, in fact, a pleasant experience. Jessie enjoyed the voyage enough to do it again.

In the meantime, the *E.C. Jones* continued to cruise from the Atlantic to the North Pacific Ocean and Bering Sea by skirting around Cape Horn at the tip of South America. After many whale catches, gams, and a return run around Cape Horn on the way back, the *E.C. Jones* returned to New Bedford on the 28 of August, 1860, with 120 barrels of sperm oil, eleven hundred barrels of whale oil and twenty-two hundred pounds of bone. This was a successful voyage for Captain Hawes as he had negotiated for 1/12 of the profits of the voyage. Furthermore, Captain Hawes, along with Jessie, had earned a welcomed vacation. They would enjoy life on shore in New Bedford with Addie until the next voyage on the *Milo* in 1863. In the meantime, the presidential election campaign was in full swing in August 1860 with Republican Abraham Lincoln going against three other candidates. They were Southern Democrat candidate John C. Breckinridge, Northern Democrat candidate Stephen Douglas, and Constitutional Union candidate John Bell.

Earlier, back in July 1859, Lieutenant James Waddell was ordered from his assignment at the Naval Academy to report to Commodore Cunningham for duty aboard the steamer, *Saginaw*, which was still under construction at Mare Island, California. In compliance with the order, Waddell took passage on a Pacific mail steamship via Panama. During this time, the *E.C. Jones* was eight months into its voyage in the southern Atlantic, and well below the equator and cruising off the coast of Africa. Moreover, Jessie had celebrated her birthday on board ship on July 4.

In the meantime, when Waddell arrived in Panama, he traveled across the Isthmus on the now famous Panama Railroad. On reaching the Pacific side, he took a steamer to California and arrived at Mare Island for duty. Upon arrival, he was completely dismayed at finding out that the *Saginaw* was six months from completion at Mare Island. Furthermore, he would be quartered on the *Independence*, the same old ship he had been on in the Mediterranean several years before. He remained on the *Independence* until the spring of 1860, when he joined the *Saginaw* and sailed to China.

Needless to say, Waddell was quite unhappy about the delay in the ship's construction and other related circumstances. He did not like being separated from his family for the six months or so during final construction of the *Saginaw*. He did not like the fact that the *Saginaw* was being built in California rather than back east where the lumber was of superior quality to that of California. Furthermore, he considered the *Saginaw* a political vessel that was ordered to be built in California by the secretary of the navy at the instigation of California Senator William McKendree Gwin, whom Waddell referred to as the "Duke of Sonora." While in the Senate, Gwin was also credited with establishing a mint in California, the survey of the

Pacific coast, and the establishment of a navy yard and station with large appropriations. He also carried through the Senate a bill providing for a line of steamers between San Francisco, China, and Japan, by way of the Hawaiian Islands. He served as a California senator until March 1861. Sonora was a gold mine town in California that had become well known in the 1849s, and by 1859 it was a growing community. Later, Gwin wanted to colonize Sonora with Southerners from Mexico, and he actually traveled to Paris in 1863, to meet with Napoleon III and present his plan. Napoleon approved Gwin's plan and coordinated it with Mexican Emperor Maximilian. Gwin ultimately traveled to Mexico, but was unsuccessful in fulfilling his plan to colonize Sonora. Waddell later wrote about Gwin's influence in the building of the *Saginaw* along with his influence in political matters, both home and abroad and thus referred to him as the "Duke of Sonora."[19]

Upon completion of the building phase, the *Saginaw* sailed from Mare Island to Hong Kong, China, with James Findlay Schenck in command and Waddell as second lieutenant, the third-ranking officer on board. The *Saginaw* succeeded in making port calls at all of the islands along the way and luckily escaped the violence of a typhoon in the China Sea just before arriving in Hong Kong. In July

103

1860, they were ordered to the Gulf of Pecheli, where they joined with English and French allied forces. They witnessed the defeat of Chinese forces at the hands of the allies at fortifications on the Peiho River. Waddell was actually a witness to the advance of an English naval brigade. He saw an officer who was gallantly leading the charge fall down from a shower of iron and leaden hail. The officer was on his feet as quickly as he was down and kept the lead. The battle lasted for only a few hours before victory was achieved. Following this, the *Saginaw* returned to Hong Kong. It was at that time that news was beginning to filter down about the political situation in the United States. Each mail brought intensified news about rumors of a civil war.

Waddell later wrote about an event that occurred ten years after this incident. He was attending a state dinner given by the governor of Maryland, William Bowie, for the captain and officers of the *Monarch*, the newest and largest ship of the British navy. The captain of the *Monarch*, Sir John Commerell, was seated to the left of Waddell. Engaging in professional talk, Waddell stated what he had witnessed on the banks of the Peiho River during the battle with the Chinese. Captain Commerell remarked, "I was that officer who fell, I was hit by a spent ball."[20]

Preceding the state dinner, the British prime minister had arranged for the *Monarch* to return the late George Peabody, the famous philanthropist, who had recently died in England, from England back to Baltimore, Maryland. Peabody was one of two persons who have been honored with the "Freedom of the City of London." The other was General Dwight David Eisenhower after World War II. In the United States, Peabody was also awarded the Congressional Medal in 1867.

The *Saginaw* remained in Hong Kong for a few months in late 1860, following the naval operations with the English and French forces. During this time, the sloop of war, *John Adams*, also in Hong Kong, had completed her service in that area and was ordered to return to the United States. Early in 1861, while still in Hong Kong, Waddell was detached from the *Saginaw* and ordered to the *John Adams*. He was pleased to receive this order and the opportunity to return to the United States. However, with the news of an impending civil war, he was determined to go with the South and assist those people if the North made war. After all, he was a Southerner and felt his obligations were with his people. However, he hoped for peace and wished that the situation would turn around. With the uncertain political situation back home, Waddell sailed on the *John Adams* en route for New York. He wrote later that the passage was good enough, but unnecessarily prolonged. The *John Adams* arrived at St. Helena Island in the latter part of November 1861, and while there they received their first intelligence of the actual war, the result of the Battle of Bull Run.

The Battle of Bull Run took place on July 20, 1861 and was the first major battle to occur after the start of the Civil War. The battlefield was near the town of Manassas Junction, Virginia, which was close to Washington, DC. It was a very hot day, but this did not stop the residents from nearby Washington who came out to picnic and watch the fight, believing that it might be the highlight of what was expected to be a very short war. Both sides were unprepared for battle, and there was utter confusion on each side most of the day. As the day wore on, the Confederates got the upper hand and the Union forces panicked and ran. By this time, the Confederates were too tired to chase them. By the end of the day, all thoughts of a short war had evaporated.

Upon the news of Bull Run, Waddell immediately wrote a letter of resignation and sent it through his commander,

John M. Berrien, to the secretary of the navy. It could not take effect until the return of the *John Adams* to the United States had been reported to the Navy Department. Their arrival at St. Helena aboard the *John Adams* was almost two years from the time the *E.C. Jones* had visited with Captain Hawes and Jessie aboard.

During the almost two years between the *E.C. Jones*' visit to St. Helena and the *John Adams*' visit there, many important events had occurred. First, the *E.C. Jones* had returned to New Bedford in the fall of 1860 providing a change of pace for Jessie and a chance to be a normal wife and mother, and also giving Jonathan Hawes an opportunity to plan his next voyage. The presidential election campaign was in full swing at that time, and the country was having serious problems with the issue of slavery. Abraham Lincoln had won the election in November 1860, and South Carolina had seceded from the Union in December 1860. Jefferson Davis was elected president of the Confederacy in February 1861, and Abraham Lincoln was inaugurated as president of the United States in March 1861. Finally, the Confederates fired on Fort Sumter in April 1861, which was the beginning of the Civil War in the United States.

After the *John Adams* departed St. Helena and they had heard the news about the Battle of Bull Run, Lieutenant Waddell pondered what he would do now that he had submitted his resignation to the navy. Under the circumstances, Waddell thought this was turning into a very long journey home, and he was anxious to get back and get into the fight for his homeland in the South, in some way. However, he had no idea what he would be doing after he arrived in the United States.

The *John Adams* finally arrived at the New York Navy Yard on January 11, 1862. Waddell immediately became aware that the war excitement was intense and the brutal languages employed by the people there toward Southerners fell upon his ears at every turn. He was shocked and appalled. He called on the navy paymaster in New York to draw money due him and was told that they had received instructions to transfer settlement to the Navy Department. He found a way to travel to Annapolis, Maryland, where his wife and child were living, and of course was happy for a reunion with them. But Annapolis was in enemy territory, and Waddell was uncomfortable in these surroundings. After arriving in Annapolis, he wrote a letter to President Lincoln on January 24, disclaiming an oath he took not to take arms against the United States. He was obliged to take the oath upon his arrival in New York in order to avoid confinement. He expected to be arrested from day to day, but was not. On January 28, he received a letter from Secretary of the Navy Welles, that his resignation was accepted and that his name was stricken from the rolls. He received another letter from Mr. Welles a few days later regarding money due for his services prior to arrival in New York. The letter went on to say that he would receive money through his state government if he would state upon his word of honor that he would not take arms against the government. Waddell, of course, would not do this. He later wrote that if he were ever paid, he hoped that the government would consider the honorable thing, and pay interest. As it turned out, he was never paid for his services following his arrival on the *John Adams*.

6. James Waddell Changes Sides

James Waddell now found himself in a quandary. He wanted to get home, but was not sure how to get there. He was a rebel in Yankee land, had not been paid by the U.S. Navy for services, and was beginning to feel like a wanted criminal. Maryland was a border state, but it was sided with the North. Waddell made arrangements to have a vessel call on the port of Annapolis at night, at which time he would go on board and head south. The vessel never showed. Then, a friend informed him that if he wanted to go south, he should visit the March Market in Baltimore, enter the market at the south end, go to the first beef stall on the right, and inquire of a fat man, "the price of beef."[21]

He followed the directions, and the fat man replied, "Do you want to go south?" Waddell said, "Yes." "I will call you tomorrow evening about eight o'clock and take you to Carroll Island. A schooner will be there to go to Virginia." Following this, Waddell met with a friend who also wanted to go south if they could find a way. Waddell did not want to leave his wife and child, but under the circumstances, he needed to go to his homeland and do whatever he could to fight for the South. He said his goodbyes to his family and met with his friend. Waddell and his friend were taken to Carroll Island in a two-horse team. On the way, the driver asked if Waddell was in the carriage. He then handed a small pellet in a tinfoil to Waddell and said, "Give that to Mr. Benjamin."[22] Waddell wondered who had sent this and who the driver was. Judah P. Benjamin was then the Confederacy's attorney general and later its brilliant secretary of state.

They arrived at Carroll Island at midnight during a rainstorm and drew up in front of a small dilapidated cabin and found ten persons inside waiting for the schooner to arrive. Waddell had paid the butcher one hundred dollars' passage for his friend and himself. At daylight, the schooner came to anchor and all the passengers boarded her. They were determined to press her into service and take them to the sacred soil of Virginia. The journey was not uneventful. They were obliged to dodge a convoy of navy steamers heading for Washington as they were heading south to the Big Wycomico River. They did not intend to enter the river while anything warlike was in sight. The schooner skipper was a Yankee, but he was in business to make money, and although a staunch Yankee, he put business before patriotism.

111

Upon entering the river, they ran into a small boat and inquired of the lone sitter, "Are you a pilot?"

"Yes."

"Come alongside."

Upon boarding, the pilot took them to a place up the river in Virginia, where they could safely leave the vessel. They landed on the north side of a creek into which the pilot had run the schooner, and Waddell was delegated to visit a house near the spot of the landing and learn the news. He knocked on the door and heard a voice from a kindly old man, "Friend of foe?"

"Friend," replied Waddell.

"Come in friends." Replied the old man, and Waddell then entered the humble home of a Southern farmer.

The old man's wife sat at one corner of the fireplace and a son, sixteen years old and dressed in Confederate Army uniform, sat across the room. When Waddell turned to address the old man about his mission, the old man told him, "The boy is my grandson. He was in the battle of Bull Run, and was sent home to die." He went on further to say that that all of their sons were gone, some to return no more. "Others are in the army where they should be,"[23] and with that said, he braced himself and was ready to listen and help. He provided the group with two carriages to take them to a place where they could board a train to Richmond. This offer was what they had been looking for, and they were all thankful for the help. After one or two stops and a change of carriages, they found themselves at a place on the York River Railroad, and were fortunate to meet the train for Richmond shortly afterward. That evening, they had dinner at the Spotswood Hotel in Richmond, and Waddell delivered the tinfoil pellet to Mr. Benjamin.

The following day, Waddell and his friend met with General Winder, who was head of the Confederacy's Secret Service, and were recognized. This led them to the next step which was to visit the Confederate Navy headquarters in Richmond and submit applications for commissions in the Confederate Navy, similar to those they had relinquished in the federal navy. A few days later, on March 27, 1862, Waddell received his commission as a Lieutenant in the Confederate States of America Navy.

Early in the next month, General Ulysses S. Grant's army was caught off guard near the town of Shiloh, Tennessee, and was on the brink of being routed by the Confederates. However, Grant rallied on April 6, 1862, and managed to counterattack and push the Confederate Army into retreat and disarray. This was a turning point for the North and helped solidify the Union Army's dominance in the West. It also focused on General Grant as a general who could win. This was what the Union needed badly. A few months later, another battle took place at Antietam Creek on September 17, 1862. The battle was fought on a narrow field between Antietam and the Potomac River in Maryland. It was General Lee's first push into Union territory and was disastrous for Lee. Lee was outnumbered and could not maneuver. This was one of the bloodiest battles of the Civil War, with twenty-two thousand killed or wounded. It forced General Lee to return across the Potomac and gave President Lincoln the "victory" he wanted to announce the "Emancipation Proclamation." On September 22, Lincoln made his proclamation public. He announced that as of January 1, 1863, "All slaves in any state still in rebellion shall be then, thenceforth and forever free." Unfortunately, this did not make everyone happy. The South knew that if they lost, they would lose their slaves, so they fought harder. The North knew that if they won, the slaves would move north and compete for jobs. Army desertions increased and enlistments decreased after the announcement. It appeared there were no winners in this contest.

After his commissioning by the Confederate Navy, things started happening rather fast for Lieutenant Waddell. He was ordered to New Orleans where an ironclad ram was being constructed and was thought to be near completion. At that time, Admiral David G. Farragut, on his flagship USS *Hartford* of the Union's West Gulf Blockading Squadron, was steaming westward along with his fleet, planning an attack to take New Orleans. The Confederates remaining in New Orleans determined that the ram could not be completed in time to disrupt Farragut, or even if the ram could be defended at all. In the meantime, Waddell found himself on a steamboat heading for Vicksburg to help defend the Confederate position there. But upon hearing about the ram, Waddell volunteered to return to the ram and destroy it. He took a boat and one other volunteer with him, and they both set up the ram for destruction. Suddenly, five men boarded the ram and one of them asked if the Zeft brothers, who were building the ram, were there. Then he added, "He is a traitor and we brought this rope to hang him."[24] Waddell said the brothers were not there, but that he had just prepared the ram to be blown up for destruction. They left quietly and immediately. In a few minutes, Waddell set off the explosions, destroyed the ram, left the scene and returned by boat to the steamship for Vicksburg.

In the meantime, Admiral Farragut made the decision to take the city of New Orleans and to run past Forts Jackson and St. Philip, below the city. He was a clever man and he came up with a plan that he thought would fool the enemy. He had the crews crisscross the hulls of the wooden ships with great chains until they were almost as well protected as the ironclads. Further, since he planned to pass the forts at night, Farragut had the hulls covered with mud from the river to make them less visible from the shore and had the decks painted white so that needed objects would stand out clearly. He even had tall trees lashed to the masts of his vessels so that the enemy would think they were trees on the opposite bank!

Farragut's strategy worked. Bombardment of the forts began on April 16 and lasted until April 24 when the *Hartford* and the rest of the fleet passed them at night. He later said, "The smoke was so dense that it was only now and then we could see anything but the flash of the cannon...The passing of Forts Jackson and St. Philip was one of the most awful sights I ever saw." His own vessel, the *Hartford*, was disabled when a raft set afire rammed the flagship and flames damaged the masts and rigging. Nevertheless, the fleet safely reached New Orleans and Farragut accepted the surrender of the city at one o'clock in the afternoon on April 28, 1862.

After arriving in Vicksburg, Waddell was ordered back to Richmond where he was involved in a strategy meeting at the Confederate Navy Department for capturing enemy ironclads that they thought were going to enter Charleston Harbor. He was then ordered to Charleston to organize the force to destroy the ironclads when they entered the harbor. The ironclads never entered the harbor, and shortly thereafter, Waddell was ordered to Europe for foreign duty. He arrived in May, 1863, without ceremony, in Liverpool, England.

During his voyage to England, the battle of Chancellorsville took place in Virginia. On May 1, General Joseph Hooker tried to surround General Robert E. Lee's army. But Lee took a brilliant gamble; he divided his smaller army and attacked first. It was a complete

Confederate victory, but a costly one. His top general, Thomas "Stonewall" Jackson, was shot and killed mistakenly at night by his own troops. This was a great loss for the Confederates.

By the time Waddell arrived in England, the CSS *Florida* and the CSS *Alabama* were out in the Atlantic Ocean, seeking to destroy any Yankee ship that showed itself on the horizon. The *Alabama* actually began its search-and-destroy mission after commissioning at sea in August, 1862. Although the *Florida* was commissioned before the *Alabama*, its service was held up due to sickness aboard ship. After a lengthy stopover in Montgomery, Alabama, for recuperation and repairs, it finally left Montgomery in January, 1863, to begin its mission at sea. So, by the time that Waddell arrived in England, both the *Alabama* and *Florida* were active on the high seas in the search of American ships.

One such incident involving the CSS *Florida* took place in mid-1863. A Yankee merchant ship, *Southern Cross*, a 938-ton medium clipper ship built in Boston and launched in 1851, was returning from a voyage to Hong Kong via San Francisco en route to New York via Cape Horn. On June 6, 1863, the ship was off the coast of Brazil in very calm waters with light rain showers occurring. Moreover, there was some concern on board about where they were actually located at sea. At about two o'clock in the afternoon, Captain Benjamin Howes and his wife Lucy were sitting in their cabin when they heard shouts from the deck that a steamer was in sight. They immediately went up on deck and saw about five miles distant a low rakish steamer with a bark rig. She sailed under the English Flag. Well, Lucy thought, at least someone else was out here, so where there was life there was hope, and she felt better for this.

Then, at about three o'clock, the *Florida* came alongside and ordered the *Southern Cross* to heave to. Shortly after, a boat came alongside and Lieutenant Stone came aboard and placed his hand on the captain's shoulder and said, "Captain, you are all our prisoners." Meanwhile, the English flag flying on board the *Florida* was lowered and the Confederate flag was sent up. At this point, Lucy knew they would have to say adieu to the ship forever. The ship had seemed like a home to her for over two years had come to an end. They were told to pack quickly and be prepared to board the *Florida* as soon as possible, as there was not much time to spare. At four o'clock, they were lowered into boats on a now rougher sea and shortly thereafter, boarded the *Florida*. The other officers and men went before them and were already in irons when they arrived. Captain Howes and Lucy were taken to the officer's ward, where they ate their first supper on board. After supper, they were taken to the captain's cabin and were welcomed by Captain Maffitt as prisoners of war. Lucy wrote that Captain Maffitt treated them very kindly and gave up his own room for her to sleep in. At nine o'clock, the *Southern Cross* was burned. Captain Maffitt advised Lucy not to watch the burning as it would make her feel so bad that she would not be able to sleep.

Captain Maffitt intended to transfer the prisoners to another ship as soon as one became available. As things turned out, Lucy was quite complimentary of Captain Maffitt and his hospitality under the circumstances. They had a number of conversations over the several days they were on board the *Florida*. Captain Maffitt even confessed to spending time in Dennis, Massachusetts, during one summer and called the girls on Cape Cod "flirts." She said, "He was fond of joking." The other officers and men of the *Southern Cross* were relieved of the chains most of the day, but were required to wear the chains at night, "for protection," said Captain Maffitt. He was referring to another case when a prisoner tried to start a mutiny from the ship, *Jacob Bell*, which was also captured and burned at sea by the *Florida*. On June 12, a ship came into view on the horizon, and Captain Maffitt steamed after the ship to overtake it. It was the French Bark, *Fleur de Para*. The *Florida* caught up and went alongside, and Captain Maffitt requested of the French captain that they take passengers from the *Florida*. The captain agreed and the passengers were transferred over to the French ship, and their journey as prisoners ended. In fact, on the *Fleur de Para*, they were actually listed as passengers, much to their liking. They were later taken to port in Brazil and found passage back to their home in Massachusetts in due course.[25] What was significant was that all prisoners were treated fairly by Captain Maffitt, and this was the case with all of the Confederate cruiser commanders during the course of the Civil War. There is no record that any private citizen, taken prisoner, was ever intentionally harmed or murdered during the course of the Confederate naval and sea operations.

By late June, Admiral Farragut was taking steps to neutralize the Mississippi River from Confederate control by providing naval assistance to the Union Army under General Grant in the battle of Vicksburg. He moved his fleet up the Mississippi River to just south of Vicksburg. He was supported by a motor flotilla under the command of his stepbrother, Commander David D. Porter, who joined him there. These forces were further joined by the Western Flotillas under Flag Officer Charles H. Davis who came down the Mississippi River from the north. Coordinating with Union Naval forces on the Mississippi River, General Grant masterfully moved his outnumbered army around the city and laid siege to it. The city surrendered on July 4, giving complete control of the Mississippi River to the Union. This was a major blow to the South, and was perhaps the beginning of the end of the Confederacy. Following this, Admiral Farragut sailed down the Mississippi, out into the Gulf of Mexico, and from there he headed home to New York for a well-earned rest.

Another major event occurred in July, the famous battle of Gettysburg took place. General Lee moved his army north into Pennsylvania in early July. The battle began on July 2, 1863 and lasted for two days. Lee's army hurled itself at Union forces led by General George Meade, but his effort failed, and the Union forces fought back and forced Lee to withdraw. This was the costliest battle of the Civil War in terms of causalities. There were 51,112 casualties, 23,049 Union and 28,063 Confederate. This led to President Lincoln's famous Gettysburg address in November 1863, which took place one week before the *Milo* departed New Bedford Harbor for its journey to the North Pacific.

In retrospect, this did not seem to be the best time for the *Milo* to venture on to the high seas away from home. On the other hand, the demand for whale oil was greater than the supply, and this condition lead men to take risks to gain the accompanying rewards. With this in mind, Jonathan Hawes decided to invest in the *Milo* venture and make the journey. Jessie Hawes also was in favor of the voyage and was anxious to take to the seas again. During their time on shore, Jonathan and Jessie Hawes added another child to their family, Frederic Blake Hawes, born on April 5, 1863. So, on this voyage, the *Milo* would accommodate the Hawes family of four, Captain Hawes, Jessie, Addie and young Fred. Addie was now five years old. Between July and November 1863, Captain Hawes spent most of his time getting ready for the long journey on board the *Milo*. This involved getting together for planning with the other owners and making financial preparations for trip. There was planning for the legal aspects involved, i.e. registration and insurance, planning for the food and ship supplies, planning for recruiting crew members, planning for provisions for the Jonathan Hawes family and all of whom would be aboard the *Milo*. There was much to be done.

123

Jessie, too, had many things to get done during this time. She would have to be mother, teacher, preacher, doctor, maid, and pacifier during the long trip. It was a rather difficult proposition for a young mother to undertake, with two young children, but Jessie took everything in stride and with flying colors. She was determined to make this a great voyage. She had no idea what would take place on the voyage and that she would be in for a great challenge. It turned out to be a greater challenge than she could have ever imagined.

Also during summer and fall of 1863, Lieutenant James Waddell was trying to adjust to life in England. In March, prior to his arrival there, the Confederate government purchased the merchant ship, *Japan*, built in 1862 as a fast commercial vessel. On April 1, 1863, the *Japan* departed Greencock, England, ostensibly bound for the East Indies and carrying a crew of fifty for a voyage to Singapore. A few days later, she rendezvoused with the steamer *Alar* off the coast of France and took on guns, ordinance, and other stores. On April 9, she was placed in commission as the CSS *Georgia* under the command of Commander W. L. Maury, CSN. Her orders read to prey against United States shipping wherever found.

On September 19, 1863, another major battle was taking place between the North and the South. This time it was at Chickamauga, Georgia, just south of the Tennessee boarder. This was the second most costly battle of the Civil War. There were 34,624 casualties, 16,170 Union and 18,454 Confederate. It set the stage for the final Union advantage. Union General George H. Thomas was the hero and became known as "The Rock of Chickamauga." He took over for General Rosecrans who was in command, but when the Confederates began to overwhelm the Union forces, Rosecrans and two senior officers fled the battlefield. Only General Thomas remained. Interestingly enough, when Rosecrans and his chief of staff, James A. Garfield, reached a point where Rosecrans could safely travel to Chattanooga, Garfield returned to the battlefield. Twenty-five years later, James A. Garfield was elected president of the United States. Even though the Union forces were defeated at Chickamauga, General Thomas saved the day and allowed the Union forces to regroup in Chattanooga, Tennessee. Following this action, the Battle of Chattanooga took place between November 23 and 25 which was led by General Grant, now commander of the Military Division of the Mississippi with responsibility for Chattanooga. The Union forces routed the Confederates this time and opened the door for General William T.

Sherman's "March through Georgia." This was the beginning of the end for the South. All of this took place during the two days before the *Milo* left New Bedford harbor.

Following commissioning in April, the CSS *Georgia* sailed to the West Indies, Brazil, and Trinidad, recrossed the Atlantic to the coast of Africa, and then sailed up to Cherbourg, France, arriving October 28 for repairs. During this short cruise, she captured nine prizes. The *Georgia* was an iron bottom, which meant she had an iron frame and an iron hull. She was not suited for long voyages and required frequent dry docking as antifouling coatings had not been developed at this time. Captain Bullock, the chief Confederate agent, would have nothing to do with iron bottoms, but Commander Maury opted for *Japan* because wood was being superseded in England by iron. Consequently, wooden ships were not easy to come by in England in 1863.

This made it difficult for adding ships quickly which was what the Confederates wanted to do to increase their fleet of cruisers. Moreover, the ironclad warships that were being constructed in England were more controversial as they would ultimately be used to enter United States ports

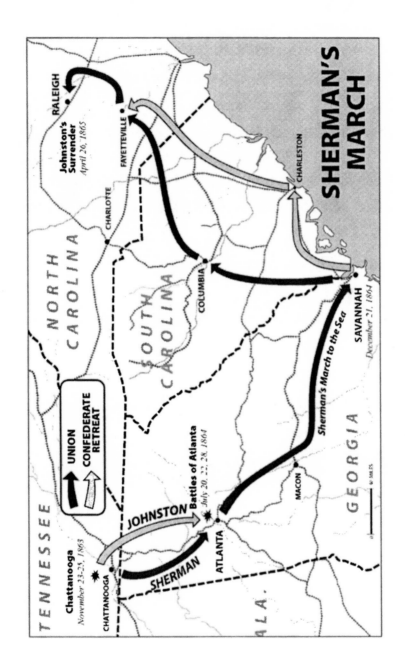

Sherman's March through Georgia

127

and cause great destruction. England, as a neutral nation, did not want to be blamed for delivering ironclad ships, and this made it almost impossible for them to allow the ironclads to leave the country.

Under these conditions, Waddell had a lot of time on his hands and for a long period of time, he had nothing positive to look forward to in terms of the South procuring, and his commanding, a new Confederate cruiser which, of course, was why he was there. By the time the CSS *Georgia* arrived in Cherbourg, Waddell was still waiting for news of a new assignment. To make matters worse for the Southerners in England, they were all instructed to stay by themselves and not mix with other Southerners whom they knew in the area. Any getting together could have aroused suspicion by United States diplomats and their agents who were constantly on the lookout for such activity. It was very lonely for Waddell and his associates.

About the time that the CSS *Georgia* arrived in Cherbourg, the CSS *Florida* was heading for Beast, France, also for maintenance and repairs. Once there, Captain Maffitt of the *Florida* relinquished command to Lieutenant C. M. Morris, who would carry on with the Confederate cruiser mission of destruction when the repair service was complete.

Also at this time, Captain Jonathan Hawes was making last-minute decisions prior to his departure from New Bedford, scheduled for November 26. The *Florida* and the *Alabama* were both very active on the high seas, and both were taking a large number of prizes. The *Florida* cruised the Atlantic Ocean while the *Alabama* cruised the North and South Atlantic as well as around the Cape of Good Hope to the Dutch East Indies. Both of these Confederate cruisers had developed a fear among Yankee shipping interests. Many Northern ships were sold to foreign interests to avoid capture on the high seas and to counter the extremely high insurance costs born by Yankee ship owners.

When Captain Hawes and the *Milo* finally departed New Bedford on November 26, James Waddell sat in England and was a very frustrated sailor. He wanted so much to join in the fight along with the *Alabama* and the *Florida*, who were the "stars" of the Confederacy. Captain Hawes had a lot to be concerned about with both of these cruisers out on the Atlantic in addition to many others, among them the *Georgia*, the *Sumter*, and the *Tallahassee*, out there as well. By this time, the South had well over five hundred ships in their arsenal, and they were stationed all around the Atlantic Ocean and Gulf of Mexico. They proved to be a significant and costly menace to the United States, and before it was all over, the Confederate Navy had destroyed well over three hundred unarmed merchant and whaling vessels. This was a dangerous and risky journey to undertake for Captain Hawes and family aboard the *Milo*.

7. Confederate Cruisers Show Their Muscle

On December 18, 1863, the *Milo* was located exactly at 30° north latitude and 30° west longitude in the Atlantic Ocean. This put her roughly four hundred miles south of the Azores and three hundred miles southwest of Madeira Island which is off the coast of Morocco. The *Milo* was headed south to warmer waters at this time of year and specifically to Cape Horn on the tip of South America for entry into the Pacific Ocean after she passed that landmark.

Back in England, life for a Confederate sailor was not the normal life you would find anywhere. Life moved very slowly and quietly. It was so quiet for a Confederate in England that it was almost unbearable. There were Confederate sailors in England waiting for an assignment to a fighting ship so they could enter the fight with the Yankees. But they had to be very quiet in order to keep from arousing any suspicion by United States diplomats and agents who were all around England and who were always on the lookout for the enemy. The diplomats knew there were Southerners in England who were preparing to get into the fight on the Confederate side, and they established a network of agents to stop such activity. The sailors from the Confederacy were instructed to remain alone and not talk about their presence to anyone else in England. This was a rule strictly enforced by the Confederate officials in England in order to reduce the likelihood of being discovered. With this in mind, Lieutenant Waddell had to remain by himself and not mix with anyone else. This was a difficult position to be in as Waddell wanted to get on with his assignment. Unfortunately, he had to wait for the right time and this was going to be a long wait. By February 1864, Waddell was going out of his mind. On the twelfth of February, the CSS *Florida* departed France and sailed for the West Indies under the command of Lieutenant Morris.

Out on the high seas, the *Milo* found herself in the South Pacific Ocean. On February 20, the *Milo* came in contact and gammed with the New Bedford whaler *Charles W. Morgan*, also heading for the North Pacific for next summer's whaling. By February 29, the *Milo* had skirted around the western side Cape Horn and was located at 54° south latitude and 80° west longitude. This put the *Milo* about four hundred miles west of the southern Chilean coast. Up until this time, the *Milo* had seen a few whales but had caught none. By March 31, the *Milo* was in the equatorial Pacific Ocean about two thousand miles west of Panama. There was not much happening. They were heading for the North Pacific and the Bering Sea where serious whaling would take place. However, they were still a long way from their destination. They were not alone as they met and gammed with a number of ships along the way. On April 20, the *Milo* arrived at the Sandwich Islands and dropped anchor in the Port of Honolulu. Captain Hawes needed to purchase provisions for the next leg of the voyage. Captain Hawes went on shore with Jessie, Addie, and Fred to mail letters and to take care of other matters requiring a personal visit. Jessie and the children enjoyed the time on shore in contrast to life at sea.

During this stopover, Jessie learned of a photographer, Henry L. Chase, who had a studio on Fort Street in Honolulu. Jessie visited with Mr. Chase and decided that he would be the person to take pictures of the Hawes family. Pictures were taken of the family and specifically of Jessie and baby Fred. After five days in Honolulu, Captain Hawes decided it was time to head north to the Bering Sea for summer whaling in the Arctic Ocean. On the evening of April 24, the *Milo* took on a harbor pilot to guide the ship out to sea. At eleven o'clock that evening, the pilot was discharged and returned to Honolulu, and the *Milo* headed north.

Jessie Hawes and Fred[26]

Gamming was truly a social function carried on by whalers around the world and was a healthy social exchange of crew, food, gossip, pleasantries and mail between whalers. More often than not, the whalers knew each other and in many cases were from the same port. New Bedford, for example, had over three hundred whaleships in its fleet, and they were scattered around the world at any given time.

Among the many whalers that gammed with the *Milo* over the couple of months in 1864, between February and June, were whalers *Emma C. Jones, Euphrates, George Howland,* and *Congress.* After leaving Honolulu, the *Milo* captured her first whale of the voyage on April 27 during a rainy and overcast day. Captain Hawes was not expecting to see whales in this location but took advantage of the opportunity and was able to put some barrels of oil in the ship's hold by the end of the day.

During this same time period, James Waddell, in England, became somewhat philosophical in his views. He later wrote of the situation as a military man. Ironclad rams were rapidly being built by English shipbuilding firms for the Confederates in 1863, and the Confederates hoped they would be ready for service in the fall of that year. It was very doubtful if the British government would allow the ironclads to escape its vigilance, like the *Florida* and *Alabama*, and be shipped to the Confederates. From the European point of view, the South appeared to be losing the war, and sooner or later, the rest of the world would have to deal with the United States, as they surmised that the Confederacy would be history. Since the British were neutral, they did not want to take the chance of breaking that neutrality. Consequently, the ironclad rams were seized, and the hope of their use by the Confederates vanished.

Waddell later wrote in his memoirs that the South had a shortage of seamen and to build fighting ships without the seamen would be a grave mistake. Most of the Southern naval officers had a lengthy service in the United States Navy. However, there were a large number who were loyal to United States Navy after many years of service at sea and decided to remain with the North even though they were sons of the South. They were not political men, but were accustomed to doing service outside of the country as opposed to home service. This excluded them from participation in the policy of government along with the internal interests of the country. Consequently most naval men chose to remain with the government to which they had been part of for most of their careers, while army men chose for the most part to join with their land of birth in the fight for their homeland. One example was Admiral Farragut who was a son of the South, born in Tennessee and grew up in Louisiana, and then entered the navy as a midshipman while still a teenager. When the Civil War broke out after many years of service in the United States Navy, he moved his family to New York out of loyalty to the North and remained there for the rest of his life while continuing his service with the navy. Farragut became the first full admiral of the United States Navy.

By June 3, the *Milo* had arrived in the Bering Sea. It was the best time of the year for profitable whaling there. Somehow, the whales seem to know where to go for food and spawning. The Bering Sea was the best place for that. Whales have been doing this from the beginning of time, and they are still doing this today. In 1864, however, it was a rough time for the whales because there were literally hundreds of whaling ships in the Bering Sea hunting for them and their precious oil. The world had discovered oil in the ground, but it had not invented the means to process that oil. It was soon to come, but in 1864, the whaleships were out there to hunt and kill the whales for their valuable materials.

A few days later on the other side of the world, the CSS *Alabama* was cruising off the coast of France. *Alabama*, a 1050-ton screw steam sloop of war, was commanded by Captain Raphael Semmes. She cruised in the North Atlantic and West Indies after commissioning at sea, and during the rest of 1862, she captured over two-dozen Union merchant ships, of which all but a few were burned. Among those released was the mail steamer *Ariel*, taken off Cuba on December 7, 1862, with hundreds of passengers on board.

The CSS *Alabama* began the next year by sinking USS *Hatteras* near Galveston, Texas, on January 11, 1863. She then moved into the South Atlantic and stopped at Cape Town in August. She then went on to the East Indies, seizing nearly forty more merchantmen during the year, destroying the majority, and doing immense damage to the seaborne trade of the United States. Later in the year, the *Alabama* called at Singapore in December 1863, but was soon back at sea to continue her commerce raiding. However, the *Alabama* was increasingly in need of an overhaul and had only captured a few ships in 1864. On June 11 of that year, Captain Semmes brought her to Cherbourg, France, for repairs.

News of her presence soon reached the USS *Kearsarge*, which promptly steamed to Cherbourg, arriving on the fourteenth. Seeing that he was blockaded, with repairs delayed and with the likelihood that his ship would not be able to resume her raiding activities, *Alabama*'s Captain Semmes challenged *Kearsarge*'s Captain John Winslow to a ship-to-ship duel. That suited Winslow very well, and he took station offshore and waited.

After four days of loading coal, painting, and other maintenance work, the *Alabama* steamed out of Cherbourg harbor in the morning of June 19, escorted by the French ironclad, *Couronne*. The ironclad remained in the area to ensure that the combat took place in international waters. On paper, *Kearsarge* and *Alabama* were well-matched, with the *Kearsarge* having a slight advantage in gun power and speed. As the *Alabama* approached, the *Kearsarge* steamed farther to sea, to ensure that Confederate cruiser could not easily return to port.

By late morning, Captain Winslow put his ship around and headed for the enemy. The *Alabama* opened fire a few minutes later, at a distance of about a mile, and continued to fire as the range decreased. As the ships closed to about a half mile, the *Kearsarge* turned and began to shoot back. Both ships had their guns trained on each other, and the engagement followed a circular course, with the ships steaming in opposite directions and turning to counter the other's attempts to gain an advantageous position. Superior gunnery on board the *Kearsarge* and the deteriorated condition of *Alabama*'s powder and shells soon began to tell. Though *Alabama* hit her opponent several times, the projectiles caused little damage and few casualties. One shell that hit the *Kearsarge*'s sternpost, failed to explode and survives today as a relic of the battle.

USS *Kearsage* Defeats CSS *Alabama*"

After about an hour of shooting, the *Alabama* was beginning to sink, with several men killed and many others wounded. Among the injured was Captain Semmes, who turned and tried to run back toward Cherbourg. However, when the *Kearsarge* headed him off and the rising water stopped his engines, Semmes struck his flag. As the *Alabama* sank, some twenty minutes after the firing ceased, most of her crew were rescued by the *Kearsarge* and by the

British yacht *Deerhound*. Those saved by the *Deerhound* included Semmes and most of his officers. They were taken to England and thus escaped capture and imprisonment. This was one of the Civil War's most significant naval actions and ended the career of the South's most destructive ocean raider.

It was during this time that James Waddell contemplated what he was doing and why he was doing it, and it was a dilemma for him. In fact, one English company offered him the command of a blockade runner, and one thousand pounds for each round trip to and from Bermuda to any Southern port in the Confederacy. He thought about this for a while, and even consulted Confederate Flag Officer Samuel Barron who offered his consent for Waddell to accept the assignment. After sleeping on this, Waddell decided to decline the offer.

Flag Officer Barron is another example of a naval career gone askew. Samuel Barron had been an officer in the United States Navy, and later became a Confederate Navy officer, acting as a representative in Europe for the Confederacy during the Civil War. Born to a prominent military family in Hampton, Virginia, on November 28, 1809, Barron was entered into the navy at the surprising age of two on January 1, 1812, presumably due to the influence of his father, a high-ranking Commodore who served at the local naval base. In 1820, Barron was allowed to begin his official service in the navy, serving in various positions until his promotion to lieutenant on March 3, 1827. From then until 1860, Barron had an impressive career in the United States Navy, rising to captain in 1855 and to a bureau chief of the Navy Department in 1860. When Virginia seceded from the Union, Barron resigned, but his resignation was not accepted by Navy Secretary Welles, and he was actually dismissed. He and Welles did not get along, and Welles had the upper hand. Barron then joined the Confederate Navy and was soon after assigned to England to oversee construction of the two ironclad rams CSS *Stonewall* and CSS *Georgia* for the Confederacy. After the ships were seized by British authorities the following year, Barron traveled to France, remaining in Paris as "Flag Officer Commanding Confederate States Naval Forces in Europe." He acted as a contact for Confederate naval officers as well as blockade runners and privateers until February 25, 1865. On that date, he resigned his commission returning to the United States shortly before the Confederacy's surrender. Until his resignation, he was the top Confederate naval authority in Europe.

Soon after his decision to decline the offer to command a blockade runner, Waddell finally received notice in October 1864 of his new assignment. This was what he had been waiting for all of this time. The notice was in the form of the following letter.

Paris, France, 5 October, 1864

No. 30 Rue Drouot

Sir:

When the vessel under your command is ready for sea, you will sail on a cruise in the region of ocean already indicated to you in personal interviews. The charts which have been sent to you are the best sailing directions which you can have.

Your position is an important one, not only with reference to the immediate results to the enemy's property, but from the facts that neutral rights may frequently arise under it; reliance, however, is placed in your judgment and discretion for meeting and promptly disposing of such questions.

It is now quite the custom of Federal owners of ships and cargoes to place them under British protection, and this may at times cause you embarrassment. The strictest regards for the rights of neutrals cannot be too sedulously observed; nor should an opportunity be lost in cultivating friendly relations with their naval and merchant services, and of placing the true character of the contest in which we are engaged in its proper light. You will not hesitate to assume responsibility when the interest of your country may demand it, and should your judgment ever hesitate in seeking the solution of any difficulty, it may be aided by the reflection that you are to do the enemy's property the greatest injury in the shortest time. Authority is vested in you to make acting appointments to fill any vacancies which may occur.

The maintenance of strict naval discipline will be essential to your success, and you will enjoin this upon your officers and enforce the rigid observance, always tempering justice with humane and kind treatment.

I am, sir, very respectfully, your obedient servant,

S. Barron
Flag Officer

Lieutenant Commanding James I. Waddell

Enclosed in the above letter was a memo from the Confederate Navy Department, dated August 19, 1864, with further instructions to Lieutenant Waddell.

A fast vessel with auxiliary steam power, leaving the meridian of the Cape of Good Hope on the first of January, would reach Sydney in Australia in forty days, adding twenty days for incidental interruptions, and leaving the coast of Australia on the first of March, passing through the whaling ground between New Zealand and New Holland, and the

> *Caroline Group, touching at Ponape, and allowing 30 days*
> *for incidental interruptions, would reach the Ladrone Islands*
> *by the first of June. She would then, visiting the Bonin Islands,*
> *Sea of Japan, Okhotsk Sea and North Pacific, be in position*
> *about the 15 of September, north of the Island of Oahu,*
> *distance from sixty to one hundred miles, to intercept the*
> *North Pacific Whaling fleet, bound to Oahu with the products*
> *of the summer cruise.*

These were Waddell's marching orders. He was ecstatic and later wrote that it would have been wholly superfluous to have tried to write specific instructions for such a vast journey with such devastating objectives. He was to make the decisions on all of the details of the journey from recruiting crew members, to guns, ordinance and ammunition provisions, to the general conduct of the cruise, and for his intercourse with the enemy as well as neutrals at sea. This was a massive assignment for such a rather young naval officer at forty years of age.

While preparing for his lengthy sea voyage, Waddell soon learned that the CSS *Alabama* had been sunk by the USS *Kearsarge*, and he realized that he would now be commanding one of two major cruisers for the Confederates, the other being the CSS *Florida*. At that time, he did not know it, but soon he would soon have the only major Confederate cruiser.

On October 4, 1864, the CSS *Florida* sailed into Bahia, Brazil for crew rest and repairs. Bahia, also known as Salvador, is located at the Bay of San Salvador which is on the east coast of northern Brazil. It was and still is one of the major ports in Brazil and was equipped to make the repairs on the CSS *Florida* as well as provide rest and relaxation for the crew members on board the ship. On the way in to port, the *Florida* was approached by another vessel and asked the name of the vessel. Upon reply, the other vessel acknowledged that it was the HMS *Curlew*.

The next morning, Captain Morris found out that the USS *Wachusett* was at anchor near his ship, but there was no British steamer in sight. He then concluded that the ship that had inquired of their name was really the USS *Wachusett*, and this put a different slant on the situation. Captain Morris made all of the official arrangements to have repairs done which included communications with the Brazilian government up to and including an interview with the governor. After the interview, the governor gave the approval for the repairs and crew rest not to exceed forty-eight hours to finish the work, but that if the repairs should take longer, the time would be extended. Furthermore, the governor was most urgent in his request that the *Florida* strictly observe the laws of neutrality as he was more concerned that the *Florida* would attack the *Wachusett* as the United States consul had assured him that the *Wachusett* would not attack the *Florida*. In fact, a Brazilian admiral who was present at the interview suggested that Captain Morris reposition his ship between the admiral's ship and shore as further protection for the *Wachusett*. Following this, Captain Morris did reposition his ship and then made arrangements to begin work and to allow one watch at a time to go ashore for a twelve-hour period of time.

On October 6, Captain Morris along with four of the ship's officers and another group of crew members went ashore for the night, as they were confident that nothing would take place between the *Wachusett* and the *Florida*. At three o'clock the next morning, with Captain Napoleon Collins in command, the *Wachusett* slipped her cable and steered for the *Florida*, about a half mile distant, and struck the *Florida* on the starboard quarter, cutting down her bulwarks and carrying away her mizzenmast and main yard. The *Florida* was not otherwise injured. A few pistol shots were fired from the *Florida*, and two broadside guns were fired from the *Wachusett*, at which time the *Florida* surrendered. During the absence of Captain Morris, Lieutenant Thomas Porter was the officer in charge. He quickly went on board the *Wachusett* and surrendered the *Florida* with fifty-eight men and twelve officers on board, and at the same time made an oral protest against the capture.

USS *Wachusett* Tows CSS *Florida*[28]

Following this, Captain Collins took a hawser to the *Florida* and towed her to sea. A weak attempt was made by the Brazilians to intercept the *Wachusett*, a few shots were fired, but the *Wachusett* was able to increase the distance in

148

a short time even though she was towing the *Florida*. Captain Collins had a plan to convert the *Florida* into a federal warship after necessary repairs were made. This put the *Florida* out of commission for the Confederacy and left the South with one less Confederate cruiser. This action took place on October 7, 1864. At that point, Lieutenant Waddell had command of the only Confederate cruiser that would be a major threat on the high seas. One would believe that he would be an easy target for the United States Navy.

8. CSS *Shenandoah* is Commissioned

CSS *Shenandoah*[29]

On October 7, 1864, the English ship, *Sea King*, left her moorings in Liverpool under the command of Captain G. H. Corbett. She was cleared for Bombay, India, or any other port in the East Indies, on a voyage not to exceed two years. This was the very same day the CSS *Florida* was captured in Brazil. Captain Corbett was a British subject and the *Sea King* flew the English flag. However, Captain

James Bulloch had purchased the *Sea King* earlier in the fall of 1864 with the intention of using her as his weapon to destroy the American whaling fleet in the Pacific and Arctic Oceans. This mission was conceived and initiated by Confederate Secretary of the Navy Stephen R. Mallory.

The *Sea King* would be the last cruiser Bulloch would buy, and she was the last hope of the Confederate Navy. In order to disguise his intentions, Bulloch sent Richard Wright, son-in-law of his English partner, Charles Prioleau, to Scotland and had him make the deal to buy the *Sea King* in his own name. Wright then ordered the *Sea King* to several English ports. Prior to her final departure from Liverpool, she slipped in and out of the ports in an attempt to make it appear that she was an innocent merchant ship. On October 7, Wright gave power of attorney to Captain Corbett to "sell the *Sea King* at any time within six months for the sum of not less than £45,000 sterling." On that same day, the *Sea King* departed Liverpool and headed for Madeira Island.

Bulloch had also purchased a large supply ship, the *Laurel*, and had loaded her to the gunwales with guns, powder, and supplies. Although she was a Confederate vessel, she flew the English flag but was skippered by Lieutenant Ramsey, a

Confederate. The *Laurel* departed Liverpool in the early morning hours on the day after the *Sea King* departed. Aboard the *Laurel* were a number of Confederate officers and seamen, some of whom had seen service on the Confederate cruisers *Florida*, *Alabama*, *Georgia*, and *Rappahannock*. Also aboard was the officer that Secretary Mallory had selected as captain of the new cruiser, Lieutenant Commanding James I. Waddell.

Each of these men arrived alone at the dock where they boarded a tugboat to take them to the *Laurel*. They did not talk to each other or even show signs of knowing each other. This was a precautionary measure to avoid any suspicion of Confederate activity that could be noticed by United States agents who were all around Liverpool. Each man's baggage had previously been sent on board, packed in dry goods boxes, and marked with a diamond and number above it by which each officer and seaman was known. At the time of departure, everyone was furnished with a receipt for thirty-two pounds for his passage in the steamer *Laurel* from Liverpool to Havana, Cuba. But, in reality, the *Laurel* was to rendezvous with the *Sea King* at Funchal, on the Island of Madeira, off the coast of Morocco, Africa.

The *Sea King* was observed by the United States agents as she departed Liverpool, but nothing was seen as a threatening sign. Her decks were clean and only two twelve-pound guns were noticed, and these were typical of any merchant vessel going to sea at that time. There was nothing in her departure to excite even passing attention. On the other hand, no one bothered to look closely at the *Laurel* when she left the scene without fanfare during the early hours of the next morning while it was still dark. As soon as the *Laurel* got under way, the Confederate officers and seamen got together, introduced themselves to each other, and had a merry time. This was their first social activity in a long time. Lieutenant Waddell, however, was rather subdued and aloof in terms of socializing with the other men. He remained that way throughout the entire voyage. After all, he was their leader, and he was the only one who knew where they were going and what they were going to do.

On the same day on the other side of the world, the *Milo* was departing the Bering Sea and heading south for the Sandwich Islands, having completed a successful whaling season. She would now be in search of winter whaling in the southern Pacific during the cold winter season in the Arctic. Furthermore, the Hawes family was ready for some rest and change of pace in Honolulu after several months of hard work in the Arctic. The *Milo* was not alone as there were hundreds of whalers heading south for the winter at this time. This was the season of the year that Secretary Mallory laid out for Captain Waddell to go after the Yankee whalers on their trek from the Arctic to the south in the late fall. Of course, this was planned to take place during the next year when Waddell's Confederate cruiser was scheduled to be there.

Meanwhile, the *Laurel* sighted the Island of Madeira on the sixth day out of Liverpool and before noon dropped anchor in the harbor of Funchal. There was no sign of the *Sea King*. In fact, there was no sign of the *Sea King* the next day, or the day after. Needless to say, there was some uneasiness among the *Laurel* passengers regarding the *Sea King*, as sufficient time had elapsed by the third day to allow her to arrive. Finally, on the evening of the third day, the absentee made her appearance and began signaling, but it was against the rules to leave the harbor after dark. Therefore, the *Laurel* waited until morning and after receiving permission from the authorities, weighed anchor and went out to meet her. With a stiff breeze and a full head of steam, as the *Laurel* neared, she signaled the *Sea King* to round the Desertas, a barren and rocky island lying near

Madeira, and to follow the *Laurel* to a place of rendezvous. The *Sea King* followed in her wake and after three hours, they found a perfect place to transfer passengers, armament, and supplies from the *Laurel* to the *Sea King*.

Time was of the essence as they were aware that United States warships were out there searching for any such activity, and they could be anywhere in any direction. Therefore, it was incumbent for them to make the transfer in as short a time as possible, since during the transfer operation, they would be like sitting ducks. Once the transfer was done, the *Laurel* would be under little threat, being an English merchant steamer to the unknowing, and the *Sea King* would be able to outrun almost any ship on the seas, particularly federal warships. So they were anxious to get this transfer done quickly.

It was on the morning of October 19, 1864, and both ships were positioned on the leeward and north side of the Desertas. Immediately before the transfer began Captain Waddell announced to all aboard that the *Sea King* was now commissioned as the CSS *Shenandoah* of the Confederate States of America Navy. Those who were to embark on the journey with the *Shenandoah* were excited with the prospects and rewards of this journey and of fighting for their homeland, or for a country that needed their help. Most of the crew members already appointed were sons of the South, and they were ready to go to battle. However there was a lot of work to be done before the *Shenandoah* was ready to embark on its mission.

The *Shenandoah* was anchored in eighteen fathoms as the *Laurel* came to and was lashed alongside of her. The waters were smooth, and the day was clear and bright, and the crew felt a harbinger of success. After about thirteen hours, her decks were loaded with all of the guns, supplies, and ammunition from the *Laurel*, and confusion reigned with all of the items scattered about the ship. Needless to say, in order to convert a merchant steamer into a warship, the *Shenandoah* had to be modified to accommodate all of the different articles of war and supplies. The guns had to be installed and cutouts had to be made to accommodate the guns. The guns had to be secured in their positions on deck so that they could be fired without disrupting other items on the deck. The supplies had to be stored below decks and the powder had to be stored in a safe place. To do all this, there was only one carpenter aboard. Under these conditions, Waddell realized that the conversion of the *Sea King* into the *Shenandoah* was going to take time, and they had to be patient. Normally this kind of work would have been done in the shipyards before going to sea, but in this situation, this was impossible, so the work had to be done at sea. Above all, the crew had to have enough men on board to properly sail this fast cruiser and accomplish its mission to destroy the American whaling fleet on the other side of the world.

The following officers were detailed to Lieutenant Commanding James I. Waddell's command:

William C. Whittle	Lieutenant
John Grimball	Lieutenant
Francis T. Chew	Lieutenant
S. Smith Lee	Lieutenant
Dabney M. Scales	Lieutenant
Charles E. Lining	Passed Assistant Surgeon
F. J. McNulty	Passed Assistant Surgeon
Irving S. Bulloch	Acting Master
O. A. Brown	Midshipman
J. T. Mason	Midshipman

In addition, there were a few men picked from the crew of the CSS *Alabama* who were specially retained and accompanied them on the *Laurel*. These men constituted the nucleus of the force which Waddell needed to organize and recruit at the place of rendezvous. Among these men was George Harwood, the chief boatswain's mate of the late *Alabama*, a good seaman, an experienced man-of-wars sailor, and one calculated to carry weight and influence with a crew composed exclusively of foreigners. Waddell determined to give him the appointment of acting boatswain as soon as the *Laurel* cleared the channel and to explain to him their mission to the North Pacific. Waddell was sure Harwood would assist materially in persuading the men intended for the cruiser to reship for the Confederate service. Once they arrived at the rendezvous place, there would be as little communication with the shore as possible, and none of the officers or men would be allowed to go ashore. Waddell took every precaution to prevent information reaching the shore as to the character of their visit and the destination of the cruise.

After the transfer from the *Laurel*, there were ten persons on the list of acting appointments, as follows:

List of Acting Appointments:

Matthew O'Brian	Chief Engineer	Louisiana
W. H. Codd	Assistant Engineer	Maryland
W. Breedlove Smith	Paymaster	Louisiana
George Harwood	Boatswain	England

John Lynch	Carpenter	New York
Henry Alcot	Sailmaker	England
John L. Guy	Gunner	England

And Petty Officers

Joshua T. Minor	Master's Mate	Virginia
Lodge Cotton	Master's Mate	Maryland
C. E. Hunt	Master's Mate	Virginia

Over and above the transfer itself, the most important immediate objective was to recruit sufficient additional crew members, so the ship could be sailed and managed properly. Waddell's first order of business was to sign up additional crew members from the *Laurel* and the previous *Sea King*, and this took place soon after the transfer was complete. Accordingly, all of the men from the *Laurel* and *Shenandoah* were called before the quarterdeck of the *Shenandoah*. There, he informed them of the changed character of the *Sea King*, read his commission to them to convert the steamer *Sea King* into the Confederate cruiser CSS *Shenandoah*. He then pictured to them a brilliant and dashing cruise, and asked them to join the service of the Confederate States of America and to assist an oppressed and brave people in their resistance to a powerful and arrogant northern government. Out of eighty present, only twenty-three men were willing to venture on such service in spite of a very good compensation offer, and most shipped for six months only. Those who declined to serve on the *Shenandoah* were directed to go on board the *Laurel*. Following this, two persons were added to the list of acting appoints, as follows:

List of Acting Appointments

| John Hutchinson | 2nd Assistant Engineer | Scotland |
| Earnst Muggufrey | 3rd Assistant Engineer | Ireland |

All told, there were a total of forty-seven persons aboard, including twenty-four officers. This was a feeble force of men to handle the work involved in sailing this cruiser on a mission around the world. There was still a great deal of work to be done to clear the desks of every conceivable item needed to conduct the mission. Confusion reigned supreme, and they realized the almost endless labor before them, but they had every encouragement in the belief that they had a well-built and fast ship under their feet, and courageous hearts to sail her. Waddell had every intention of adding additional men to those already aboard by adding men from captured ships as well as men from various ports along the way. In the meantime, they had to do first things first. They had to get the vessel in shipshape condition as soon as possible, but Waddell wanted to leave the rendezvous area right away. The *Shenandoah* left on October 20 after the entire crew of men and officers worked hard to weigh the anchor. The officers had in most cases never had to work this hard before, but now they were needed help raise the anchor as there were not enough men to get the job done without the added manpower.

The guns and cannon were put into place the next day. They mounted two eight-inch shell guns and one thirty-two pounder Whitworth rifle. The following day the second Whitworth rifle was installed. Whitworth guns were made in England, were very accurate, and were used extensively by the South during the war. These guns constituted their battery of firepower along with two twelve pounders, aft, which were already in position when the ship left Liverpool. The carpenter, supported by Lieutenant Lee, pierced the side of the ship for the portholes to accommodate the weapons, and otherwise all officers and seamen worked together to transfer items above and below deck as things began to look shipshape. Still there was much to do in temporarily disposing of the ammunition in a place of safety and giving the ship a general cleaning up.

At this time on the other side of the world, the *Milo* was cruising close to the Sandwich Islands, and all those aboard were looking forward to a change of pace in Honolulu. The *Milo* crew had worked hard during the summer season in the Bering Sea, and the result was a ship's hold filled with barrels of whale oil and whalebone. The *Milo* needed to offload its whale harvest, and Honolulu was the place to do it. They needed to do this in order to make room for future oil and bone products, as they planned to continue this voyage for at least another year or so. On October 26, the *Milo* dropped anchor in the Port of Honolulu and spent several days there on business and pleasure. Captain Hawes made arrangements with the whaleship *Helen Mar* of New Bedford to load over five thousand pounds of whalebone for delivery in New Bedford upon her arrival there. He also made arrangements to offload some two thousand barrels of oil to be sold on the open market in Honolulu. After these arrangements, the *Milo* was ready to start a new whaling voyage. Jessie, along with Addie and infant Fred, spent most of the time ashore in Honolulu.

They visited stores for shopping, parks for relaxation and the Chase Gallery on Fort Street, to have more pictures taken while in Honolulu this time. After all, most parents want pictures of their children, and this was not possible in those days aboard ship on the high seas. Addie was now six years old, and baby Fred was a year and a half. Jessie and the family treasured all of the pictures taken during their visits to Honolulu. Also during this stopover, Captain Hawes arranged for an extravagant luau for the entire ship's crew under the palm trees. This was a fitting contrast to the frozen Arctic and a sailor's fare of "salt horse." Needless to say, the ship's crew had a delightful time of it with food of every kind they could eat and with plenty of time to eat, tell sea stories, and just relax.

Meanwhile, back in the southern Atlantic, the *Shenandoah* was sailing south, and at the same time, the crew continued the work of preparing the cruiser for her mission of destruction. By October 22, four days after the commissioning, the guns were all in their carriages and the decks were clear for the most part. Some items were missing and they would have to be supplied by captured ships at sea. Waddell's orders were to get supplies from captured ships during the voyage. He was well aware of this requirement and based his planning on being able to use this procedure to accommodate his needs. One of the items missing was the gun tackles which were used to position the guns. Waddell planned to find these from captured ships, but, in the meantime, he had to improvise until they were on hand. Consequently the gun carriages were secured fore and aft of the deck, close to the ship's side, and in the absence of bolts, straps were passed through the scuppers and toggled outside to which the guns were lashed.

On October 25, the powder was removed from Waddell's cabin to a small apartment under the cabin. It was also on a deck which was below the surface of the ocean, and divided from the steerage deck by a strong open lattice work with a heavy canvas cover tacked to the partition. The powder was better protected there than in Waddell's cabin, but still in an insecure place. This was one of the problems associated with converting a merchant steamer into a wartime cruiser. Waddell later remarked that only those who have done this work on a broad and friendless ocean can appreciate the anxieties accompanying such a task. Another area lacking was the furniture for the officer's quarters. There was a shortage of everything one would like to have in his quarters, such as dressers, chairs, and so on. These would also have to be procured from captured ships along the way. This was the plan. Everyone aboard accepted these shortcomings, but were comforted by the excitement of the voyage they were taking and the possibilities of military success and prize money.

Captain Waddell was the only anxious person aboard. At the times he was amused by the actions of his officers and men. He would be distracted a moment later by the thoughts of the nature of his command and the important interests confided in him. No one had ever been given this much responsibility on the world scene to make legal and ethical decisions based upon his own best judgment. He was to be responsible for making decisions as the situations developed. The outcome of his decisions would determine the success or failure of the mission. This was a very demanding responsibility for one man.

On October 26, the same day the *Milo* dropped anchor in the Port of Honolulu, the *Shenandoah* was putting on the final touches of becoming operational as a Confederate cruiser. Coal which had been dumped in the berth deck by the *Laurel* was finally removed to the side bunkers on the ship until they were full. The remaining coal was then moved to the aft berth deck and out of the way, and a cover was placed over the coal to keep it out of sight and as dry as possible. By now, it was found that there was ample room to berth two hundred men comfortably, exclusive of that area converted into a coal bunker. The complement of men for the *Shenandoah* was fixed at 120, even though they were well short of that number on this day in October, 1864.

Waddell took to the offense immediately. He later wrote that he was convinced that it was the only way for the feeble to act toward a strong foe. He knew it may be called audacity, but it was pluck, and your enemy knows he may be hurt some way; and the very respect it engenders is very often the safeguard.

The ship had now reached a point in the southern Atlantic off the coast of Africa and was constantly receiving heavy rain and violent squalls of wind. To the horror of those on board, the decks leaked like sieves, and the seams of the hull were open enough to admit a fine spray from the sea which had spent itself on her sides. Aside from these inconveniences, there was still much to do in the temporary moving of ammunition to a place of safety and in giving the ship a general house cleaning

9. Heading South and Taking Prizes

On October 28, the *Shenandoah* began her first chase. The lookout aloft reported a sail and in an instant, there was a great deal of excitement.

"Where away?" Yelled the officer of the deck as he looked hurriedly around the horizon.

"About two points on the lee bow, sir, standing the same as we are."

"Can you make her out?"

"Aye, aye, sir, a square rigged vessel. We are approaching her fast and I see her better now. A barque with long mast heads, and she looks American."

"Very good. Let me know when she shows her colors."[30]

This was a very exciting time for this skeleton crew on the first few days of its voyage. From every part of the ship, the limited crew took positions in the rigging and anywhere else to observe what was going on and passed spy-glasses from hand to hand in the moments that followed. Opinions were anxiously exchanged as to what the stranger would prove to be. Within an hour of the first observation, it became clear that she was flying the English ensign flag from her peak, but she looked so American that Captain Waddell concluded that he should board her and have a look at her papers.

A blank cartridge was fired across her bow, and she understood the signal. She immediately hove to, after which an officer from the *Shenandoah* was dispatched to board her and ascertain her true nature. She proved to be the barque *Monque*, American built, but she had been sold to the English, as had been the case for many of the American-built merchant ships during that time, mainly due to the threat from Confederate cruisers. The captain had his wife and family with him, and they were quite content in their little home on the sea. Under the circumstances, the *Shenandoah* crew was satisfied to the man to see that this little ship was protected by the flag she flew and was safe from capture.

Immediately after allowing the *Monque* to proceed on her voyage, two sails were spotted by the lookout. One sail was on the starboard quarter and the other on the port beam. Waddell decided to cautiously avoid a confrontation with these two ships as the *Shenandoah* was understaffed and could only man two of the eight-inch guns leaving two-thirds of the battery unmanned. Under these conditions, it was probable that the two strangers were much stronger than the undermanned *Shenandoah,* and so it was determined to avoid the confrontation. Waddell reluctantly decided to permit these two ships to proceed on their way unmolested and, without fanfare, the *Shenandoah* continued on her southerly heading along the western African coast.

On October 30 about nine o'clock in the morning, another sail was reported off the port bow. It was positioned to be heading southward and westward and within easy reach of the *Shenandoah.* Waddell ordered steam and the *Shenandoah* began its chase. In about two hours, the barque *Alena,* displaying the American flag from her peak, was brought to a halt after firing a blank cartridge across her bow. On reaching the vessel, the captain was informed that his craft was a prize of the Confederate States of America and ordered him to get his papers and proceed on board the *Shenandoah.* Shortly thereafter, the *Alena*'s captain arrived on board the *Shenandoah,* accompanied by one of the

Shenandoah's officers, with a tin box containing his documents. He was told that his ship was to be condemned and that he should gather his clothing and other personal property that he might wish to preserve. The *Alena* was on her first voyage, well equipped, beautifully clean, and nicely built as reported by the boarding party. At this time, the *Shenandoah* was in the northern Atlantic at 15° north latitude and 26° west longitude, in the vicinity of the Cape Verde Islands.

The captain took it very hard and remarked to Cornelius Hunt, the Confederate officer escorting him, "I tell you what, maty, I've a daughter at home that this craft was named for, and it goes against me cursedly to see her destroyed."

Hunt replied, "Neither myself nor my brother officers have any disposition to do you a personal injury. Our orders are to prey upon the commerce of the United States and in carrying them out, private individuals have to suffer, as the widow and orphans of the South have done and are doing from the invading armies acting under the instructions of your government."[31]

The captain answered, "I know it is only the fortune of war, and I must take my chances with the rest, but it's damned hard, and I only hope I shall have an opportunity of returning your polite attentions before this mess is over, that's all."

The *Alena* was the first capture for the *Shenandoah* and more importantly, a valuable prize in that she furnished the blocks for the gun tackles, a variety of other blocks that were also needed, and cotton canvas which was suitable for sail making. In addition, an assortment of furniture and dining utensils were taken on board along with a supply of provisions that would supplement items missing at the time of commissioning. They would be useful during the remainder of the voyage. Moreover, five seamen and a coal passer entered their names on the shipping articles making the crew number for the *Shenandoah* now at twenty-nine. The rest of the *Alena* crew were confined in the top-gallant forecastle while the officers were accommodated in the wardroom and treated with much respect. Needless to say, the officers greatly appreciated their treatment, especially the captain, who remarked that he "little anticipated such kindness from an enemy." The captain, however, remained aloof and refused any offers of refreshment from his captors. On the other hand, during the next several days, he was quite talkative and told many stories of his own experiences to anyone who would listen.

On the night of the *Alena*'s capture, Captain Waddell contemplated on methods to destroy this valuable ship and later wrote that it is better to leave a prize so disabled and injured as to be formidable enough to endanger the navigation of the ocean. More frequently, he wrote, fire must be resorted to and that there is no escape from that ruthless element. In this case, he elected to destroy the *Alena* by knocking a hole in her bottom just below the waterline. This caused the vessel to sink rapidly and finally disappear, leaving only a few pieces of plank floating over the great abyss which closed over her in a very short time.

To prepare a vessel for destruction by fire, he later wrote, first remove all living animals, take out all useful equipment which may be wanted, discover what combustibles are in her hold, such as tar, pitch and turpentine, and see to the removal of all gunpowder. Combustibles should then be scattered throughout the vessel, bulkheads torn down and piled up in her cabins and forecastle. All hatches should be open and all halyards let go, so that the sails may hang loosely and the yards counter braced. Fire should then be taken from the cooking stove in the galley and deposited in various parts of her hold and on the deck. If the vessel is very old, she will burn like tinderbox.[32] Waddell later went on to write that this painful duty could have been avoided if they had been allowed to take their prizes into port for adjudication. He did not like this part of doing his duty, but it was necessary under the rules of war at that time in order to accomplish his mission.

Apparently, the first capture produced a marked difference in the bearing of the crew. The work pressed steadily upon them, but they were now supported by an enhanced crew, gaining strength in numbers from their captives. Whenever they heard the cry of "Sail Ho!" the crew reacted by manifestations of joy. After working hours, those who looked for amusement collected in gangways and gave themselves up to dancing, jumping, singing, or spinning yarns, in which the narrator was the hero. "Jack is easily entertained and simple in his tastes,"[33] wrote Waddell in his memoirs later on. "Jack" is a term he used to refer to the seamen in general on his ship.

From this first encounter with the enemy, the *Shenandoah* continued on its journey southward heading off the coast of Africa, always on the lookout for sails on the horizon. Excitement took over the ship and the crew was anxiously prepared for another encounter. Between November 5 and 13, the *Shenandoah* successfully chased, captured and destroyed the following merchant ships: the schooner *Charter Oak* of Boston, the bark *D. Godfrey* of Boston, the brig *Susan* of New York, and the American schooner *Lizzie M. Stacy* of Boston. She was able to transfer numerous provisions from these vessels into her own stores as well as hardware, furniture, and navigational equipment. By this time there were ten men who had signed on with the *Shenandoah* from the captured vessels, bringing the total to thirty-five new crew members. During this period, the rebel ship made contact with the Danish brig *Anna Jane* and made arrangements with her captain to take prisoners from the first capture, the *Alena*. She also chased and captured, but ransomed the American clipper ship, *Kate Prince*, out of Whales. This ship was ransomed because women were on board, and Waddell did not want to increase his prisoner roster with more women. All remaining prisoners on board at that time were transferred over to the *Kate Prince* as part of the ransom agreement. On the same day, Waddell chased and captured the bark *Adelaide Pendergrast* out of Baltimore. However, the *Pendergrast* was simply ransomed when it was discovered that she had been sold to non-American parties in Rio de Janeiro. At the end of the day on November 13, the *Shenandoah* approached the equator

174

and headed into the South Atlantic Ocean. She had already proven to be a worthy investment for the South, and she was already beginning to increase her crew roster from captured vessels.

Still later on that day when darkness was approaching, the *Shenandoah* crossed the equator, and although this was a ship of war, certain ceremonies having to do with his majesty, Neptune, were taken according to the laws of the sea at their rightful place on board. Some of the men had been over the line before, but there were a good number of novices, officers, and seamen alike, that had to go through the rituals, and they were all submitted to the initiatory rites. Needless to say, the event was anticipated with more than an ordinary interest by all on board.

This continued until the late hours, and all hands had a frolicking time singing, dancing, and joking around. It was even more enjoyable to most of the crew when it was learned that two or three of the younger seamen actually believed they had been in the presence of the veritable Neptune. It was only after a considerable period of time that they discovered that they had been duped by some of their own shipmates. This was a day no one would forget.

On this very same day on the other side of the world, the *Milo* weighed anchor in the Port of Honolulu for winter whaling off the coast of California. Jessie Hawes was thankful for the three-week stopover in Honolulu with the hotels, restaurants, shopping, and sightseeing that the island offered. The children, Addie and young Fred, really enjoyed being on land where they could run and play without the rolling and constant up and down motion of being at sea. Addie and even young Fred enjoyed some time on the beach playing with the constant waves coming in and going out. Jessie was glad that she was able to have more pictures taken during this stopover at the Cosmopolitan Photographic Gallery, as the family had been at sea for such a long time, and the children were quickly growing older. The children took it in their stride and had fun with the picture taking. Captain Hawes was not overly anxious to go through all the various poses and other whims of the photographer, but after a number of objections, he went along with the request from Jessie and had some pictures taken. Jessie was dressed in the latest fashion, so that the portraits would reflect that of an aristocratic lady, which she was. It also served as a record of their visits to Honolulu and one that would be of historical value in the future. All in all, it was a great time for the children as well as for the parents. However, business before pleasure was the decision by Captain Hawes, so on that fifteenth day in November the *Milo* weighed anchor and went back to sea. At 4:00 PM in the afternoon the harbor pilot went on board, guided the *Milo* out of the harbor, and was discharged at 5:00 PM.

Jonathan and Jessie Hawes[34]

The *Milo* took a course that would take her to the southern coast of California where there would hopefully be some good winter whaling. Two days later, still amongst the Sandwich Islands, the *Milo* gammed with a whaler out of New Bedford, the ship *Wollastan*, for a social visit and exchange of news. The *Milo* would spend the next several months in the southern Pacific, off the coast of California. When the next spring approached, the *Milo* would head back to the Bering Sea for the best whaling of all, in terms of productivity and profitability.

Back in the United States, a week earlier on November 8, President Abraham Lincoln was reelected president, defeating Democrat George B. McClellan. Lincoln carried all but three states with 55 percent of the popular vote and 212 of 233 electoral votes. "I earnestly believe that the consequences of this day's work will be to the lasting advantage, if not the very salvation, of the country," Lincoln told his supporters. Moreover, Union General William Tecumseh Sherman had captured Atlanta in July 1864, and this is believed to have helped President Lincoln get reelected.

On November 15, the day that the *Shenandoah* crossed the equator and the day that the *Milo* weighed anchor in the Port of Honolulu, General Sherman began his march to the sea from Atlanta, Georgia, to Savannah, laying a sixty-mile swath of destruction all the way and letting the world know that war is hell. By that time, the South was on its last legs, and the war was nearing an end. However, the signals of the war's end were not heard on the CSS *Shenandoah* and Captain Waddell set the course for Australia by way of the Cape of Good Hope, South Africa. He knew his objective was the Yankee whaling fleet that would gather in the Bering Sea the next summer. His mission was to destroy the American whalers and cause a significant impact on the economy of the North, one that could help the Confederacy succeed. This was a bold maneuver for one single Confederate cruiser to accomplish, and one that was ultimately doomed to failure. But, at that time, Captain Waddell was in no mood to think negative. He was determined to go forward in order to achieve the objectives of his mission of destruction. And so, he pressed onward to do just that to the best of his ability, to the detriment of those Yankee whalers who would come within his sight.

Coincidently, at Newport News, Virginia, on November 28, the CSS *Florida* reached the end of her strange career when she sank under dubious circumstances after a collision with the USAT *Alliance*, a troop ferry. A court order had been issued to return the *Florida* to Brazil following the capture in Brazilian waters, as Brazil was a neutral nation.

Following the capture of the *Florida*, it was the intention of the United States to convert her into a federal cruiser, which the Union Navy sorely needed. The sinking was most likely done at Admiral David Dixon Porter's encouragement, if not his behest. The *Florida* could therefore not be delivered to Brazil in satisfaction of the final court order and could not rejoin the ranks of the Confederate Navy. Furthermore, it could not be converted to a federal cruiser either. This also meant that the Confederates had only one cruiser of significance out there on the seas, the CSS *Shenandoah*.

On the same day, November 28, fourteen days after crossing the equator, the *Shenandoah* found itself at nearly 27° south latitude, below the equator and midway between Brazil and South Africa. They came in contact with many sails, but none were Yankee. Finally, they came in sight of white sails ahead that took on a Yankee profile. Captain Waddell increased steam to pick up speed in order to overtake the ship. The ship turned out to be the Yankee whaleship, *Edward*, out of New Bedford, and just what Waddell was looking for. After a shot from the *Shenandoah* over the *Edward*'s bow, the *Edward* came alongside and surrendered, having no weapons with which to fight. The skipper of the *Edward*, Captain Worth, was most cordial under the circumstances, and upon arrival on board the *Shenandoah* with his ship's papers, he immediately won the respect of all on board the *Shenandoah*.

He greeted the officer of the deck with these words, "Good afternoon, gentlemen, you have a fine ship here for a cruiser."

"Yes sir," replied the officer of the deck, "and that ship of yours appears to have sailed the seas for many a year."

"Her keel was laid before you or I was thought of," replied the skipper.

He continued to carry on with the men of the *Shenandoah* as though this was a social event, or gam, and talked about whaling and life at sea. The men felt badly about having to destroy his ship, but these were the things that happened in a war. Since whalers were known to have more provisions on board than other ships at sea, there were a number of these provisions that were transferred over to the *Shenandoah*. The prisoners helped with the transfer of these items. By the end of the day, all of the provisions that were to be transferred were on board the *Shenandoah*, and Captain Waddell ordered the *Edward* to be destroyed by fire. A few hours later, there was nothing left of the *Edward*; it had been burned and scuttled. The prisoners taken on board had been put in irons for the night and the skipper and officers of the *Edward* were guests of Captain Waddell in the ward room. All other prisoners were put on three whale boats that were towed by the *Shenandoah* as there was not sufficient room on board to house all of the prisoners. As soon as this arrangement was stable, the *Shenandoah* took course for the island of Tristan D'Cunha, where Captain Waddell planned to discharge the prisoners.

Tristan D'Cunha is an island almost midway between the coast of southern Brazil and the coast of southern Africa. The island has a volcanic mountain over eight thousand feet high, so it can be seen from a great distance away. It is about the same latitude in the southern hemisphere as the Cape of Good Hope, but over a thousand miles to the west. It lies about 15° west longitude and 40° south latitude and is a long way from anywhere else in the world. The day after the *Edward* was scuttled, the mountain on Tristan de Cunha could be seen in the distance. Captain Waddell ordered a course for the island and was anxious to get there and discharge the prisoners. Upon arrival at the island, the *Shenandoah* steamed for a suitable location to drop anchor and take care of any business at hand. They soon caught sight of an English flag close to shore and dropped anchor a short distance from the shore. This took place on the December 6, 1864.

The Island of Tristan D'Cunha encompassed mainly the mountain and surrounding low-lying plains which offered a place to raise domestic animals and grow plants for food for the inhabitants. The entire island was only a few square miles in area, and one could not travel far without running into the ocean. There were about forty inhabitants living there under the rule of an exiled Englishman who had been there for many, many years. He was the ruler and self-appointed king of the island.

Upon nearing a place to drop anchor, a boat appeared close by, and the principal occupant was offering for sale, fresh eggs, milk, chickens, meat, and other commodities that were, needless to say, readily desired by the *Shenandoah* and its crew. The islanders did not recognize the flag being flown by the *Shenandoah* and inquired as to its origin. When informed that this was a Confederate cruiser and that they had thirty-five prisoners to contribute to the population.

"Where the devil did you get your prisoners?" asked one of the astonished natives.

"From a Yankee whaler not far from here," responded one of the officers.

"And may I ask what happened to the ship?"

"We burned and sunk her!"

"Oh my, is that they way you get rid of vessels you fall in with?"

"Only if they belong to the Yankees, not otherwise."

"Well, that's your business, but I would say that the United States would not go along with your methods, and I guess they will be out there looking for you to give you the same treatment."[35]

After this exchange, it was business as usual. The prisoners were transported to shore along with supplies of coffee, tea, sugar, and other articles necessary for their temporary relocation. It was also observed that were a good number of the gentler sex on the island that could use some friendly relationships with the prisoners and that was probably something certain to happen to the delight of the native girls as well as the prisoners. Along with the prisoner settlement, the business of procuring the supplies offered by the natives went rather smoothly, and as soon as all supplies were transferred on board, Captain Waddell ordered the anchor weighed. On December 7, the *Shenandoah* sailed out of the harbor. A short time later, only the tip of the mountain of Tristan D'Cunha was in view, and very shortly after that went out of view altogether.

10. Around Good Hope to Australia

It was discovered during the stopover at Tristan D'Cunha that the propeller shaft was cracked and needed repair. Captain Waddell elected to sail to Melbourne, Australia, without steam in order to avoid further damage to the shaft. Steam would not be needed between Tristan and Australia, but would certainly be needed later on when they reached the North Pacific. Captain Waddell considered having repairs made in Cape Town, but decided against that option due to the possibility of a federal cruiser being in the vicinity during a stopover there. Melbourne also had facilities that could be used for maintenance and repair prior to her venture into the Pacific, and this would be a safer place for the *Shenandoah*. Consequently, Waddell elected to press on to Australia.

Captain Waddell later wrote that after departing Tristan D'Cunha, he learned that the USS *Dacotah* made a stopover there and rescued the prisoners who were left on shore. The *Dacotah* left Tristan and immediately headed for Cape Town in search of the *Shenandoah*. The *Dacotah* was a steam sloop during the Civil War. She was named for the Dakota Indian tribe. *Dacotah* was launched March 23, 1859, at the Norfolk Navy Yard and commissioned May 1, 1860. During the time she was a commissioned vessel, the USS *Dacotah* was involved in many different naval operations during the Civil War from blockade work to searching for Confederate cruisers like the *Alabama* and *Florida*. She participated in the search for the captured steamer *Chesapeake*, turned raider, during December, 1863. During the search for the *Shenandoah* following her arrival in Cape Town, the *Dacotah* was unable to gain any knowledge of the whereabouts of the *Shenandoah* and therefore was not able to help in any way to interrupt the mission of the *Shenandoah*. In the end, the USS *Dacotah* was decommissioned on May 30, 1873, and no other U.S. Navy vessel has ever been named the *Dacotah* since. Needless to say, the *Shenandoah* continued on her way to the Pacific Ocean without interruption.

Granted, the United States Navy did manage to destroy both the *Alabama* and the *Florida*. However, the American commanders were lucky to learn at the time that each Confederate vessel was being serviced for maintenance and repair and was in a harbor and unable to maneuver. The advantage was with the federal warships, and they had the upper edge in both cases. The *Alabama* was destroyed by

187

superior weaponry, and the ability to choose the battle site was enjoyed by the USS *Kearsage*. The *Florida* was captured after the surrender by a junior officer while the vessel was docked in the absence of the captain. These two Confederate vessels were a menace to Yankee shipping and by neutralizing both of them, the United States Navy was able to rest easier. Now, they had mainly the CSS *Shenandoah* to contend with. One would believe that this would be an easy task for the federal navy, but this was simply not the case.

Northern intelligence had no clue as to the whereabouts or the intentions of the *Shenandoah*. Although there was knowledge of the *Shenandoah*'s victims and her limited port calls, no one was able to guess where she was at any given time or predict where she was going. Communications were slow compared to today's standards; and intelligence gathering was sporadic at best and never produced a rational plan to defend against Confederate ships at sea. The size of the federal navy was insufficient to provide effective blockade coverage of the southern coast, not to mention intercepting Confederate ships on the high seas. In other words, the United States was not prepared to neutralize Confederate naval initiatives, and therefore the Civil War lasted much longer than it would have otherwise.

The lesson here is that we should never again allow the naval forces of the United States to be unable to protect United States interests, wherever they are, on the oceans of the world.

In this case, the *Shenandoah* was essentially free to travel without any disruption to anywhere it wanted to go on the Pacific Ocean side of the world, and destroy any merchant vessel or other unarmed target in its sight. Secondly, the *Shenandoah* was not even a formidable warship and could have been destroyed easily by any federal warship in a one-on-one contest. Even Captain Waddell was not completely aware of the freedom he had at his disposal, particularly as he was approaching his target area, the Pacific Ocean. But, he was aware of his advantages: the fact that his targets were essentially unarmed, the federal navy could not locate his position, and the *Shenandoah*'s speed could outrun the federal warships. However, now that his speed was compromised with the crack in the propeller shaft, he knew he must sail on to Australia where he would have the shaft repaired and consequently regain his speed advantage.

The run between Tristan and the Cape of Good Hope was not an easy sail. The weather began to go from bad to worse just days out of Tristan. Those aboard could hardly believe that the *Shenandoah* could withstand the beating it was taking from the volatile sea. The waves were mountainous and frequently covered the main deck with ocean water. Eating was a disaster, as the ship heaved and rolled to such an extent that it was impossible to keep food and dishes on the galley table. As soon as food was served, water would flow into the ward room and as the ship heaved and recovered while disrupting all articles on the table. It was a very disheartening experience for all aboard, and it lasted for days and days. Most of those on board were certain the ship would be torn apart and leave them in the mighty ocean with no means to survive. It was an experience that no one ever wanted to relive or even think about again. It was a terrifying time for all on the *Shenandoah*, and they all hoped for some relief as soon as possible. On December 11, the *Shenandoah* crossed the Greenwich Meridian and was halfway to Cape Town from Tristan D'Cunha, but still about five hundred miles away. Waddell's initial instructions were to pass south of the Cape of Good Hope by the first of January, 1865, but on December 17, the *Shenandoah* was east of that meridian with a west wind following fast. The speed of the *Shenandoah* varied with the speed of the wind. The wind was from the west and helped them with good speed in spite of the lack of steam. Captain Waddell felt he had gone through a bad dream, but was now going to make a heading change to get into better conditions. They were approaching a point to the south of the Cape of Good Hope which put them off the coast of South Africa on December 25, Christmas Day. A Christmas dinner had been prepared with captured supplies, but it was impossible to sit long enough to enjoy the meal under the circumstances. Most of the dishes were scattered off the table, and the food went everywhere, but there was still enough left to feed those on board and also for them to consider this an unfortunate incident in a sailor's life.

During this holiday season on the other side of the world, the *Milo* was located off the coast of California where the weather was warm and the whales were close by. This was the time of year that the whalers vacated the northern Pacific and headed south for the winter. Whaling was not as good, but it was acceptable and profitable, and it was certainly the best option for that time of year. Captain Hawes did not want to waste time and lose any opportunity to make the trip more rewarding from a profit point of view.

On December 25, Christmas Day, the *Milo* crew was busy cleaning up after whaling activity during the several days

191

before. But, since this was a very special holiday and one that was observed by most of the crew, they were somewhat laid back and reflective on that day. Captain Hawes acted as a minister and performed a Christmas service for the entire crew and family at eleven o'clock in the morning, and this put everything in a proper perspective. Back home in Massachusetts, Captain Hawes was a member of the Congregational Church and served on the church vestry; he was certainly qualified to perform the service. A Christmas dinner of turkey and all the dressings were prepared by the cook, and it was a special meal enjoyed by all. Addie and young Fred received Christmas presents that Jessie had purchased during the last stopover in Honolulu. Addie was now nearly seven years old, and Fred was almost two. They were growing up fast and learning more and more each passing day. Jessie made sure to teach the children during the time at sea. As a consequence, the children were quite well educated for their age, because she was able to concentrate on the subjects that were important to them during their younger years.

Later on during Christmas Day, the *Milo* and the *J.D. Thompson*, a whaler out of New London, got together for a gam, and exchanged news along with social pleasantries for

192

a couple of hours during visits to each other's ship. This was a good time for both parties and one that would be remembered for a long time. Later on, in 1871, the *J.D. Thompson* was lost in the ice on the Bering Sea during a severe freeze which also caused thirty-two other whalers to be destroyed by the ice. The year 1871 was a terrible year for the whaling fleet. Also lost in that freeze was the ship *Roman*, which was the first ship that Captain Hawes sailed on to begin his whaling career. It was also the ship for his second voyage.

By December 29, Captain Waddell decided to head in a new direction, and soon the weather turned for the better as rapidly as it had gone bad many days before. Waddell decided to head more north and east to find relief from the bad weather in the lower latitudes. He later wrote that if he ever took this route again, he would stay above the weather one finds below the south fortieth parallel.[36] The next day, a sail was spotted astern of the *Shenandoah*. Captain Waddell ordered the ship to slow down in order to have the stranger catch up and be recognized. Soon thereafter, the stranger was close to the stern of the *Shenandoah* and flew the flag of the United States, just what Waddell was looking for. It was the *Delphine*, out of Bangor, Maine, and heading to Akyab, Burma, to take on board a load of rice intended for the use of the federal armies. Waddell ordered the Confederate flag to be raised on the *Shenandoah*, thereby showing its colors to the *Delphine*. Following that, he then fired a shot across the bow of the stranger. Shortly thereafter, Captain Nichols of the *Delphine* came on board and was advised that his vessel was a prize and would be destroyed. He pleaded with the officer on deck that his wife was taken ill by the shot that was fired and would probably die if subjected to transfer at sea to the *Shenandoah*. Waddell's surgeon visited the lady and reported back that she was in good health and would not be at risk if transferred. The transfer was accomplished without fanfare. Soon two women and a child were safely landed on deck.

After arriving, Mrs. Nichols confronted Captain Waddell and asked in a very loud voice, "What do you intend to so with us, and where are you taking us?"

Waddell replied, "To St. Paul Island, madam, if you like."

"Oh no, never, I would rather remain with you."[37]

Waddell was surprised to see that that the sick lady was a tall, finely proportioned woman of twenty-six years, in robust health, evidently possessing a will and voice of her own. That evening, all livestock was taken from the *Delphine* and the ship was burned and scuttled. Captain Nichols and family were treated like passengers and took over Captain Waddell's quarters, although no one on board thought the prisoners appreciated the good treatment they received. Most of the crew from the *Delphine* joined the *Shenandoah*, increasing the crew to forty-seven. This all took place on December 31, the last day of the year, and the forth year of the Civil War. Waddell contemplated the devastation the war had caused so many people and wondered when it would end and what good would come from it. He decided to make a stopover at St. Paul Island in order to search for any Yankee whalers and take appropriate action if any were found there.

On January 2, the *Shenandoah* came into view of St. Paul Island. As they approached the island, Master's Mate Cornelius Hunt noticed that Mrs. Nichols appeared somewhat disturbed and apprehensive and had tears in her eyes.

"Did you suppose," he asked, "that you would be stranded on this out-of-the-way spot?"

"That was my husband's expectation," she said, "and I presume that his fears were not without foundation."

"Let me assure you to the contrary, madam, and please be good enough to explain how you and your husband came to imagine that the commander of the *Shenandoah* was capable of leaving a whole ship's company in such a place."

"Well," she replied, "they tell terrible stories at home about the outrages committed upon helpless men and women by your rebel cruisers. The papers have been full of them and I naturally supposed that the stories were based on fact, at least."[38]

Following this discourse, Mrs. Nichols went to her stateroom and returned with a copy of an article written by a lady correspondent for a New York publication. The article was written about the encounter of a Yankee vessel with the Confederate cruiser CSS *Alabama*, and told of horribly evil and sadistic results, totally made up of falsehoods. After all, the Confederates did at least treat all unarmed prisoners with utmost respect, always. That was simply the way they went about their business throughout all of the encounters they had with Yankee shipping.

Officer Hunt was quite amused and took the article to the wardroom where the entire crew had many a laugh for the several days of reading the article over and over. Needless to say, Mrs. Nichols was quite relieved to learn that they would not be stranded on this desolate island in the middle of nowhere.

St. Paul is a small volcanic island about forty miles south of the main island of Amsterdam and both are far away from any other place on earth. These two islands are part of a group of three French colonies, with the main island, Reunion Island, located far away off the coast of Madagascar. St. Paul Island is located in the Indian Ocean midway between Africa and Australia. Reunion Island is the seat of government of the three islands and, at the time, was governed by Governor Rondoney, who was a former officer in the French Army. Rondoney fit in very well in this position and governed this very small but widespread island group with class. The islands conducted most of their business with Madagascar and other ports in Africa by supplying seafood and also by repairing chronometers. The repair service was used by many merchant vessels that made port calls at Madagascar. Otherwise there was very little other activity going on there.

St. Paul Island is another story. Captain Waddell had sent a team ashore to search for evidence of any Yankees and to make plans to neutralize them, if found. The team reported that it had met two Frenchmen during their search for Yankees. They appeared to be quite happy with their life there while waiting for their own ship to return. They had been left on the island by a French whaler some time before while the whaler visited the island of Amsterdam to the north.

Following the report of the search party, there were several officers and men on the *Shenandoah* who asked permission to go ashore and do some fishing and exploring. After all, they had been at sea for almost three months and had only been on land for a short time at Tristan D'Cunha. Permission was granted by Captain Waddell, so they took a boat and rowed ashore. There they met with the two Frenchmen, exchanged pleasantries and learned how the inhabitants were living and discovered that the two really enjoyed what appeared to be the life of Robinson Crusoe while they remained on the island. The tourists from the *Shenandoah* also did some fishing while ashore and then returned before sunset. Needless to say, on this tropical island, they took in a lot of sunshine and returned quite sunburned from the fishing and blistered from the rowing to and from the island. Later on, the Frenchmen took a small row boat to the *Shenandoah* and brought a number of chickens along with a penguin from the small settlement on the island to exchange for some civilized items, in particular, handkerchiefs which were in short supply. The exchange was welcomed by both parties. Captain Waddell, however, was ready to move on to Australia and wanted to waste no more time. Early the next morning, Waddell ordered the anchors weighed and sails set, and the *Shenandoah* left St. Paul Island. It was January 3 and Australia was a few weeks away by sail. He wanted to get there as quickly as possible in order to arrive in time for letters to be sent on a mail steamer heading back to England from Melbourne on January 26. If they missed that steamer, there would not be another opportunity to send letters to England for a long time.

The weather had changed for the better and the sail out of St. Paul Island was uneventful. The sea was more or less calm, but neither the winds nor sea current were favorable to Waddell's schedule. Steam was used on the way out of St. Paul Island, but in order to protect the propeller shaft, Waddell decided to continue with sail only after leaving the vicinity of the island. Needless to say, the prisoners on board were anxious to arrive in Australia and gain their freedom. In the meantime, they had nothing to do but pass time, and this can be very boring at sea. Captain and Mrs. Nichols had the privilege of and spent a lot of time walking on the poop deck, enjoying their relative freedom, but not showing much appreciation. The crew was not fond of Captain or Mrs. Nichols, who made themselves continuously disagreeable. It became such a feeling that the entire ship's complement was anxious to have them depart the ship as soon as possible. This was true for the prisoners as well.

After a few days on course, a sail was spotted, and it was hoped to be another Yankee vessel. This was not to be the case. Upon coming alongside the stranger, the *Shenandoah* raised the English flag and then recognized the flag of the Netherlands flying high on the overtaken vessel. It was the *Nimrod*, an American-built vessel that had been transferred to Dutch owners, and this was certainly out of respect to the Confederate Navy. The papers were all in order and Waddell, of course, honored the change in ownership and showed respect to the captain of the intercepted vessel. On a return call to the *Shenandoah*, the *Nimrod* captain, a grand-looking, white-bearded, old fellow, presented Captain Waddell with a dozen bottles of Otard cognac. This pleased Waddell greatly. Following this visit, the *Nimrod* was free to continue on its own course, and the two ships separated, once and for all. The *Nimrod* captain was long remembered by the entire crew for his colorful, high-spirited and jovial nature.

At the same time, on the other side of the world, the *Milo* was sailing off the coast of Mexico in search of whales. Captain Hawes was certain that this would be a profitable side venture during the winter months as the option of fishing in the Bering Sea at this time of year was impossible. It was too cold and the ice was too dangerous. There was no way to be successful in the North Pacific during the winter season. Jessie and the children enjoyed the rather pleasant weather and the frequent stopovers at ports of call in Mexico as well as Southern California. Furthermore, there were many gams to take place and many friends to revisit out on the high seas. The life of a whaler was not all that bad. During the month of January 1865, the *Milo* captured a rather large number of whales and spent much of the time in processing the whale harvest on board the ship. By the end of January, Captain Hawes began to plan for the next summer's visit to the Bering Sea and was looking forward to a successful harvest. He was not concerned at all about meeting up with a Confederate cruiser as the news about the expected ending of the Civil

War left him with confidence that nothing like this would happen. He first would have to make another stopover in Honolulu in order to sell off the harvest from the winter whaling in the southern Pacific. He had to do this to make room for the storage of the expected catch to be taken from the Bering Sea. A good captain was also a good businessman, and one who spent time on the details. Captain Hawes was a good captain.

By January 25, the lookout on the *Shenandoah* spotted Cape Otway on the southern coast of Australia, and soon thereafter the shoreline leading to Port Phillip became visible. Port Phillip, also commonly called Port Phillip Bay or just "the Bay," is a very large bay measuring 745 square miles in area located in southern Victoria, Australia. Geographically, Port Phillip is a large marine bay which has a coastline perimeter length of 164 miles. At the northern end of the Bay is Melbourne, the largest city in Australia in 1865, with a population of about one hundred and fifty thousand at that time. At the entrance to the bay is a narrow channel, about two miles across, that leads from the Indian Ocean into the bay. Just outside the bay, the *Shenandoah* was met by a pilot boat whose pilot, a Mr. Johnston, inquired why the *Shenandoah* wished to be taken into Melbourne.

Before Captain Waddell could reply, the pilot continued, "My orders are peremptory about Confederate vessels."[39] This, of course, meant that he could refuse to allow the *Shenandoah* into the bay, if he did not feel comfortable about the situation.

Waddell apparently gave a satisfactory reply and following that, the pilot boat directed the *Shenandoah* to the rather small channel providing entrance to the bay. Following instructions from the pilot boat, the *Shenandoah* then steamed for over thirty miles to a location about two miles from the city itself, and dropped anchor near the small town of Williamstown, about two miles from the center of Melbourne in Port Phillip Bay. Thus began a two-week stopover in Melbourne, Australia, which would never be forgotten by anyone on board the *Shenandoah*.

Immediately upon dropping anchor, the authorities from Melbourne arrived to make a routine inspection of the foreign vessel. However, not only the authorities, but also most of the inhabitants of Melbourne were excited by the arrival of this vessel from the Confederacy. From the moment the Confederate vessel arrived at anchor near Williamstown, there began a steady stream of boats, yachts, and sightseers steaming or sailing close by to have a good look at the visitor. This was an opportunity for the American consul and affiliates to have a thorough inspection of the vessel and to draw conclusions about its reason for being in Australia, and its intentions after leaving. Many were sympathetic to the South, while others were loyal to the North. Those loyal to the North made the situation tense for those on board the Confederate ship, as it was believed that there were those who would take action to destroy this ship, if given the chance. There were demonstrations by both sides with gatherings and flag waving and shouts and cheers. Waddell made sure that the ship was well guarded and allowed no strangers on board. Some of those who had recently arrived in Melbourne from England actually recognized the outline of the *Sea King*, out of Liverpool. Needless to say, they were somewhat confused as this vessel was supposed to have sailed to Bombay, India. It was almost like a circus had come to town by the attention given to the *Shenandoah* and her officers and men, along with the related activities.

During this time, there were many communications between Captain Waddell and the civil authorities in Melbourne. Waddell was anxious to have the repairs made to the propeller shaft, so the ship could proceed on its mission as soon as possible. The authorities were unsure of what to do and what rules applied to this situation. Captain Waddell was extremely forceful and clever with his arguments to the governing bodies and after many exchanges was able to convince the authorities to go ahead and make arrangements for the needed repairs. Once the

Shenandoah in Dry dock[40]

approval was given, plans were made to get the ship ready for dry dock, so the underneath hull could be accessible and the propeller shaft repaired. This meant removing all the items not tied to the ship such as furniture, equipment, supplies, and so on, in order to lighten the ship in preparation for dry dock. The authorities gave Waddell two more weeks to get the job done and no longer, unless absolutely necessary. In the meantime, the officers and crew were treated like visiting dignitaries by the citizens of Melbourne. There were parties at the local hotels. A dance was given to the officers and men of the *Shenandoah*, and the ladies were all impressed by these sailors and their uniforms from the Confederacy.

The American consul and agents were well aware of the goings-on and made numerous demands to have the *Shenandoah* seized and taken out of commission. However, the Australians were steadfast in their determination to judge the situation without taking sides and held on to their rights to handle the situation as they saw fit. Their position was that they were a neutral nation and the *Shenandoah* was a distressed ship at sea needing repairs, and they would provide the services. On the other hand, they were not passive in their relationship with the Confederate vessel, and organized a police force to oversee the goings-on at the dry dock repair facility in Williamstown, as well as to offer protection to the ship from those who would like to see the ship destroyed, essentially the American sympathizers. Captain Waddell had been warned that there were plots to destroy his ship, and that was why he had requested protection from the Melbourne authorities.

In one case there was a request by the Melbourne authorities to make an inspection of the *Shenandoah* in search of alleged stowaways on board, which had been reported presumably by American interests. In addition, there were suspicions that the *Shenandoah* had recruited crew members from the local area in violation of neutrality, and several instances were reported to the civil authorities. Captain Waddell was certain that these accusations had come from the American consul and its supporters. In all instances, Captain Waddell was firm in his refusal to allow any authority to board his ship as he claimed that a vessel of war was part of the territory of the country to which it belongs, and therefore not subject to search by civil authorities of a foreign country. He stood firm and the Australians backed off.

At the end of ten days in dry dock, repairs had been completed and the *Shenandoah* was returned from dry dock to the bay and there dropped anchor to prepare for departure the next day. Stores, furniture, and supplies were placed back on board, and a load of coal was delivered from an English coal barge, enough to last the entire journey into the Pacific Ocean. All officers and men returned to the ship and were ready to depart the next morning, Sunday, February 19.

11. *Shenandoah* Disappears

The next morning saw the anchors of the *Shenandoah* on her deck, and at 8 o'clock she steamed from the mooring near Williamstown to the Heads of Port Phillip, thirty miles away to the south. The pilot was the same Mr. Johnston who had directed them into the bay three weeks earlier. It seemed that Mr. Johnston had been so unfortunate as to run a vessel on a shoal after he had worked the *Shenandoah* perfectly upon her arrival at the entrance to Port Phillip Bay. This incident had injured him in the opinion of many shipmasters and his career was in jeopardy. His brother called upon Captain Waddell to explain the situation and ask for a chance to redeem Johnston's reputation by taking the *Shenandoah* out of the bay.

He added, "If you will again let him take your steamer out, he will be on his feet again."

Waddell accepted and Mr. Johnston took the *Shenandoah* safely out. Soon they were out of Port Phillip Bay, through the channel and into Bass Strait, a body of water between Australia and Tasmania. The pilot was discharged soon thereafter as Waddell did not want to extend his employment any longer and let him find out any more about what the *Shenandoah* was up to. They had already made communication with more than one vessel heading into Port Phillip Bay, and these vessels would certainly report on the heading and what they guessed about the intentions of the *Shenandoah*. The pilot left them with a farewell and good wishes, but it was not the kind of parting one would have with close friends or comrades. Waddell was also suspicious of Mr. Johnston and what he would have to say on his return to Melbourne. After discharging the pilot, Waddell continued heading south. At nightfall, he took a turn to the east, and headed for Round Island in Bass Strait, one of the many islands between Australia and Tasmania. Tasmania is a fairly large island south of Australia where the original settlers arrived from England in the early 1800s, before moving on to the mainland of Australia.

As he was departing Bass Strait and heading for the southern Pacific Ocean, Captain Waddell later wrote that he was not the least concerned about federal cruisers based on their lackluster showing in their search for the *Alabama* and *Florida*. He knew that he had spent too long in Melbourne and that the Americans certainly had sufficient time to gather intelligence and pass it along to federal authorities across the oceans. However, that service could not have been avoided, as the repairs were needed and time consuming, and could not have been done quicker under any circumstances. Regardless, he had no choice but to continue with his mission in spite of the unfortunate delay in Melbourne.

Also, there were some positive consequences from the stopover in Melbourne. First, the *Shenandoah* received thirty-four young Americans and eleven others of different nationalities in exchange for those former crewmen who had decided to leave the Confederate service in Melbourne. One deserter was offered a promise of $100 by the American consul, according to Waddell. These new sailors had smuggled themselves on board the night before leaving Melbourne. Waddell was mystified as to why these men would align themselves with a Southern cruiser in the destruction of property belonging to their fellow countrymen. On the other hand, he was pleased that the *Shenandoah* now had a full complement of men to handle the many tasks before them in their search for and destruction of Yankee whalers. At this point, there were enough extra hands on board to provide a sergeant, a corporal, and three privates to form the nucleus for a marine guard. The sergeant represented himself as having been aide-de-camp to Lieutenant General Leonidas Polk, an Episcopal bishop and a West Point classmate of Jefferson Davis. He had been called to duty by Davis to serve as a major general for the South. Unfortunately, he was killed when hit by enemy fire during a battle with General Sherman's army in Georgia. The sergeant, thought Waddell, would be the perfect leader for the marine guard on board.

Waddell was still concerned that they had been discovered and the word was out that they were heading into the Pacific. As it turned out, there is no evidence that the Americans were able to get the word out that the *Shenandoah* was well-armed, was in good condition, and was heading for the Pacific whaling fleet. In this regard, Waddell had never disclosed his mission target area in the Bering Sea to anyone in order to keep this information totally secret and known only to himself. This discipline paid off, as no one knew where they were going and therefore no one was able to tell. There is no record that any special alerts or notices were sent to any of the American stations in the Pacific that were more than of a routine nature. The situation was better for Waddell than even he realized. In the meantime, Waddell pressed onward and soon found himself south of Lord Howe Island and Norfolk Island, well off the coast of eastern Australia. These islands were in close communication with Sidney, and they would certainly have been notified of any suspected Confederate cruiser activity. Both islands were also normally visited by whalers from all countries to procure provisions and to exchange goods with the natives. Waddell was convinced, however, that these islands had not seen any whalers for the past few months at all, and that a warning had been provided to all whalers about the presence of the *Shenandoah* in these parts. He was certain that the alarm had been given to the whalers to avoid the southern Pacific, as there was no evidence that any whalers had been in the vicinity. He was sure they were all in the northern Pacific by this time, and that the delay in Melbourne had thwarted his mission to destroy the Yankee whalers in the southern Pacific. Again, no evidence has ever been verified to support this assessment.

The *Milo* remained off the coast of California during this time, leaving this area on February 25 and again heading for the Sandwich Islands and Honolulu. There, the *Milo* would prepare for the next summer on the Bering Sea and look for another profitable whaling harvest. Life was never dull on a whaling voyage, as there was always something that had to be planned for the next day. There was a lot of work to be done when whales were captured and processed, and there was a lot of planning to do to get ready for the next phase during a long voyage like the *Milo* was undertaking. There was also the business of offloading oil and bones stored on board after a long period at sea. Captain Hawes intended to sell his harvest in Honolulu upon arrival there in order to make space available for the summer's catch. At this point, the *Milo* had been at sea for almost a year and a half. Captain Hawes was looking forward to the next summer where he expected a large catch and if things went well, he would return to New Bedford after the summer. He was not aware of the whereabouts of the *Shenandoah* and was not aware of the danger lurking down the road. It looked like they were going to have a very successful whaling venture this time, and if things worked out well, he thought he would retire from whaling after this summer and start building a new career back home. Furthermore, the news about the war was positive, and most people thought it would be over soon, as the Confederates were running out of soldiers and ammunition, and were beginning to show signs of defeat.

Back in the United States, President Lincoln attended inauguration ceremonies in Washington, DC on March 4,

214

for his second term as president. He gave a short speech prior to the swearing-in ceremony and essentially set the stage for a peaceful future between the two warring sides in the final words of his address by saying:

With malice toward none; with charity for all; with firmness in the right, as God gives us to see the right, let us strive to finish the work we are in; to bind up the nations wounds; to care for him who shall have borne the battle...to do all which may achieve and cherish a just and lasting peace, among ourselves, and with all nations.

What he was setting up was to unite the nation in peace without vengeance or punishment to anyone on either side of the conflict in order to instill a sense of respect for both North and South, and avoid hate and further bloodshed. The crowd that had gathered around for the ceremonies was looking forward to peace in America, and following the speech, Lincoln was cheered and applauded and some even had tears in their eyes. However, not everyone shared his vision and some wanted revenge, and even hangings, as punishment for those who instigated the conflict.

Lincoln's Second Inaugural Address[41]

On this same day, General Robert E. Lee rode into Richmond for a meeting with Confederate President Jefferson Davis. He had a plan to discuss with his boss. The plan was based on the predicament the Confederacy was in, having been outmanned and out supplied by the Union. The situation was dire and Lee wanted to improve on the strategy of the war. He wanted to give up Richmond, join forces with General Joe Johnston and move the Confederate headquarters to another location farther south. It was taking too many resources to hold Richmond and at the same time be isolated from the main Confederate Army of General Joe Johnston, currently located in North Carolina. Lee's strategy was to pull out of Richmond and move south and join up with General Johnston. From there they could put up a better stand against the armies of General Grant and General Sherman. General Sherman had recently marched his army from Savannah. From there he turned north and laid a swath of destruction through South Carolina, laying waste to its capital, Columbia. His argument was that South Carolina had started the war, and they would pay the price for this. From there, he went on into North Carolina and settled his army east of Raleigh, near Goldsboro, in a position to attack General Johnston's army. Sherman had destroyed everything in sight during his march from Atlanta to Savannah and then through South Carolina into North Carolina, and the South paid dearly.

Lee's meeting with Jeff Davis was productive and Lee convinced Davis to go along with his plan. Richmond would soon be evacuated and the citizens would be left to the mercy of the Union. The next several weeks would be eventful for both sides as well as for events in the Pacific Ocean.

On March 15, 1865, the *Milo* dropped anchor in the Port of Honolulu and was ready to spend the next few weeks getting prepared for the sail back north to the Bering Sea and the summer's work ahead. There were many tasks to be accomplished during this stopover. The ship needed painting, food, and other supplies for the long voyage north. Also, whale oil and bones needed to be offloaded and sold on the open market in Honolulu in order to make room for the fishing harvest expected in the Bering Sea. The Hawes family and the entire crew were looking forward to another restful time in Honolulu. Jessie, in particular, wanted more new pictures of the children and made arrangements with Henry Chase to have this done. Jonathan was anxious to take care of business first, and then to enjoy the pleasures of the best hotel and restaurants in Honolulu with Jessie and the children. This was also a time to purchase new clothing as the children had outgrown their old clothes and Jessie and Jonathan as both could use a change in dress for the many social events they would encounter later on during the gams while at sea. Life was good and they all enjoyed the time they could spend in Honolulu. Of course, many of their whaling friends from New Bedford and other ports in New England were also there doing essentially the same things in preparation for the Bering Sea. They were not alone by any means, and there were many social events for those from the many whaling vessels anchored there. The Hawes family was well entertained throughout their stay in Honolulu.

Out in the Tasman Sea, the *Shenandoah* was sailing east from Australia and then north upon reaching sight of New Zealand. Soon, the Three Kings Island just north of New Zealand came into view. By the middle of March, now in the southern Pacific Ocean, she had passed by the Fiji Islands, and was heading north toward the equator. Around March 21, she approached Drummond Island, close to the equator. Drummond Island was a popular stopping place for whalers and Waddell knew this. Upon approaching the island, Waddell ordered steam and even brought down the sails so he could maneuver better. As they approached the harbor, there was no activity at all, and Waddell was now completely convinced that an alert had gone out about the *Shenandoah*, and that all Yankee whalers had left this part of the Pacific. He was also completely in the dark about the situation back home as to the progress of the war. He had no idea that the Confederacy was on its last legs and in deep trouble. Communications were slow at best in those days, and news was spread by newspapers and mouth. Waddell would learn the news from other ships that he came in contact with on the high seas, or whenever he was in port. Since Waddell had been mostly on the high seas and had had little or no contact with any other ship, he was not aware of news from anywhere. Consequently, Waddell did not know what was going on back home at any given time. He was further handicapped by the fact that he would not believe anything he heard from American ships, and he did not have the opportunity to exchange a great deal of news with ships flying other flags. In terms of the telegraph, these services did not exist between continents until 1866, when the first Transatlantic telegraph cable was laid.

A day or two after leaving Drummond Island, the *Shenandoah* met with the schooner *Pftel* from Honolulu on a trading mission among the islands for tortoise shell, and the two ships exchanged information. The *Pftel* was the only sail the *Shenandoah* had seen from February 20 to April 1, which was evidence to Waddell that the South Pacific whaling fleet had taken flight. After demanding papers from Captain Hammond of the schooner, Waddell discovered that this schooner was not American, but also learned that American whalers may be in port at Ponape Island, called Ascension Island by Waddell, just north of the equator in the Caroline Islands, and only a few days away. After discovering that this vessel was from Honolulu, Waddell gave the name of his ship as the British warship, "*Miami*." It was later surmised by government officials that the *Miami* was in fact the *Shenandoah*. Today, the city of Palikir on Ponape Island is the capital city of the

Federated States of Micronesia, made up essentially of all of the Caroline Islands in the Pacific Ocean.

On April 1, 1865, the *Shenandoah* arrived at Ponape Island and was met by a small boat with a single occupant. He was an Englishman, Thomas Harrocke, and a pilot to Lea Harbor in which four vessels were at anchor. Harrocke was an escaped convict from Sidney, Australia, who had lived there for over thirteen years and had married a native woman. When questioned about the safety of the harbor for anchorage, he said the harbor would be too confining for a ship the length of the *Shenandoah*. With this information, Harrocke, the pilot, was instructed to anchor the *Shenandoah* inside a long reef which extends almost across the entrance to the harbor, rendering the approach very narrow. At that time, the flag had not been shown and the pilot had no idea of the nationality of the visitor, nor did he ask any questions. Waddell stayed with the pilot until the *Shenandoah* was anchored inside the entrance of Lea Harbor. As soon as the *Shenandoah* was secured in position, three of the vessels in the harbor hoisted the American flag and the forth hoisted the flag of Oahu. The scene was set and Waddell was ready to go into action. Waddell then dispatched four armed boats, each with orders to board the vessels and to send their officers, ship papers, logbooks, charts, and instruments for navigation over to the *Shenandoah*, and the boat crews were to remain in charge of their respective prizes until further orders were given by Waddell.

Officers in charge of the four boats from the *Shenandoah* were Lieutenants Grimball, Chew, Lee, and Scales. The boats were all of different sizes, but none over thirty-two or less than twenty-eight feet in length and having less than six-feet beam. They were strongly built and carried water and provisions for thirty persons for twenty days. They had masts, sails, oars, a compass, lanterns, and a hatchet and small chest for pistols and cutlasses. Each boat had a prize crew of seven men, and each lieutenant had one or more subordinate officer, each with a special duty assigned to him independent of the others. From that moment on, it was a classic exercise of a warship taking on four unarmed whaleships all contained in a small harbor and with no means to escape. They were like sitting ducks. The ships were the *Edward Cary* of San Francisco, the *Hector* of New Bedford and the *Pearl* of New London. The forth ship flew the flag of Oahu, but its registry bore the name of *Harvest* of New Bedford, and the master of the vessel could not prove otherwise. Captain Waddell considered all vessels American and would soon destroy them accordingly.

Once the boats had left the *Shenandoah*, the Confederate flag was raised and the gun was fired giving notice to all in the harbor and everyone on the island who this vessel was and that they meant business. The natives who were gazing at the vessel sought shelter in the bushes and the American whalers hauled down their flags. Thomas Harrocke who had brought them to the anchorage was asked if he knew the Confederate flag. He replied that he had heard about the "big war" in America and knew about Jeff Davis and had heard that the South had "whipped" the Yankees in all the big battles. When Waddell told him they were a Confederate cruiser, Harrocke replied, "Well, well, I never thought I would live to see Jeff Davis's flag." The popular abbreviation of President Jefferson Davis's name was common on Ponape Island as it was in most other Pacific Islands, and it bore the significance of their own king. The natives were familiar with the name of Jeff Davis through conversations with the many whalers who had visited the islands over the past few years. Harrocke told Waddell that the natives on the island had heard about the American war through him, and that he had received his information from newspapers given by visiting whalers and conversations with whalers themselves.

The four whaleships were boarded by the *Shenandoah* boat crews and boarding officers received surrenders from the mates and crew aboard. None of the masters were aboard, as they had arranged a joint visit to the local missionary post which was located nearby on the island. They were captured later on when they returned together from the visit to the missionary minister and were brought over the *Shenandoah* for a conference with Captain Waddell. Here, they were advised of their prisoner status and the ultimate destruction of their vessels. Needless to say, they were not happy about this, but no one put up a fight. All of the masters knew exactly what was going to happen in their confrontation with the Confederate cruiser, and there was nothing they could do about it.

Some of the prisoners elected to join the *Shenandoah* as crew, but the majority chose to decline. The charts that were captured were most important because they showed all of the navigational charts used by whalers in the Pacific Islands, the Okhotsk, and Bering Seas, and the Arctic Ocean, and where they had been most successful. With these charts in his possession, Waddell had the key to all the likely places where the New England whaling fleet was most likely to be without any guessing or tiresome search. These charts would be the most valuable information Waddell could expect to have and this would be a great advantage to him. This bit of information gave him a road map for the next few months, and he would set his course accordingly, first north from the Caroline Islands, then north to the Okhotsk Sea on the eastern coast of Siberia, and then east into the Bering Sea.

Thomas Harrocke became Waddell's interpreter and also his introduction to the king of Lea Harbor. His Majesty the King Ish-y-Paw was fascinated with the power of the Confederate cruiser and became very respectful of Waddell. A deal was made with the king to leave all prisoners on the island to be picked up later by visiting vessels. His Majesty agreed to this arrangement but was puzzled by the fact that the prisoners were not just killed. Waddell explained through the pilot that he did not kill unarmed prisoners, but saw to it that they were treated humanely and were left with the ability to return to a normal life when possible. The king did not understand this, but he accepted it. The king also agreed to allow the four whaleships to be destroyed at a location in the bay, away from the harbor, so that any remaining bits and pieces would not interfere with the harbor. He also liked the idea that his people would be able to take anything off the ships before the ships were put to fire. Everyone liked this idea, and on April 2, the natives began their search for their new treasures aboard the four ships. They swarmed over the ships all day and took everything they could get their hands on, until they had taken everything in sight. Following this, they put their new possessions into their canoes and went ashore.

On April 3, the destruction began and the *Pearl* was the first ship set afire. Before the flames had reached their heights, the *Hector* and *Edward Cory* were also blazing and the bay was alive with a bright and huge bonfire of whaleships. The *Harvest* had not been put on fire as yet because there were still items to be contributed to the *Shenandoah*, and this did not take place until April 10. This ship was brought alongside the *Shenandoah* on that morning, so that the transfer of items could be made. In the meantime, there were several ceremonial visits between His Majesty, King Ish-y-Paw, and Captain Waddell, on shore as well as on board the *Shenandoah*. The king visited the *Shenandoah* along with his entourage in a large fleet of canoes. His Royal Highness drank freely of the alcoholic beverages provided by Waddell and became very friendly and communicative using the harbor pilot as interpreter. The king, of course, had a very narrow vision of the world, and it would be difficult to try to analyze just what he thought about all of the subjects discussed during the ceremonies.

The Burning Ship at Ponape[42]

The prisoners from the whaleships that did not transfer over to the *Shenandoah* elected to remain on Ponape Island rather than be transported to Guam, which Waddell offered as an option. At this point, Captain Waddell was more prepared than ever to continue his mission with the new charts and information on American whaling fleet operations. The *Shenandoah* would remain at Ponape Island for a few more days to prepare for their voyage north. Waddell had no idea that back in the United States, the Confederates were on the verge of defeat.

12. The Beginning of the End of the War

While the *Milo* was still at anchor in the Port of Honolulu and the *Shenandoah* was sailing toward its destructive stopover at Ponape Island, a significant meeting took place at City Point in northern Virginia on March 24. City Point no longer exists as a city, but as a partition in the city of Hopewell, now a separate city in Virginia. In 1865, City Point, located on the James River, was General Grant's supply depot for the Union siege of rebel forces at Petersburg where ships by the thousands loaded and unloaded. Some sunken ships still remain on the bottom of the river as wrecks, at a location known as Shipwreck City. Lincoln arranged to meet with his two top generals, Grant and Sherman, to discuss what he hoped to be the beginning of the end of the war. That meeting took place on the *River Queen*, a floating headquarters for Grant's army on the James River at City Point. On the day after Lincoln's arrival at City Point, General Lee planned and executed an attack to overrun the Union's post at Fort Stedman, south of Petersburg by several miles. After an initial success by the Confederates who succeeded in taking possession of the fort, the Union troops with overwhelming numbers counterattacked and forced the Confederates to retreat after loosing nearly five thousand soldiers. After the ensuing Union victory, President Lincoln could not restrain himself and made arrangements to see the Fort Stedman battlefield the next day. He viewed the area by railroad car at close range after the Union forces had retaken the fort. This loss forced General Lee to accelerate his withdrawal from Petersburg and make an attempt to join forces with Confederate General Joe Johnston in North Carolina.

Lincoln spent two weeks at City Point presumably on a vacation, but actually, to lay out his strategy with his top generals for ending the war. Pure and simple, his vision was to bring everyone together, Union and Confederate alike, to forgive and forget. He hoped to bond everyone in the nation together with respect and dignity for all. He wanted a definite end to hostilities, without further bloodshed. He was aware of and had studied insurgencies and its effect on nations from the beginning of recorded history. Insurgencies had never solved anything and always extended the bloodshed over many years, sometimes, it seemed, never to end. Somehow, he knew that it would be possible for the South to take to the hills, and to continue the fight for independence. He was not wrong, as this option had been discussed many times among the leaders of the Confederacy and was a distinct possibility. Generals Lee and Johnston had considered insurgency as a possible strategy, but neither wanted to seriously take that course. Other leaders in the Confederacy, however, had pushed hard to do just that. They wanted go to the hills and strike the enemy from time to time, until the enemy got tired of it and gave up. These were Confederate leaders like Nathan Bedford Forest, John Mosby, and Cherokee Chief Brigadier General Stand Watie, all of whom became famous for guerrilla activities throughout the war. And last but not least, there was also Confederate Navy Captain James I. Waddell, skipper of the CSS *Shenandoah*, who was also prepared to fight an unconventional insurgent naval operation for however long it would take to gain independence. Waddell had already made his mark and had brought on considerable destruction to Union property. If Jeff Davis gave the word, Waddell would take the bait and continue the fight. Even though President Davis considered taking this course and even made announcements promoting an insurgency, he ultimately decided against this approach. Interestingly, Jeff Davis had never sought the Confederate presidency and never wanted the job, but somehow he was elected in absentia and did not turn it down.

Lincoln feared an insurgency more than anything else, and he wanted to avoid such a happening at all costs. He continued with his thoughts outlined in his speech at his second-term inauguration ceremony on March 4. He wanted to make sure that Grant and Sherman understood what he wanted to accomplish and that they would both do their best to carry out his vision of bringing everyone together in harmony after the end of hostilities and to forgive those responsible for the insurrection. Both Grant and Sherman were in favor of the idea, as both had been concerned about Confederate forces going to the hills and waging a hit and running war for a lengthy foreseeable future. They did not want this to happen either. Consequently, this vision of Lincoln's shaped the outcome of events that were to come in the ensuing weeks ahead. This meeting at City Point was perhaps the most important meeting of Lincoln's presidency, as it articulated the ultimate outcome of the war and the Reconstruction. The spring of 1865 was a momentous time for America; many events were taking place in different places around the world that would shape the destiny of this great country.

And so, after a nine-month siege by General Grant at Petersburg, General Lee was ready to move his Army of Northern Virginia on a march that would ultimately allow him to join up with General Johnston in North Carolina. His strategy was to join forces with General Johnston and together they could take on both Grant and Sherman, and with the enhanced force of both armies combined, they had a good chance to overcome the Union forces and win their independence. Lee felt that if he stayed where he was, at Petersburg protecting Richmond, he had no chance to win the war.

The siege had actually begun at the battle of Wilderness in northern Virginia during May, 1864, where Lee was victorious. Even though victorious, Lee was always clever in reestablishing his forces for the next battle without giving any hints to Grant, who had the superior forces. Regardless, Grant continued to pursue Lee's army and after battles at Spotsylvania, North Anna, and Cold Harbor, Grant had his army dug in surrounding Petersburg for the long siege. On March 29, after Lee's loss at Fort Stedman, General Grant sensed Lee's weakened condition and decided it was time to strike again, quickly. He met up with Lee's forces at Five Forks, about ten miles southwest of Petersburg, on April 1, and the battle began. This was the same day that the *Shenandoah* arrived at Ponape Island and began its destruction there.

At Five Forks, the Union forces were simply overwhelming, and this became Lee's first real disaster since his victory at Wilderness, nearly a year earlier. Lee knew he was in trouble, as he had now lost nearly one-forth of his Army of Northern Virginia. Lee began his retreat to Amelia Courthouse, forty miles to the west, where he expected to pick up provisions and supplies for his troops. In the meantime, he sent telegraphs to Confederate President Davis to begin the evacuation of Richmond immediately. At first, Davis responded that there was not enough time to save valuable documents and material. Lee was then beside himself, as he knew the situation was dire and time was short. Richmond had to be evacuated now!

The next morning, Sunday, April 2, while the *Shenandoah* was taking action against the four American whalers at Ponape Island and General Lee was retreating to Amelia Courthouse, President Jefferson Davis was attending church services at St. Paul's Episcopal Church in Richmond. During the service he received another message, delivered by a courier from General Lee, requesting that he leave the city immediately, as Lee had started to move his army to the south to join with General Johnston in North Carolina. Jeff Davis rose from his pew, and quietly walked to the front of the church and made an exit with two of his aides by his side. The congregation was unnerved, but most remained seated and quiet. They knew that something significant was happening. At the same time, similar messages were delivered to other churches in town as well. The congregations were advised to go to their homes and trust in God. The white people knew what was going on; they went to their homes, closed the doors and hid inside as they were fearful of the Yankees. The black people were out on the streets, dancing and cheering and feeling liberated and thanking God for this moment. It was quite a sight.

Soon after, some of buildings were burning in the city and then things went from bad to worse. Fire and smoke surrounded the city as there were those who wanted to destroy everything in sight. Jeff Davis managed to pack all of his belongings as well as government documents and had these loaded on a government train made up of cars labeled: "War Department," "Quartermaster Department," "Treasury Department," and so on. The train was scheduled to depart at 8:30 PM, but it was not until 11:00 PM. when it pulled out of town, just in the nick of time. He was heading south to Danville, Virginia, on the Richmond & Danville Railroad, to a more secure location and out of harm's way. Richmond, a city that was once the center of the Southern revolt and a city of beauty, had changed in a moment. Now it was a city of destruction and chaos. With all the smoke and fire, it looked like things would never be the same again. Next would be the entrance of Union soldiers and their takeover of the city, and this began quietly at nightfall. When this actually happened, the Richmond citizens feared for their lives and began their evacuation to the hills or wherever they could feel safe. The blacks, however, remained and danced with joy. Who could blame them?

While this was going on, General Lee continued his retreat to Amelia Courthouse, with Grant in hot pursuit. Amelia Courthouse was only a stopover place; Danville, Virginia, was the initial goal. That was where the railroad would be used to supply Lee's army with more food and provisions in order to join up with General Johnston in North Carolina. Grant did not want to continue to chase Lee, but wanted to surround Lee and force a surrender before Lee was able to travel too far. He did not want Lee to become an insurgent force and be able to continue the war any longer. This, of course, was also President Lincoln's wish.

Early in the afternoon of April 4, President Lincoln with his high silk hat and long black coat arrived at the Port of Richmond on the James River, accompanied by a naval guard of ten sailors, and set foot on Richmond soil and made the two-mile walk to the center of the city and Capital Square. From his first step onto Richmond soil, he was cheered and praised by all of those whose were gathered around, mostly black and mostly in awe of this president. He was considered almost a God by those present. "Bless the Lord," they shouted. "Glory to God!" "Glory Hallelujah!"[43] The cheers and prayers went on and on as Lincoln worked his way through the crowd. The people wanted to touch him and transfer some of the godliness to themselves, and they did. His security guard was on the alert for any attempts of assassination, and they were constantly looking into the crowd and into the surrounding buildings for any sign of guns. There was no attempt on his life although he was in close contact with all of the people who were there. There was no official welcoming party to greet the president, and he did not want this. He had come to visit in peace, and he wanted to demonstrate his peaceful intentions. Lincoln pushed on toward the center of the city in spite of the heat while hundreds of white citizens hidden inside the buildings gazed upon this towering president. At last he arrived at the Confederate executive mansion, now a Union military headquarters. He was pale and utterly worn out and wandered around the deserted rooms. Only forty hours after

Jeff Davis had left, he arrived in the study of the president of the Confederate States of America; he sat down and asked for a glass of water, while the Union troops cheered.

"Thank God I have lived to see this," Lincoln exclaimed. "It seems I have been dreaming a horrible dream for four years, and now the nightmare is gone." But he knew it was not finished yet and that there was still a long way to go. In spite of this, he was there to lay the foundation for eventual reconciliation, and to ensure that the occupation of Richmond was not to be a repeat of Sherman's march to the sea or any other destruction of property that had taken place during the war by the Union forces. He knew that the war was not over and that it could take months, or even years, before peace could be attained. But at this time, he wanted to show that his intentions were for peace and reconciliation for all to see and believe. He came "as a peacemaker" his escort, Admiral David Porter said, and "his hand is extended to all who desire to take it." Porter hoped that the Richmonders would see Lincoln as a peacemaker and not as a monster, and there was less of a devil about him than in Jefferson Davis

From the day Lincoln arrived in Richmond, there were no rapes, looting, fires started or anything destructive. On the contrary, there was a sense of peace in the air and this could be felt by everyone. Union soldiers acted professional, and they were courteous to the citizens. In one case, Mrs. Robert E. Lee had remained in Richmond and could not travel due to health problems. A black guard had been placed at her front door for security reasons. When she complained about the black guard, a white soldier was immediately sent over to replace the black. This was a direct result of Lincoln's presence. Lincoln wanted the nation to unify in peace and he did his best to set the example. He wanted to immobilize Robert E. Lee and his Army of Northern Virginia as soon as possible, and he was getting close.

On the same day that Lincoln arrived in Richmond, General Lee and his army reached Amelia Courthouse, and settled in for a night's sleep and some food. Lee was still confident that he had the advantage and would be able to ultimately stand up to and defeat General Grant. Lee continued his march westward and arrived at Saylor's Creek on April 6. There, Grant caught up with Lee and began with a viscous attack on Lee's army. This turned out to be the bloodiest battle of the entire Civil War and ended up in hand-to-hand combat between the two sides. Both sides resorted to using bayonets, knives, and just plain clubbing with rifle butts when their ammunition ran out to kill their enemies. At the end of the day, Grant had captured six thousand rebels, including Lee's son, Custis, and Lee had lost eight thousand more, killed or wounded. Lee was visibly shaken and wondered if his "army had been dissolved." This single day would be known forever in history as "Black Thursday."[44] However, what would take place in the next thirty-six hours would enshrine General Lee in immortality as much as his accomplishments of the past four years.

Grant then called on General Sheridan to move his calvary out ahead of Lee's army in order to surround Lee in a pincer movement and offer resistance to Lee's forward march westward. He was almost at the point of putting Lee into a trap that could not be bridged. As General Sheridan continued his sweep around the flanks of Lee's army, he wired Grant, "If the thing is pressed, I think that Lee will surrender." When Lincoln read this, his spirits soared. He then telegraphed Grant, "Let the thing be pressed!"[45]

On the evening of April 6, Lee's army arrived in Farmsville, midway between Amelia Courthouse and Lynchburg, and just east of Appomattox Station. At Farmsville, where the first full rations of the march awaited them, the troops were fed, campfires were built and Lee

240

began to feel a sense that he could prevail if he could make it to the north side of the Appomattox River. There his troops could eat and rest and then try to either make a run to Danville or otherwise continue west to Lynchburg and be protected by the terrain of the Blue Ridge Mountains. The river was swollen by spring rains and would be difficult for Union troops to cross, and this would give Lee more time to rest and regroup. Fortunately for Grant, Lee made a poor decision when he opted to continue on the longer route through Lynchburg rather that the shorter route directly to Danville.

A visit to Lee by John Breckenridge, confederate secretary of war, and a discussion of the strategy caused Breckenridge to telegraph Jeff Davis that "the situation is not favorable." The next morning, April 7, Lee pulled out of Farmsville and marched westward toward Appomattox Station. Before noon, General Grant and his staff rode into Farmsville and set up a temporary headquarters in the village hotel. Grant began contemplating his next move. During this time, he had a discussion with a Doctor Smith, formally of the regular army and a native of Virginia, who was a relative of Confederate General Richard Ewell who had been captured at Saylor's Creek and was now a prisoner of Grant's forces. He told General Grant that

241

Ewell had told him that the Confederates had lost the war when they crossed the James River some time before, and that further hostilities would be in vain. He went on to say that someone had to bring a halt to the war and that any further action would be murder.[46] When Grant heard this, he sensed more than ever that General Lee was in dire straights and thought that now may be the time step up the hot pursuit and also to make a proposal for Lee to surrender.

That evening, around ten o'clock, Grant composed a message to General Lee that would begin a dialog to end to bloodshed and to end the war. In order to deliver the message to General Lee, Grant asked his adjutant general to deliver the message under a white flag of truce. This was Brigadier General Seth Williams who rode to the Confederate front lines with an aide. There, they were met with a volley of gunfire; the aide was killed, but Williams was able to get away. He tried again a short time later, and this time was successful, and he delivered the message to the Confederates. The message was shortly thereafter handed to General Lee, who received it at 10:00 PM that evening.

This began a series of exchanges between Grant and Lee over the next two days. It became obvious to General Lee that his army was in dire straits and that his capability in battle was severely diminished. He did not want to quit, or surrender. so he continued to respond to Grant's requests with that message. Lee coordinated all along with his staff on the options available. All the officers on his staff were most loyal and respective of General Lee, and none wanted to see him in defeat. General Lee was certainly not a quitter, but he was pragmatic and realized that he was not capable of continuing the fight any longer and simply could not win. On the morning of April 9, after several exchanges between the two opposing generals, General Lee requested a meeting per the following short memo to General Grant to discuss the surrender options.

> *April 9th, 1865*
>
> *LIEUTENANT-GENERAL U.S. GRANT*
>
> *GENERAL: I received your note of this morning on the picket line, whether I had come to meet you and ascertain definitely what terms were embraced in your proposal of yesterday with reference to the surrender of this army. I now ask an interview, in accordance with the offer contained in your letter of yesterday, for that purpose.*
>
> *R.E. LEE, General*[18]

This resulted in an agreement to hold a meeting at Appomattox Courthouse around noon on April 9 between the two commanding generals to discuss the terms of surrender.

By late morning on April 9, General Grant rode his horse "Cincinnati" from Farmville toward Appomattox Courthouse not knowing the whereabouts of General Lee. The road was filled with men, animals, wagons, and so on, and it was somewhat difficult to move forward with all of these distractions. However, General Grant and his party pressed on. Finally, about one o'clock in the afternoon,

Grant and his party arrived at Appomattox Courthouse and about that time, encountered General Sheridan. Grant asked Sheridan if he knew the whereabouts of General Lee. "Yes, he is in that brick house."

"Well then, we'll go over," said Grant.

General Lee had arrived earlier and had requested the use of a house from one of the residents of the village, William McLean. The first house offered did not suit Lee, and he requested another more appropriate setting for the occasion. At that point, McLean offered his own house which was the best one in town. That was the house that Lee entered and waited. The house had a comfortable porch and stood at little back from the street with enough room to accommodate horses and carriages and a roadway leading to a stable to the rear of the house. They spotted a fine large gray horse belonging to General Lee and a fine-looking mare belonging to an aide of Lee. General Grant dismounted his horse and entered the building. The other members of his party including General Sheridan waited as they thought Grant would prefer to be with Lee alone at the beginning of their meeting. Shortly after, the entire party was called in to be a part of the discussion between Grand

and Lee. Introductions were done and all participants met each other.

Grant sat at one table and Lee sat at another, although they faced each other. The other participants stood around the walls of the room and listened. General Lee was dressed in his best attire along with boots, spurs and sword. He was immaculate in appearance and impressive in character. On the other hand, General Grant was just the opposite. He had been in a hurry for the past several days, and did not have time to "dress for the occasion." His clothes were wrinkled and his trousers muddy and he did not have a sword or clean boots with spurs. He worked hard at what he did, but he did not try to impress anyone with the way he was dressed, but he was impressive in his own way. On the other hand, he was the victor and the one who called the shots. Lee knew that and did not try to outshine Grant in any way. Just the opposite, Lee was very respectful and cordial. After a brief getting-acquainted time remembering previous times they were together, Lee wanted to get directly to the point. "I suppose, General Grant, that the object of our present meeting is fully understood. I asked to see you to ascertain upon what terms you would receive the surrender of my army."

General Grant replied, "The terms I propose are those stated substantially in my letter of yesterday—that is, the officers and men surrendered to be paroled and disqualified from taking up arms again until properly exchanged, and all arms, ammunition and supplies to be delivered as captured property."

Lee nodded in assent, and Grant went on to say that he hoped that this meeting would lead to a general suspension of hostilities and be the means of preventing any further loss of life.

Lee nodded again in agreement, but he was anxious to get on with the formal work of the surrender and brought up the subject again by saying, "I presume, General Grant, we have both carefully considered the proper steps to be taken, and I would suggest that you commit to writing the terms you have proposed, so that they may be formally acted upon."

"Very well," replied Grant, "I will write them out." With this, he proceeded to write the terms on notepaper. He wrote quickly and halfway through, looked up and took notice of General Lee's handsome sword which hung by his side, and thought about the humiliation of an officer normally having to surrender his sword as a consequence of surrender. He thought he would not ask that officers' swords be surrendered, but that they should be able to keep them in their possession after the surrender, and so he wrote this into the terms of the surrender. The draft version presented to General Lee read as follows:

APPOMATTOX CT.H., VA

April 9, 1865

GENERAL R.E. LEE

Commanding C.S.A.

GENERAL: In accordance with the substance of my letter to you of the 8th inst., I propose to receive the surrender of the Army of Northern Virginia on the following terms, to wit: Rolls of all the officers and men to be made in duplicate, one copy to be given to an officer to be designated by me, the other to be retained by such officer or officers as you may designate. The officers to give their individual paroles not to take up arms against the Government of the United States until properly exchanged, and each company or regimental commander to sign a like parole for the men of their commands. The arms, artillery, and public property to be parked, and stacked, and turned over to the officers appointed by me to receive them. This will not embrace the side-arms of the officers, nor their private horses, or baggage. This done, each officer and man will be

> *allowed to return to his home, not to be disturbed by the*
> *United States authorities so long as they observe their*
> *paroles, and the laws in force where they may reside.*
> *Very respectfully,*
>
> **U.S. GRANT,**
> *Lieutenant-General[19]*

General Lee was given a copy of this surrender proposal and carefully read it, showing agreement, and actually was quite pleased with the way things were going. He did ask one other favor from Grant, however, and that was to allow all men who owned their own horses to keep the horses as they would be needed back home to carry on with their work after they returned. Grant volunteered that he had not thought of this, but being reminded of the condition would not change the words of the terms of surrender, but would instruct his officers to allow all men who claimed to own their horses to keep them and return home with them. This satisfied all parties, and General Lee took his pen and wrote a letter of acceptance as follows:

> **HEADQUARTERS, ARMY OF NORTHERN VIRGINIA**
> *April 9th, 1865*

> *GENERAL: I received your letter of this date containing the terms of the surrender of the Army of Northern Virginia as proposed by you. As they are substantially the same as those expressed in your letter of the 8th inst., they are accepted. I will proceed to designate the proper officers to carry the stipulations into effect.*
>
> *R.E. LEE*
> *General[50]*

Following this, there was an exchange of congratulations and good wishes among all those present. There was also a gathering of officers from both sides renewing old friendships as they had been together prior to the Civil War, particularly those from the Military Academy at West Point. Officers and men alike were generally ecstatic that the fighting was over. After so many years of fighting, the end was abrupt, but welcomed by all. There were cheers and shouts, and dancing in the streets! The relief was so significant that it was difficult to control one's emotions. After the shouting, the generals parted with cordiality and with respect for each other. General Lee headed for home in Richmond and General Grant headed for Washington. It was April 9, and this part of the war was over, but yet, there were many things to be resolved before a complete peace would come. Among these were the surrender of General Joe Johnston's army in North Carolina, the surrender of President Jefferson Davis, the surrender of the various Confederate raiding forces, and the surrender of the Confederate Navy and particularly, CSS *Shenandoah.* Moreover, April 1865 still had many more surprises in store. Let us not forget, however, that the surrender by General Lee was in no doubt enabled by the generous terms which were visualized and stated to Generals Grant and Sherman by President Lincoln at City Point a few weeks earlier. Lincoln had it right, for the Union to survive, the Union had to come together. For the Union to come together, the Union had to forgive and forget what those who wanted to secede did, and bring them back into the fold. This worked very well with General Lee. Could it work with General Joe Johnston in North Carolina, or Jefferson Davis, president of the Confederacy, or others? Time would tell.

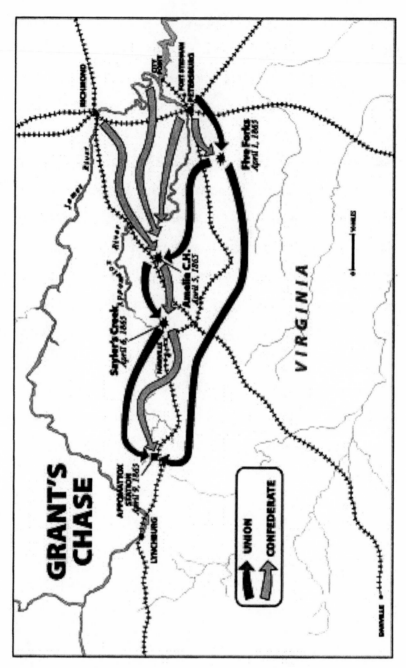

The Chase to Appomattox Courthouse

13. Hostilities Continue on Land and Sea

On April 13, all prisoners from the four captured American whaleships were removed from the *Shenandoah* and put ashore on Ponape Island. Food and other provisions for a long stay, along with two whaleboats, were made available for their use by Captain Waddell. This gesture was in line with the policy of the Confederate Navy to destroy Yankee property, but not the lives of noncombatants. Waddell did not want to have blood on his conscience. Once the prisoners had been transported to their temporary home on this savage island, a brief farewell ceremony was held on board the *Shenandoah* in honor of His Majesty, the king of Lea Harbor, and some gifts were exchanged. One gift, a dead chicken for cooking, was presented to Waddell by His Majesty for delivery to Jeff Davis, "king" of the Confederacy. His Majesty considered that he and Jeff Davis were both "kings," and otherwise equals. There is no record of what happened to the chicken after that.

Following the ceremonies, the *Shenandoah* steamed out of the harbor and set a course for new opportunities to the north. The weather was pleasant after leaving Ponape

Island and remained that way for the next several days as the ship headed first east, then north toward the Okhotsk Sea. Once the ship had cleared Ponape Island and was several miles out, Waddell ordered the steam down, propellers up, and sails unfurled, as they would use the wind for the next portion of the voyage and save coal. The weather would be perfect for the next several days and Captain Waddell decided to spend some time cruising within the shipping lanes for merchant ships that traveled between San Francisco and Hong Kong. This area was between the 17° and 20° parallels in north latitude. The *Shenandoah* remained between these parallels for several days but did not see one sail. This led Waddell to believe that there must have been some knowledge of the presence of the *Shenandoah* in the Pacific Ocean, and that was keeping the shipping lanes free of merchant ships. This was simply not the case. No one was aware of the location of the *Shenandoah* or even that it was sailing in the Pacific Ocean at all. However, this period gave the *Shenandoah* plenty of time to prepare for the action expected in the North Pacific later on. As Captain Waddell later wrote, "The delay was not without its own reward, for the executive officer, Mr. Whittle, had time to get things in good condition in his department."[51]

While the *Shenandoah* was still feeling the excitement of the events that took place on Ponape Island, President Lincoln, back in Washington, DC, was enjoying the new feeling of victory at hand and of uniting the country. On the afternoon of April 13, the president took a carriage ride out to his favorite retreat, a cottage set up exclusively for the president at the Soldiers' Home, about four miles north of the White House.[52] The president and Mary Lincoln had spent many a night at the cottage during his term in office, as it was their way of getting away from the hectic goings-on at the White House and the rather steady flow of visitors. Lincoln also enjoyed the carriage ride to and from the cottage and met many friends and acquaintances on the way each time. Mary Lincoln was the first to visit the Soldiers' Home in March 1861, shortly after the president's inauguration. Although they both preferred the Soldiers' Home to the White House, they did not spend the night there on April 13.

The next day, April 14, the president was still in great spirits after the news of General Lee's surrender to General Grant at Appomattox Courthouse a few days earlier. On that evening, he had planned to attend a show at Ford's Theater with his wife, Mary, and had asked the Grants to join them at the theater. This would provide a welcome break from being commander in chief and running a war. General and Mrs. Grant, however, had other plans and had already committed to visit their son in Burlington, New Jersey, and planned to take the train there. Several other people were invited, but all had commitments. Finally, Mary was able to secure a handsome young couple, Major Henry Rathbone and his fiancée, Clara Harris, daughter of Senator Ira Harris of New York, to accompany them.

In the meantime, something sinister, unbeknown to anyone, had been taking place. The actor John Wilkes Booth was a well known and popular actor who had a strong following in Washington as well as in other cities on the east coast. What was not known about Booth was that he was a stanch and dedicated believer in the Southern cause and in slavery in particular. He liked things the way they were and did not want change to come about. He would do anything to prevent change from taking place, and he was about to prove that to everyone. He had become a self-appointed leader of a conspiracy that intended to disrupt the government and lead to an overthrow. For several weeks he had actually been plotting to assassinate President Lincoln, Vice President Andrew Johnson, and Secretary of State William Seward. This would have eliminated all of the possible successors to the presidency, and it could have caused a great deal of chaos and disorder in the country. It would have provided a way for the Confederates to take advantage of the disruption and be able to win their independence. Booth and the other conspirators met at the boarding house of Mary Surratt, on the corner of H street and Sixth Street in the District of Columbia, not far from Ford's Theater. They also met from time to time at the Surratt Tavern which was about twenty miles south of the District, in Maryland. Her son, John, who had been one of the five original conspirators, had backed out of the conspiracy prior to the final assault. This time it was no joke, it was for real, and Booth put the plan into action on the night of April 14, when he knew that Lincoln would be attending Ford's Theater. No other attempt this bold has ever been carried out, before or since.

Booth had recruited five conspirators including John Surratt, but by April 14, only two remained on board. One was a shifty, low-browed Alabama native who was wounded at Gettysburg, and was known, among other aliases, as Lewis Powell. Powell deserted, and later rode with John Mosby, also known as the "Gray Ghost," who led a group of insurgents in Virginia, known as Confederate Partisan Rangers, during the Civil War. Mosby was noted for his lightning-quick raids and his ability to successfully elude his Union Army pursuers. He would disappear "like a ghost" with his men, blending in with local farmers and townspeople. Powell left Mosby under clouded circumstances, and somehow came under the watchful eye of John Wilkes Booth. The other conspirator was a German immigrant and carriage maker who also ferried Confederate spies across the Potomac. In his rental room, he had an arsenal of arms and ammunition. His name was George Atzerodt. On the night of April 14, Powell was designated to assassinate Secretary of State William Seward, in his home, while Atzerodt was chosen to murder Vice President Andrew Johnson in his quarters. Booth would take care of President Lincoln. If they were successful, the South could be victorious yet. It was a gamble, but it could happen. If it had happened, it would have changed history and who knows what would have been the outcome?

Booth had been suspicious of George Atzerodt and was uncomfortable with Atzerodt's ability to get the job done. With this in mind, Booth had visited the vice president's residence at Kirkwood House earlier that day, and left a short note for Vice President Andrew Johnson. "Don't wish to disturb you," he wrote, "Are you at home? J. Wilkes Booth." This was no doubt, an attempt to throw suspicion on Andrew Johnson. It also happened that earlier on that day Lincoln had met with Johnson for the first time since the inauguration. Lincoln and Johnson did not get along well. There was a great difference between the two men. Lincoln was a Republican and Johnson was a Democrat. Lincoln wanted a peaceful solution to the war to bring the Union together; Johnson wanted revenge across the board, with punishment and hangings. They did not see eye to eye on hardly any subject. The note left by Booth could have been interpreted to mean that Johnson was in league with the conspirators, but no one ever found out.

What happened that evening was frightening, deadly, bizarre, nearly catastrophic, and earthshaking, to say the least. President Lincoln and First Lady Mary Lincoln were delayed about fifteen minutes getting started to Ford's Theater due to last minute visitors at the White House. After the visitors left, they quickly stepped into the presidential carriage and headed to Senator Harris's home to pick up Clara and Major Rathbone. They arrived at the theater about twenty minutes after the performance had started and immediately stepped into the theater. Lincoln led the way up to the president's balcony, and as soon as he was recognized, the audience gave him a standing ovation and the band played, "Hail to the Chief." The president's box was decorated with a colorful flag, banners, and a picture of President George Washington, along with other decorative artwork. The party then sat down and the play continued. About five minutes later, during a humorous moment in the play, a man's hand was on the door to the president's box. There was no latch on the door. The man pushed the door open to reveal President Lincoln and Mary close to one another. At this moment, the star of the play made a foolish statement, and the audience burst into laughter along with a round of applause. At the same time, a muffled sound of a loud noise, like a firecracker, was heard. Then Lincoln's arm jerked up convulsively, nobody else moved in the presidential box, and Clara's dress, hands, and face were saturated with blood. Then pandemonium broke out. The audience reacted but had no idea what happened. Then smoke was seen rising from the president's box. Suddenly a man jumped from the box onto the stage, and he was recognized by almost everyone there. It was the actor, John Wilkes Booth. The jump onto the stage injured his leg quite severely, and he immediately had difficulty walking. At that moment, the audience went wild and erupted with screams. Then, a very loud shout was heard from a woman in the audience, "The president has been shot!" Booth ran off the stage in spite of his injured leg, went out to the back of the theater, and escaped into the night on his horse.[53]

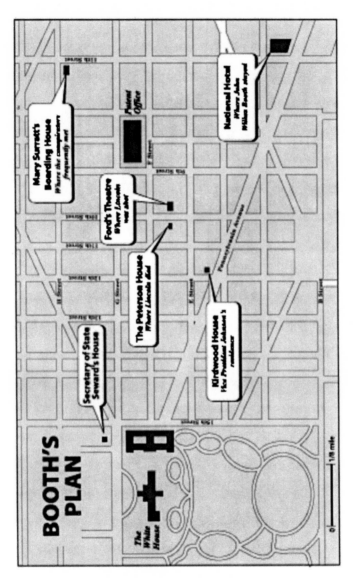

Booth's Assassination Plan

The situation then became chaotic and somewhat out of control. This was the worst possible thing that could have happened, and no one was prepared for what to do next. People were scrambling everywhere not knowing what would happen and wondered if this would become a general massacre. They were not far from wrong. At this very moment the two other assassination attempts that had been planned were under way, one to murder the vice president, and the other to murder the secretary of state. Fortunately, both Vice President Johnson and Secretary of State Seward were spared, but not without incident.

Lewis Powell, one of the accomplices, was accustomed to being shifty and ordering people about, so he simply acted like himself. He arrived at Secretary Seward's house with a package of medicine that had been presumably prescribed for the secretary. Seward had been injured earlier in the week and had facial lacerations suffered during a carriage accident and as such, it was appropriate to have medicine on the list of expected items. Powell knew about the accident and dreamed up the delivery of medicine as a ploy. After entering, Powell confronted a servant in the hallway who had been instructed to let no one in to see the patient. But Powell convinced the servant that he had special medicine for the secretary and was instructed to give it to him personally. He convinced the servant that there was no other option. The servant gave in and let Powell go into the secretary's bedroom. Next Powell was confronted by three other people, Seward's son Frederick, his daughter, and a male nurse. He pistol-whipped all of them leaving them unconscious, and then confronted Secretary Seward in bed. He pulled out his Bowie knife and began to slash away, but hit a steel brace that had been placed around Seward's neck following his accident, and this prevented a fatal cut. Seward remained alive, but injured extensively with lacerations on both sides of his neck. Powell was not sure if he had finished the job, but he was in a hurry at this point, and managed to escape from the quarters and run out into the night. But the plot had failed, and Seward remained alive, although in very critical condition.[54]

Finally, the associate with whom Booth had reservations, George Atzerodt, proved again to be completely unreliable. He simply got cold feet and did not carry out the assassination attempt on Vice President Johnson. His plan was to enter Johnson's quarters, sink a knife deep into the vice president's chest and finish him off. About fifteen minutes before he was to begin the feat, he entered a local tavern and began nursing his nerves by getting drunk. He spent the rest of the night imbibing and then wandered about the streets of Washington. This substantiated the suspicions about Atzerodt that Booth had already feared. Johnson remained alive and well. President Lincoln was the only victim that night which, by itself, was an enormous setback for the country. After being shot, President Lincoln was moved to a suitable room in the Peterson house across the street from the theater, as the doctors present did not want to move him any farther away under the circumstances of his deteriorating condition. The White House was simply too far away. The next morning on April 15, after nine hours of intensive struggle, Lincoln died at 7:22 AM.[55] This, unfortunately, was the beginning of new leadership in Washington, but it was not the same caring leadership as Lincoln had offered. The new leadership under President Johnson would make things more difficult for the country. The Confederates were still a very real threat, and they would likely be less inclined to surrender to conditions demanded by President Johnson, who sought revenge and punishment for the traitors. This would also tend to stretch out the period in which the different Confederate factions would surrender and cloud the exact time that the surrender would become official. These issues would also have an impact on the operations of the *Shenandoah* out in the Pacific Ocean, where it was difficult, at best, to know what the official status was on anything at any time.

On April 17, the *Milo* was prepared to weigh anchor and depart Honolulu to head for the Bering Sea.[56] She had been anchored in the Port of Honolulu since March 26, a little over three weeks before. On this morning, she was immaculate after spending several weeks in Honolulu, offloading the whale harvest for shipment back to New Bedford, and getting the ship painted and ready for the summer months up north. The news about the Civil War was good, and there was a feeling that the war was actually over. No one was now concerned about running into a Confederate cruiser at this point as the news of General Lee's surrender had already been received by telegraph in San Francisco and this news had spread to Honolulu. Captain Hawes was prepared for one more summer in the Bering Sea, and then he had planned to return to New Bedford and call it quits. Jessie liked this idea also, as she was ready to settle down and raise her family on land from this point on. Life at sea had been exciting and profitable, but now it was time to think about life at home in New Bedford. Both children had spent most of their lives at sea and naturally thought this was the way people lived. They did enjoy the time on shore in places like Honolulu, but they also enjoyed the life at sea where things changed from day to day. However, they would adapt to life back in New Bedford rather quickly when the time came. For now, they were prepared to spend more time on the *Milo* and looked forward to the summer on the Bering Sea. Jessie would make life interesting for them with school, games, and the chores at sea. After all, this was a family of the sea during this period of time, and they had become quite accustomed to this life.

This was an exciting morning for Captain Hawes, as the *Milo* left Honolulu and headed for the Bering Sea. At this point, the *Milo* and the *Shenandoah* were both heading north in the Pacific Ocean, but they were about four thousand miles apart. Captain Waddell was in hot pursuit of American whaleships, but Captain Hawes had no idea that a Confederate cruiser was in the same ocean at this time looking for anyone, particularly American whalers. That was the situation for the *Milo* as well as all other whaling ships in the northern Pacific at that time. The United States Navy in the summer of 1865 was also out of touch with the facts and had no idea where the *Shenandoah* was or where it was going.

To make matters worse, there was great confusion in Washington and throughout the country as to the succession of Vice President Andrew Johnson to be president after the Lincoln's death. Nothing in the Constitution covered this issue. There was a matter of precedence stemming from the succession of previous vice presidents to the presidency in two prior cases. John Tyler succeeded the first president to die in office, William Henry Harrison in 1841, and Millard Fillmore succeeded Zachary Taylor in 1850. In both cases, the decisions were not based on what was written in the Constitution, but on consensus of those in the decision-making body. These two cases set up the precedence. Constitutional scholars have generally concluded that the delegates who approved the Constitution probably contemplated that in case of the death of the president, the vice president would only perform the duties of the president until a new election was held and that he would not ipso facto become president. After Lincoln was shot and he lay dying, the argument arose again, but in this case, less than three hours after Lincoln's death, precedence prevailed and Andrew Johnson was sworn in as president on April 15, 1865. Needless to say, this was not a popular outcome, as there were many citizens who did not like Johnson and were alarmed that he would be president.[57]

Johnson and Lincoln were very different. Lincoln was a man of peace and forgiveness. Johnson was a man of revenge and punishment. Both men coveted the concept of Union and wanted the United States to be one nation, not two. Johnson showed no mercy at all, and this was significant in the way he and Lincoln differed in how the Reconstruction of the Union would be handled. Lincoln's way was reconciliation, and Johnson's way was punishment. General Lee surrendered to General Grant under the terms laid out by Lincoln during the meeting at City Point with Generals Grant and Sherman. Lee surrendered because the terms were better than he ever thought possible and they were fair to all, officers and men alike. If he had not been favorable to the terms of surrender, he may have elected to retreat into the hills and become an insurgent force. If that had happened, the outcome certainly would have been different than it was, and probably would have altered the restoration of the Union in an unfavorable way. As it turned out, with Johnson now president, the new leadership would shape things to come, albeit differently had Lincoln not been assassinated. This new leadership would change the way that peace would come about, and perhaps extend and confuse the order of events in the official peace settlement across the country. After all, there were still Confederate forces in place under General Joe Johnston in North Carolina, as well as in a number of other Confederate renegade forces scattered about in different parts of the South and West.

However, the next order of business in the minds of everyone was to hunt down and capture John Wilkes Booth and his associates. The assassination of President Lincoln had caused a feeling among all people in the North to capture and punish all of those Confederates who they thought were in back of the assassination plot. No one knew for sure how many people were involved in the plot, and everyone wanted revenge for this horrible act. The country was in shock, and there were issues on the table that needed immediate attention. In order of priority, these were the capture of John Wilkes Booth, the surrender of the Confederacy, and the restoration of the Union. Needless to say, these issues affected many different happenings that were taking place around the world. One issue was the continuing operation of the CSS *Shenandoah* as it homed in toward the American whaling fleet in the northern Pacific Ocean, the Okhotsk Sea, and the Bering Sea. If the Confederacy surrendered across the board, when would the *Shenandoah* get the word and cease further destruction of American ships at sea? Of course, no one knew the whereabouts of the *Shenandoah*, so no one really had this question in mind at that time. But the *Shenandoah* was out in the Pacific Ocean and it was homing in on the American whaling fleet. Would the word of the Confederacy's surrender, whenever it actually took place, get there in time?

The hunt for John Wilkes Booth and his accomplices went into high gear. Both the secretaries of war and navy worked tirelessly getting personnel and resources together to hunt, capture, and punish Booth and his conspirators. Booth had escaped on horseback from Ford's Theater after the shooting and quickly rode over to Navy Yard Bridge, about twenty minutes away. He arrived before any news of President Lincoln's assassination attempt. He was stopped at the bridge by a guard who questioned him closely, but remarkably, Booth gave his real name and was allowed to cross the bridge over the Anacostia River into Maryland. After all, everyone knew John Wilkes Booth; he was a popular actor; and no one would ever have thought he would cause any kind of trouble, least of all murder. After crossing the bridge, Booth rode into the Maryland countryside at high speed and was accompanied by his accomplice who had also avoided capture, Davy Herold. About midnight on April 14, they stopped at Surratt

Tavern, south of the District, to pick up carbines, ammunition and field glasses, where they had been stashed during the assassination planning stage. After this, they continued on to the Maryland home of Dr. Samuel Mudd, a sympathizer to the rebellion, arriving there about four o'clock in the morning. Booth was tired and in pain with his broken leg. Dr. Mudd set the leg, and allowed Booth and Herold to sleep in an upstairs room. Nothing was said about the assassination attempt on the president's life, so Dr. Mudd was completely in the dark. By the next day, there were literally thousands of Union troops moving about the countryside looking for the conspirators. When Mudd heard Union Calvary moving about close by, he immediately ordered the conspirators to leave his house. Mudd was later questioned and arrested. He provided the Union troops with some vital intelligence, that he had set Booth's broken leg, so now they knew to look for a man with a bad leg. Booth and Herold spent several days and nights in the woods in hiding and ultimately crossed over the Potomac River into Virginia where they thought they had a better chance to escape. They continued to a farmhouse in Port Royal, Virginia, owned by Richard Garrett, arriving there on April 24. Union troops were still in hot pursuit and arrived at the Garrett farm area on the twenty-fifth and were noticed by Garrett. He was certain now that the two men in his house were troublemakers, and he ordered them out. Booth talked him into letting them stay in the barn behind the house for another night. That night, Union troops knocked on the front door, and questioned Garrett and his sons. One of the sons blurted out that the men they were looking for were in the barn. After that, things happened fast.

Union soldiers went to the barn and loudly ordered the men inside to come out with their hands up. Davy Herold came out, but Booth stayed inside and yelled back that he would never come out alive. Herold surrendered and was taken prisoner. About 4:30 AM in the morning of April 26, one of the soldiers lit a torch and threw it into the barn, setting the barn on fire. Booth started toward the barn door and a shot rang out. Booth fell to the ground face first, then pitched and rolled over by the door. He had been hit in the spinal cord and was paralyzed; he could not move and was dying. The soldiers dragged him away from the barn door and placed him on the porch of the Garret farmhouse. A doctor who had been called arrived as the sun was coming up over the horizon. He looked at Booth and said there was nothing he could do. Booth died two and a half hours after he was shot; it was less time than Lincoln took after he was shot. It was Booth's twenty-seventh birthday, April 26. Make no mistake; John Wilkes Booth was one man that, all by himself, had an enormous impact on the direction the country would take at that time. If he had been able to pull off the three assassinations, it would have been even a more disastrous situation. It proves that one man can make a significant difference in the direction of a nation. It has happened too many times in the history of civilization, and it will probably happen in the future. This points out that we must always be on guard to place good men in high places and be vigilant for those men who would do us harm.

Lewis Powell, George Atzerodt, and Mary Surratt had already been captured before the end of the first week after Lincoln's death, and were in chains on an ironclad ship anchored on the Potomac River. Davy Herold joined them as soon as he was returned to the District after capture. By the time Booth was cornered and met his death and the news made public, there was a feeling of closure across the country and relief that the assassins had been promptly caught and punished. Then, it was time to concentrate on the end of the Civil War and the Reconstruction.

This was not an easy task under the new Johnson leadership with different points of view from those previously espoused by Lincoln. It would take focused leadership and good teamwork before peace would be at hand and for the official news to spread out to the world. In the meantime, there would be more destruction and disappointment for a lot of people here and there across the country, not to mention the American whalers in the northern Pacific Ocean.

On April 26, the day John Wilkes Booth was captured and shot, the *Milo* was heading west in the Pacific Ocean and was about seven hundred miles northwest of Honolulu.[58] The *Shenandoah* was north of the Caroline Islands and had been sailing back and forth along the shipping lanes between the 17° and 20° parallels in north latitude and unsuccessfully searching for merchant ships sailing along this shipping lane which accommodated vessels traveling from San Francisco to China. Continuing northward, the *Shenandoah* found the shipping lanes between the 35° and 45° parallels for vessels traveling west to east and spent several days along these lanes. As the ship headed north from the 43° parallel, the weather took a turn for the worse and the *Shenandoah* spent several days in and out of violent storms that tossed the vessel unmercifully.

By April 26, the *Milo* and the *Shenandoah* were about three thousand miles apart, both ultimately heading for the Bering Sea. Both of these ships were out of touch with news of the day and had no idea what was happening anywhere else in the world, particularly in America. However, Captain Hawes had heard about the surrender of General Lee to General Grant during his stopover in Honolulu. He was comfortable with the news about the war and continued to relax his vigilance for Confederate cruisers. He was furthermore looking forward to a profitable summer of whaling in the Bering Sea. Captain Waddell had not heard any news at all since leaving Melbourne and was completely in the dark about the status of the Confederacy. He had not had contact with anyone except the schooner from Honolulu, the *Pfiel*, and the whalers on Ponape Island, who were out of touch with the current war news also.

Now that John Wilkes Booth had been captured and shot to death at the Garrett farm and the other conspirators were also caught and awaiting punishment, the next order of business for the United States was to press for a Union victory and a Confederate surrender across the board. This would not be an easy accomplishment under the conditions existing by the end of April 1865.

On April 14, General Joe Johnston sent a communiqué to General Sherman asking for a meeting to discuss "exterminating the existing war."[59] Sherman was ecstatic; he could hardly believe this. Sherman answered immediately and agreed to meet with Johnston on Monday, April 17, between the picket lines of the two armies. The next morning, on the way to the meeting place, Sherman received an urgent message, in code, announcing the death of President Lincoln, the attempt on Secretary Seward, and the wider plot to kill Vice President Johnson. Sherman was aghast and swore the telegraph operator to secrecy, and told no one else. He then proceeded on his way to meet with Johnston, and like Grant, let Johnston select the place for the meeting. This turned out to be a farmhouse belonging to a local farmer, James Bennett. Unlike Appomattox, the two men went into the house alone with no one else present. They were both West Pointers and had mutual respect for each other. After some introductory small talk, they got down to business. Sherman then disclosed the news about Lincoln's death, and Johnston was shocked and also honestly and visibly upset. Sherman presented the initial terms of surrender, and these were even more generous than Grant had offered Lee. Johnston was ecstatic but wanted to do even more, he wanted this to be not only his surrender to Sherman, but the complete surrender and ending of the war across the board. Sherman asked if he had that authority, and Johnson said he would bring John Breckenridge, vice president of the Confederacy, into the discussion, and asked for three days to get things in order. Sherman gave him one day. The next morning, Johnston was accompanied by Breckenridge who had the credentials to make this happen and more importantly had the influence over all Confederate commanders to convince them to follow his advice on this matter and lay down their arms. However, the outcome of the meeting was subject to the approval of higher authority for both Sherman and Johnston. The results of the review were that Jeff Davis approved, but President Andrew Johnson did not. He was violently opposed to the generous terms and ordered Sherman to continue the fight. Following this decision, Davis ordered Johnston to essentially retreat into Georgia, and continue the fight as an insurgent force for as long as it would take to achieve victory. Jeff Davis did not agree with General Johnston or Vice President Breckenridge, and by April 15, ordered all-out guerrilla warfare. Things were not going well at all. It looked like the war was starting all over again.

Then, things took a turn for the better. Johnston thought hard about guerrilla warfare and further bloodshed, and it did not take long to come to a decision. He elected to disobey Jeff Davis and then contacted Sherman for the third time. They met on the same day the John Wilkes Booth was captured and killed, April 26, and this time, the two men quickly disposed of the matter. Sherman offered the same terms that Grant had offered Lee, and Johnston accepted.[60] It was an amiable surrender and the beginning of the end of the war. With General Grant running . interference and gaining influence with the Union leaders back in Washington, the surrender was accepted by the United States, and the country was on the way toward peace.

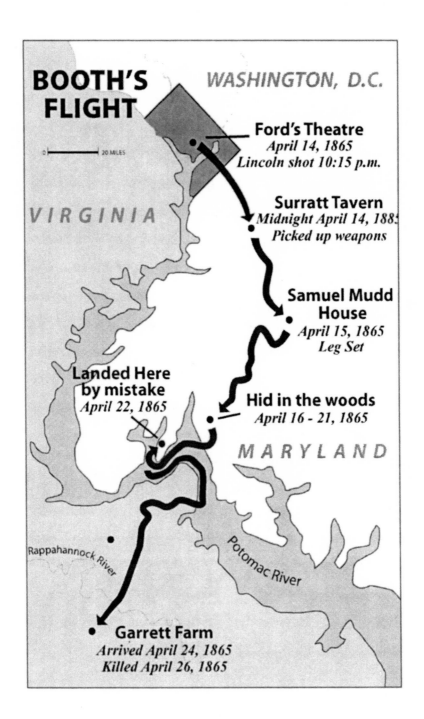

Booth's Flight to Virginia

279

14. A Drawn-Out Civil War

By the end of April 1865, the country still had some serious problems to overcome. First, of course, was the Civil War itself, which looked like it was over, was not over by a long shot. Generals Lee and Johnston had surrendered and a large Confederate force of over fifty thousand troops out of both armies had been disbanded. However, there were a multitude of Confederate forces in various parts of the South and West that were still active and very much wanting to fight for independence. Confederate President Jefferson Davis did not want to give up, and he was the loudest voice promoting a long drawn-out fight even to the extent of a guerilla campaign against the Union.

Farther south, General Richard Taylor had about ten thousand men located in Alabama, Mississippi, and Louisiana. Supporting Taylor was General Nathan Bedford Forrest who commanded a large cavalry force located in Alabama and was known for his never giving up and always giving his utmost to attain victory

Colonel John Mosby commanded the Forty-third Battalion Virginia Cavalry, Partisan Rangers, which later expanded into Mosby's Command, a regimental-sized unit of partisan rangers operating in Northern Virginia. Mosby was highly respected by Union commanders for his tenacity and skilled military leadership, and had been a thorn in the side of Union forces throughout the war.

Farther South and West, General Kirby Smith commanded some thirty-six thousand troops that composed the Trans-Mississippi Department. In the Midwest, Colonel J.Q. Chenowith was commander of the Department of Western Kentucky; and in the Deep South, Major General Sam Jones, commanded the District of Florida. In the Western region, Brigadier General M. Jeff Thompson led the rebel veterans in Missouri and the West.

Also, among still other commanders, there was Brigadier General Stand Watie, a Cherokee Indian Chief, and the only American Indian to achieve the rank of general in the Confederate Army. Watie operated mostly in Indian Territory and saw service in Kansas, Missouri, Arkansas, and other surrounding states and territories.

Last, but not least, was Lieutenant Commanding James I. Waddell, commander of the Confederate cruiser, CSS *Shenandoah*, who was at the time destroying American property in the Pacific Ocean, and who would continue doing this for as long as he had a country to represent and defend. At that time, the *Shenandoah* was a very real threat and the most destructive Confederate naval threat to Yankee shipping on the high seas.

At the end of April 1865, Waddell was out of touch with the rest of the world, but had no reason to believe that the Confederacy had ceased to exist or was even in trouble. He believed he was simply doing the work that was in support the Confederacy and President Jefferson Davis. All of the Confederate commanders and their men collectively were a great threat to the Union, and they were all in a position to hold out for years and years as insurgent forces, if that were the chosen course.

It was a difficult time for both the Union and the Confederacy in coming to terms for a peaceful settlement. This was made more difficult by the fact that President Lincoln's assassination was believed by many to be part of a conspiracy sponsored by the Confederate leadership, up to and including Confederate President Jefferson Davis. In this regard, revenge was the call of the day throughout the Union, including those in the executive and legislative branches of the United States government. It was not an easy time for anyone. Furthermore, there was a belief in the Confederacy that the Union would be merciless in their dealings with the Confederacy. They expected that punishment would be handed out to those who were thought to be behind the assassination of Lincoln, as well as anyone who took up arms against the Union during the Civil War. These thoughts made it difficult to consider the likelihood of peace and made it more likely for the South to consider a long and drawn-out insurgency that would offer the best chance for independence, however long that would take. Guerilla warfare was a distinct and likely possibility except for one person who, alone, turned everything around and made a significant difference to the outcome of this great dilemma. This person was none other than General Robert E. Lee, the idol and popular military leader of the Confederacy.

General Robert E. Lee, the patriarch of the Confederacy, could have blown the bugle that set off guerrilla warfare that could have lasted for years. He had that much influence over the South; if he gave the word, he would have been supported and the insurgency would have begun. But, he did just the opposite. When Lincoln closed his eyes for the last time on April 15, Lee denounced the assassination in the strongest possible terms and further, celebrated the end of slavery. Shortly after Lincoln's death, a scout from John Mosby's rangers slipped into Richmond and made his way to a home that Lee happened to be visiting. He had a message from Mosby, "What should the rangers do? Surrender, or fight on?"

"Go home," was Lee's blunt response, "All you boys who fought with me, go home and help build a shattered nation. The time for fighting is over."

Soon after Lincoln's death, in an interview arranged with Thomas Cook, of the *New York Herold*, General Lee called it a despicable act. The interview was published by the *Herold* and was read by loyal readers from the North as well as the South. Lee knew that many Southerners read the *Herold* to get their news. Lee wanted everyone to know his thoughts, and with this initiative, he changed the viewpoint of the nation. His vision was the same as Lincoln's in terms of bringing the Union back together in peace. He saw the folly of a widespread gorilla war that could last indefinitely and bring havoc and destruction to the nation. Lee had a new message for everyone, and that was "to make any sacrifice or perform any honorable act that would tend to the restoration of peace."[61] The fact that General Lee took this position was significant, since he had previously been associated with the top leadership of the rebellion. At this juncture, Lee single-handedly brought the country together by the public statements he made, and these were published throughout the country, during this emotional time. The last thing he wanted was a protracted and long drawn-out guerilla war.

After the fall of Richmond, Jeff Davis and his entourage had been on the run with twelve railroad cars seeking a safe and permanent location for the Confederate government. The first stop was Danville, Virginia, for a short stay. Then the train headed south to Charlotte, North Carolina, again for a short stay. The train rolled on farther to Abbeville, South Carolina. At all of these stops, Davis did everything in his power to ignite the spirit of the Southern heart, but to no avail.

Just the opposite took place among the Confederate commanders. Following General Joe Johnston's surrender on April 26, the remaining Confederate commanders, one by one, surrendered to their Union counterparts across the South and West. General Richard Taylor, commander of the Confederate Army in Alabama, Mississippi, and East Louisiana surrendered to Union General Edward Canby in Citronelle, Alabama, on May 4, in an amiable ceremony of food, camaraderie, and music. On May 9, General Nathan Bedford Forrest told his men to go home and meet their responsibilities "like men," after he had been requested by the Confederacy to go into the hills for a "long fight." Colonel John Mosby simply disbanded his rangers after General Lee's surrender, and never formally surrendered himself. During May 1865, General E. Kirby Smith surrendered his force of twenty-six thousand troops that made up the Trans-Mississippi Department; likewise Colonel J.Q. Chenowith, commander of the Department of Western Kentucky, and General Sam Jones, commander of the District of Florida, followed that path. Also, among others, the brilliant Brigadier General Jeff Thompson, leader of rebel veterans of Missouri and the West, surrendered in late May, 1865.

Jeff Davis's rolling railroad government's final stop was Irwinville, Georgia, where he planned to rally the South and put together a stand that would bring victory and independence. Jeff Davis was still shocked and distraught that General Joe Johnston had disobeyed his orders, and he felt at this point that the Confederate cause was almost lost. On May 2, he held a council of his military aides for those who were still among his entourage. It was his last council of war. He pleaded with them with more fervor than judgment to continue the fight. At this point, his aides politely shook their heads sadly and told him, "It is time."[62] It was time to give up the fight as any attempt to continue the war would be a "cruel injustice." At that point, Davis stood up and said, "Then all is lost." Still, Davis did not give up and he refused to quit. He never did surrender.

His effort did not last long. He was captured by Union forces in Georgia on May 10, 1865, ridiculed unmercifully by his Union captors and put into confinement. On that same day, President Andrew Johnson issued a formal proclamation, stating, "The armed resistance to the authority of this government may be regarded as virtually at an end." This news was quickly picked up in the North which had faster communications media, and more slowly in the South which had far less communication media capability, and even more slowly in the rest of the world which had essentially no transcontinental communications media at all. There was, in fact, no official cessation of the Civil War. There was no treaty and no exact time that the war ended. This was why there was confusion as to the status of the war for the many weeks before it was recognized by the country that, in fact, the Civil War had ended. There was also confusion as to how to punish the leaders of the rebellion, or whether to punish them at all.

This was a long and drawn-out debate which would take years to resolve. Jefferson Davis would spend over two years in confinement before being released and set free. This was certainly a change of heart from the initial "hang him" attitude among many leaders in the North.

In the meantime, news arrived from England on May 13 that the *Shenandoah* was on her way to the Arctic. Its whereabouts were not known, but there was concern that the rebel raider would do harm to American shipping somewhere in the Pacific region. On this day, a group of New London merchants and ship owners got together and requested that Secretary Welles protect whaling vessels from destructive raids by the CSS *Shenandoah* in the Pacific and Arctic Ocean regions. Following that request, there is no evidence that any such order was given at that time by Secretary Welles. However, in a three-day period, the leading maritime insurance company in New England did a booming business with ship owners for additional coverage on their vessels. During the course of one day alone, the company received almost $119,000 in premiums, the largest sum written by the company during a one-day period until the start of World War I.

On May 22, all of the emblems of mourning for President Lincoln were taken down and after this period, came pageantry. Washington prepared itself for the Grand Review of the Armies of the Republic, and the city was filled with people from all over the land. Flags all over, including the White House, went from half-staff to full staff. All of the Union forces that could make the trip to Washington were there for the great Military Review. President Johnson, Generals Grant and Sherman along with many other high-level government dignitaries were there for the Review. Military bands gathered from around the country, civic groups arrived from many cities of the North such as Boston, New York, Philadelphia, Chicago, and so on. The Review lasted two days and nights with much social activity including dances, parties, and other social events. It was a time of celebration, not only for the victory, but even more so for the end of the bloodshed, the reunification of the nation, and the beginning of peace. The country was ecstatic.

Cherokee Indian Chief and Brigadier General Stand Watie was the last Confederate commander to surrender. On June 23, he surrendered his battalion, a diverse mixture of Confederate Cherokees, Creeks, Seminoles, and Osages, at Doaksville, the Choctaw capital near Fort Towson in Indian

Territory, now in the State of Oklahoma. The Civil War was ended by the separate surrenders of individual Confederate commanders, one after the other. There was no single overall ceremony that signaled a cessation of the war, only individual surrenders. The result was that although the war was over, not everyone knew it, and there was no written document signed by both sides of the conflict to substantiate the end. Captain Waddell did not know and had no means to find out the status of the war. He was out of communication with the rest of the world, and was completely in the dark. Moreover, no other men of the sea, including Captain Hawes and all other whaling or merchant masters, knew with certainty the status of world events either. Even though they made port calls where news was available, they were only able to receive what was available. Up-to-date news was not always available on all subjects at any time in any port and certainly nothing was definite on the status of the Civil War during the summer of 1865. Regardless, most of the American whaling fleet knew that the war was taking a turn for the better, and most had heard of Lee's surrender to Grant by this time. But, they did not know that the Civil War was actually over, and this was a significant problem for the whaling fleet in the Northern Pacific at that time. More importantly, no whaling captain knew that the CSS *Shenandoah* was even in the

Pacific Ocean, and certainly, no whaling captain ever expected the Confederates to travel north to the very cold Bering Sea, not to mention an even colder Arctic Ocean. Consequently, no whaling captain ever expected to have a confrontation with the Confederate cruiser during the summer of 1865.

15. The Pacific Squadron

From the outset of the Civil War, the United States Navy did the best it could to protect American commerce and enforce the blockade of Confederate ports. The Atlantic Ocean and Gulf of Mexico were covered as well as could be expected with the limited number of warships, but there were many holes in the blockade that were penetrated by ships from mainly Europe and England that supplied goods and services to the Confederate establishment. The federal government was certainly short of warships that would have made it more difficult for "blockade busters" to penetrate, but in spite of a shortage of ships, the navy was able to perform its blockading mission with some success, particularly on the Atlantic and Gulf coasts of the United States. It was not as successful protecting American shipping and whaling interests at sea.

The Pacific coast of the Americas was a different story. The mission of maintaining peace in the Pacific fell upon the Pacific Squadron of the U.S. Navy, which was under the command of Commodore J.B. Montgomery at the outset of the Civil War. When the war began, the squadron consisted of only six relatively small wooden armed sloops to patrol the entire Pacific Ocean. The six sloops of war, USS *Lancaster*, USS *Saranac*, USS *Wyoming*, USS *Narragansett*, and USS *Cyane* and one other unnamed sloop of war comprised the entire Pacific Squadron of 1861. These ships cruised along the coast from San Francisco to Panama, and as far north as Alaska and as far south as Chili. They visited Honolulu to guard the whaling fleet, and they protected American commerce along the coasts of China and Japan, and they even cruised to Australia and the South Seas as conditions dictated. This was a very large territory for such a small fleet of warships. All of these ships were steam-powered sailing sloops except the USS *Cyane* which was the oldest ship, having been commissioned in 1838. It was a three-masted sailing ship and boasted a 22-gun battery of firepower.

Navy Secretary Welles was well aware of the defenseless position of the Pacific coast and sought the assistance of War Secretary Simon Cameron. Cameron served as war secretary from March 1861 to January 1862, when he resigned following corruption charges. Together they issued orders to the commanders of navy and army forces on the Pacific coast to aid each other in preventing the Confederates from gaining a foothold in California or elsewhere on the Pacific coast. The two secretaries were particularly concerned about protecting ships from the Pacific Mail Steamship Company. They saw to it that the army and navy jointly provided men and arms for the protection of these mail steamers that were sailing between San Francisco and Panama with their heavy shipments of gold and other valuable goods. As a further precaution against possible Confederate activities, Commodore Montgomery ordered the *Wyoming*, *Narragansett*, and *Cyane* to cruise along the coasts of California and Mexico for protection of these merchant steamers as well. Commodore Montgomery also sailed regularly to Panama on his flagship, USS *Lancaster*, to meet dispatches from the navy department on a timelier basis.

In 1862, the USS *Wyoming* was detached and sent to the East Indies thereby reducing the fleet by one fighting ship. This decrease in strength along with the increased activity along the southern coast left the Columbia River and northern coast vulnerable to attack. Also in 1862, Commodore Montgomery, after serving in this capacity for three years, was replaced by Rear Admiral Charles E. Bell as commander of the Pacific Squadron.

Around this time, the Confederate forces under General Sibley were moving up the Rio Grande from Texas and a Colonel John R. Baylor had established his rebel government at Mesilla in the Arizona territory of the Confederate States of America. Colonel Baylor issued a proclamation establishing the rebel government to a receptive population there and was secretly negotiating with the Mexican governments of Sonora and Chihuahua to secure their cooperation. The Pacific Squadron was alerted and the USS *St. Mary's* was ordered to the Mexican port of Guaymas to seek the support of the Mexican government. The *St. Mary's* had been operating out of Panama and was one of the older vessels cruising the Pacific. She was strictly a sailing ship without steam power, built in 1843, and possessed armament of sixteen thirty-two pounders and six eight-inch guns.

The USS *Saginaw* and the storeship *Farallones* were added to the fleet in 1863. This was a year of anxiety for the small squadron, the forts on shore, and the citizens as well. A plot was discovered to outfit and arm the schooner *J.M. Chapman* for use in the service of the rebellion to cruise the high seas and commit hostilities upon the citizens, property and vessels of the United States. President Jefferson Davis was behind this plot and had issued a letter of marque[63] and a form of bond with instructions on how to use these documents if any of the prizes were bonded. The plans were quite ambitious and included the capture of one of the Pacific Mail steamers, the recovery of a two million dollar treasure from the sunken SS *Golden Gate* which was wrecked off the coast of Manzanillo, Mexico, and then to continue to cruise the Pacific Ocean as far away as the China Sea and Indian Ocean. On March 15, 1863, the *J.M. Chapman* lifted anchor and slowly sailed away from the wharf, while under the watchful eye of Commander Paul Shirley of the USS *Cyane*, who had been keeping a twenty-four-hour daily watch on the activities of the *Chapman*. As soon as the *Chapman* was about three hundred yards from the dock, two boatloads of armed seamen from the USS *Cyane* rowed toward the schooner. The *Cyane* seamen then boarded the *Chapman* and captured her without resistance. The instigators were tried before a judge, convicted, and sent to prison at Alcatraz. In December of 1863, President Lincoln issued a proclamation granting all political prisoners full pardon providing they took and kept an oath of allegiance. Following this, all of these traitors demanded their release from Alcatraz and they were granted freedom in February 1864.

Other events also took place during this time on the West Coast that had nothing to do with American Civil War operations. For one, a fleet from the Russian Navy was anchored in San Francisco harbor in November 1863, on a goodwill mission ordered by Alexander II of Russia. Both Czar Alexander and President Lincoln had a common bond of sympathy and understanding as both were opposed to slavery. The Russian officers were entertained by the mayor of San Francisco as well as many of the prominent citizens. This was in contrast to her Far East neighbor, Japan. At that time, certain elements in Japan were against any contact or commerce with outsiders, including United States, European or other foreign countries that had signed a treaty with the Japanese imperial government. The Japanese rebel warlord in charge was intent on getting rid of all foreigners from Japanese soil, as he felt that the treaties were unfavorable to Japanese interests. The center of the opposition was in the city of Shimonoseki, on the Japanese island of Honshu, and involved commerce on the Strait of Shimonoseki, a passageway between the main islands of Japan, Honshu, and Kyushu, and a shortcut for sea vessels cruising between eastern Japanese waters and western Japanese waters.

In June of 1863, the American merchant steamer *Pembroke* was at anchor outside Shimonoseki Strait when it was fired upon by two European-built warships belonging to the rebel Japanese forces. Fortunately, the *Pembroke* managed to get away with only slight damage and no casualties. In short order, the Japanese warlord had managed to fire on most of the nations with consulates in Japan. In response to the action against the steamer *Pembroke*, on July 16, 1863, under the sanction of U.S. Foreign Minister to Japan Robert Pruyn, the U.S. frigate USS *Wyoming*, under the command of Captain David McDougal, sailed into the strait and single-handedly engaged the U.S.-built, but poorly manned, Japanese rebel fleet. While the *Wyoming* was cruising thorough the straits of Shimonoseki, the Japanese land and naval guns opened fire. The *Wyoming* returned the fire, and the battle continued for an hour or so. The Japanese bark *Daniel Webster* and the brig *Lanrick* were sunk and the steamer *Lancefield* was damaged. There were forty Japanese casualties, while the *Wyoming* suffered extensive damage with fourteen crew members dead or wounded. This demonstrated that the Pacific Squadron at that time had more on its hands than just a Confederate threat alone.

There were also plans to build up the defense capabilities against hostile acts by foreign gunships or other forces. One plan was to construct revolving iron towers on both sides of the Golden Gate that would draw up massive steel chains across the entrance to the harbor with steam power to prevent foreign ships from entering the harbor. This was a bold plan that required extensive engineering to develop a successful design. Also, the first ironclad ram, USS *Camanche*, was delivered to San Francisco in November 1863, but was sunk along with the delivery vessel, *Aquila*, during a violent storm. It was later recovered and reassembled and finally launched in November 1864, one year after its initial arrival. The presence of the ironclad in the Pacific allayed the fears of the people and gave assurance of their adequate protection.

In the spring of 1864, another conspiracy to capture Pacific mail steamers was discovered. Confederate Navy Secretary Mallory had ordered Captain T. E. Hogg and his command to take passage on board the SS *San Salvador* and to capture her as soon as she reached the high seas. Upon securing the steamer, he was instructed to arm her and attack the Pacific merchant steamers and the American whalers in the North Pacific. Captain Hogg went to Havana, and while there his plans were discovered by American Consul Thomas Savage and relayed on to Rear Admiral George F. Pearson at Panama. The passengers boarding the steamer in Panama were closely observed, and when the Hogg party was discovered aboard the *San Salvador*, a task force from the USS *Lancaster* arrested them and brought them to San Francisco where they were tried and convicted. They were all sentenced to be hanged, but this was later changed to life imprisonment for Hogg and ten years for the others. In the fall of 1864, Rear Admiral Pearson replaced Rear Admiral Bell after three years in the job as commander of the Pacific Squadron.

There were also other demands on the Pacific Squadron that were brought on by foreign influence. Following the Mexican-American War of 1846 to 1848, Mexico entered a period of national crisis during the 1850s. Years of fighting not only the Americans but also a civil war within the country had left Mexico devastated and bankrupt. Unable to pay its obligations, President Benito Juarez issued a moratorium on July 17, 1861, announcing that all foreign debt payments would be suspended for a brief period of two years, with a promise that, after that period, payments would resume. The English, Spanish, and French refused to allow Juarez to do this and instead decided to invade Mexico and get payments in any way they could. The English and Spanish withdrew from this stance, but the French refused to change course. The outcome was an invasion of Mexico by the French in January, 1862; the ultimate victory by the French; and the installation of Maximilian I as emperor of Mexico in 1864, under the authority of Napoleon III of France. This occupation continued through the end of the American Civil War and even into 1867. In 1867, the French withdrew from Mexico. During the withdrawal, Maximilian, while trying to escape through enemy lines, was captured and promptly executed under orders of President Juarez. This ended the French occupation. However, during the last year of the American Civil War, the situation in Mexico had a great deal of influence over the effectiveness of the Pacific Squadron to concentrate on Confederate naval activities. Associated with this occupation was armed activity along the Pacific coast by Mexico at a number of strategic ports including Acapulco, Guaymas, and Mazatlan.

Furthermore, the Spanish had interests more to the south in Peru and Chili. Spanish warships from time to time blockaded a number of ports along the coast of Peru and Chili, namely Callao and Valparaiso. In order to protect American interests and commerce all along the western coast of South America, the Pacific Squadron located ships of war at ports where they were needed for protection of Americans and American commerce. The most important of these ports in terms of military protection were Acapulco, Callao, and Valparaiso. All of these ports were active during 1865, and that was the period when the *Shenandoah* was cruising on the high seas.[64]

By early 1865, the Pacific Squadron had been increased to eleven vessels by the addition of the USS *Powhatan*, USS *Nyack*, USS *Mohongo*, USS *Tuscarora*, and the storeship *Fredonia*. Secretary Welles recommended even a greater increase to protect the increasing commerce of the Pacific. Then, in the summer of 1865, as peace came to the Atlantic coast at the close of the Civil War, the roar of the French guns at Acapulco and those of the Spanish at Valparaiso and Callao signaled that peace had not come to the west coast. This was in direct contrast to the "hands off" and "non-interference" policy of the United States government as promulgated by the Monroe Doctrine. Rear Admiral Pearson had his hands full trying to cover all the bases with such a small force. He would find the situation more difficult when the whereabouts of the *Shenandoah* became known.

16. The *Shenandoah* Comes to Life

On May 21, the *Shenandoah* arrived in the North Pacific off the coast of Kamchatka Peninsular in Siberia, Russia, and proceeded through a pass between islands in the Kuril Islands, and entered the Okhotsk Sea. The weather was cold, and the violent storms they had gone through had passed and the sky was clear. Sailing north in the Okhotsk Sea, the snow-covered mountains of Kamchatka became visible, and the men aboard were absorbed in taking in the scenery. It had been a long time for some and the first time for others to view snow-covered mountains anywhere. These were spectacular and a pleasant change from simply viewing the ocean around the ship as well as the sails that came into view occasionally. Executive Officer Lieutenant Whittle later wrote that he observed the most beautiful optical illusions he had ever seen before or since. When it was not foggy, the atmosphere was a perfect reflector. He was able to see clearly prominent points seventy miles away. He told of seeing a peak on the mountains and in the sky above the peak, a perfect reflection of the peak directly above it. The same phenomenon took place if they saw a ship in the distance, a perfect reflection of the ship inverted above the ship could be seen. It had something to do with the atmosphere there, and it was unique and striking.[65]

The *Shenandoah* sailed north, and the daylight lasted longer and longer, until finally, it remained daylight all day long. The sun simply reached a low point in the horizon but never went out of sight, and then it gradually rose up during the day. It was a strange daylight all day long. The *Shenandoah* had been encountering thick fog and heavy ice in these waters, even though it was well into May and approaching the summer months. On May 27, a sail was spotted on the horizon. Gradually the sail appeared closer and closer until it finally came into clear view. The *Shenandoah* then raised a Russian ensign which appeared appropriate since they were inside Russian waters, and this was done to trick the other vessel. Soon the other vessel came into clear view, and it raised the Stars and Stripes. This was exactly what Waddell expected, an American whaler! Immediately, the Russian ensign came down and the Confederate Stars and Bars went up. Waddell ordered a blank shot to be fired across the bow of the other vessel which turned out to be the brig *Abigail*, a whaler out of New Bedford. After the shot, the *Abigail* came to a halt and went alongside the *Shenandoah*. Waddell then dispatched Lieutenant Lee to board the whaler and inform the captain that his vessel was a prize to the Confederate State Steamer *Shenandoah*, and that he must at once proceed with his papers. After that, the following dialog was heard:

"Well," said Captain Ebenezer Nye, the old skipper, "I never thought I would see one of you Southern Privateers up here in the Okhotsk Sea. I've heard some of the pranks you fellows have done, but I thought I was out of your reach."

"Why, the fact of the matter is," replied Lieutenant Lee facetiously, "we have entered into a treaty with the whales, and are up here by special agreement to dispense of their mortal enemies."

"All right, my friend," said Captain Nye, "I never grumble at anything I can't help, but the whales needn't owe me much of a grudge, for the Lord knows I haven't disturbed them much this voyage, although I have done my share of blubber hunting in years gone by."

Since it was very cold outside on the deck of the *Abigail*, the nonchalant old skipper then invited the boarding officer inside to get something warm for his stomach while getting his papers in order. Soon thereafter, Captain Nye announced that he was ready and along with Lieutenant Lee they went on board the *Shenandoah* and the skipper then prepared to meet with Captain Waddell and learn his fate.[66]

Shortly after that, the *Abigail* crew of thirty came aboard the *Shenandoah* in their own whale boats and soon learned that they would be taking a different voyage home. It would be steam and not sail. They were all similar in nature to the skipper, and one said, "He had not expected to take steam home, and would just as soon trust to sail." However, they all accepted their fate in a good-natured way and even single irons and confinement in the forecastle did not seem to depress their spirits.

As it turned out, Captain Nye had lost a ship three years earlier when he had been confronted by the CSS *Alabama*. That ship was destroyed by the Confederate ship, but Captain Nye was able to find return passage home and subsequently find the current whaling ship, *Abigail*. Captain Waddell informed Captain Nye that he had no option but to destroy this ship as well and furthermore that his officers and men would search the ship for any provisions that were needed by the *Shenandoah*. Captain Nye had made space available for a large supply of corn whiskey to use for trading for furs with the coastal Siberians during the cruise. At the time of the capture, there was still a large supply of the alcohol aboard, and this was transferred over to the *Shenandoah*. In fact, this was about the only material transferred over to the *Shenandoah* as there was practically no whale oil in the hold.

As soon as a cask of whiskey was discovered by the crew, it was quickly opened and shared by a greater part of one watch. Those participating in the frolic were soon as drunk as men can be. As soon as this was discovered, the men were put into the ship's forecastle and the more inebriated were put into irons. This went on for a while and gradually, as more men found out about the discovery, there was more drinking until almost the entire ship was drunk and disorderly, except for the prisoners who were confined and chained. By the time control was established, there were not more than a dozen sober men on board the ship. Acting Master's Mate Cornelius Hunt later wrote that this was "the most general and stupendous 'spree' he had ever witnessed." The remainder of the beverages, consisting of twenty-five barrels of the corn whiskey, was stored away aboard ship only to be used *"in case of sickness,"* by order of Captain Waddell.[67]

The *Abigail* was put to flames and left burning while the party continued. Captain Waddell was angry, but was able to rather quickly gain control of the situation by putting the drunkards under arrest until they regained their normal senses. Following this event, Captain Waddell decided to cruise around the Okhotsk Sea in search of more Yankee whaleships, as this was a favorite location for many whaling masters. The weather was terribly cold at this time of year anywhere in the world, but here it was brutal. "If this is what summer weather is like," wrote, Lieutenant Whittle, "then winter must be terrible, and I feel sorry for all of those Russians sent to Siberia for crimes committed, as their lives must be awful." Next, Waddell discovered a group of some fifteen to thirty Yankee whaleships that had been known to be whaling at a particular spot around Jonas Island near the center of the Okhotsk Sea during this time. If he had targeted this group, it would have been a very large prize, perhaps the largest of all so far. However, ice on the Okhotsk Sea had been building and had become very thick and made it difficult to navigate. It also was a danger to a ship not built to withstand thick ice. With this in mind, Captain Waddell reluctantly gave up the chase to capture these ships.

On June 10, the *Shenandoah* was still cruising about the Okhotsk Sea where the ice had become less of a problem. On this day, several of the *Abigail* crew decided to sign up with the Confederates, and this turned out to be a bonus for Captain Waddell. One of those was the disreputable Thomas S. Manning who had shipped as second mate on the *Abigail* in San Francisco, but had been born in Baltimore and claimed to be a Southern sympathizer. He was enrolled on the *Shenandoah* as the ship's corporal. Manning was a traitor and a menace to his old shipmates. He was experienced as a whaler and knew his way around the North Pacific. To everyone's amazement, he volunteered not only to join the Confederate cause, but also to guide the *Shenandoah* to the location where they would find the Yankee whaling fleet in the Bering Sea, which included a ship that he had once served on. This was something that Captain Waddell did not expect but was glad to have available, in spite of Manning's reputation as a traitor and a reprobate. It was like having a harbor pilot aboard to steer the ship into uncharted waters. On June 13, the *Shenandoah* cruised out of the Okhotsk Sea and headed east and then north through the Aleutian Islands toward Cape Navarin, off the Siberian coast, all under the experienced navigation guidance provided by Thomas Manning, the newly acquired "pilot."

The day after the *Shenandoah* entered the Okhotsk Sea on May 21, the *Milo* arrived in the Bering Sea, having passed through a channel in the Aleutian Island group and was located about fifty miles northwest of Unalaska Island. Between May 22 and June 13, the *Milo* was actively searching for whales in the Bering Sea along with a number of other whaleships from New England, many from New Bedford. The *Milo* had caught only two whales during this time. The *Milo*'s hold was more or less empty of oil due to the fact that it had only been there for a few weeks, and all of its oil and whalebone from the winter months had been offloaded in Honolulu prior to her departure.

The *Milo* arrived along with the *Euphrates* of New Bedford and other American whaleships that had departed Honolulu about the same time. All of these ships were getting adjusted to the relatively cold weather in the Bering Sea after having spent the winter months in the southern Pacific where it was warm and less violent. The whales were also arriving from the southern Pacific; it was the season for such activity, as they were driven by some inner spirit to make the journey to the Bering Sea. Everyone knew about this natural phenomenon, and it was exciting for all of those present. When the summer season was over, it was expected to be profitable for all unless something unforeseen happened, like the arrival of an unwanted adversary.

By June 13, the *Milo* had sailed north and west toward the Siberian coast and was joined by a fleet of whalers from America, Honolulu, and Australia as well as other European countries. Life was not as lonely as one would believe during these voyages. The whalers visited each other frequently during voyages at sea. This occurred almost every day, particularly when they were not engaged in working on a captured whale. The gams continued to be enjoyable and entertaining for the entire Hawes family, as it gave Jessie a chance to visit with other ladies in each other's quarters, and the children to play with young friends whom they had met from time to time during the long voyage. Of course, it gave Captain Hawes a chance to discuss business and strategy with his fellow captains. Life was not that bad, and to make it even better, they all had a chance to return with a profitable catch at the end of the season.

During this period, while sailing north and west along the Siberian coastline, the *Milo* gammed with many vessels out of New Bedford almost on a daily basis including the whaleships *Euphrates, John P. West, Mercury, Leonidas, Corinthian, Gov. Troup, Mount Wollaston, Brunswick, Camilla, Congress, and Cleone.*[68] The *Milo* also gammed with whaleships from other ports including the *Covington* of Rhode Island, the *Hae Hawaii* and *Victoria* of Honolulu, and the *John Robert Towns* of Australia. On any given day, the *Milo* may have gammed with one of more of the above ships which included news, gossip, and meals.

The whaleships were not out on the sea alone by any means, and they had over time developed the habit of visiting each other as a matter of course. Much of the talk during these shipboard visits was about news back home and the status of the Civil War. In fact, by this time, it was assumed by all that the war was over after the news had spread to this part of the world of General Lee's surrender to General Grant at Appomattox Court House on April 9. Consequently, the American whalers were not concerned, or even gave a thought about a Confederate cruiser causing any trouble, particularly in the damp and cold Bering Sea at this time of year.

There were literally hundreds whalers in these waters ready for the summer harvest of whale oil and bones. On many days, the *Milo* spotted a large number of sails on the horizon, and on one day as many as forty. As the *Milo* proceeded north and west in the Bering Sea, patches of ice began showing up even though it was summertime, and it was very cold for late spring and early summer. During this time, the *Milo* spotted many whales, some of them, humpbacks, and on several days, boats were lowered and chases were made. The whalers did not chase the humpback whales, because when they were killed, the humpbacks sank and could not be recovered. During this time, most of the chases were unsuccessful, and the whale boats returned empty. However, on June 12, the *Milo* captured one whale.[69] This was the first whale caught since leaving Honolulu. All aboard were excited by this first catch, and the entire crew was busy going through all of the steps necessary to process a whale, from bringing the whale alongside the ship, to cutting and boiling the blubber. This was a long process and was hard work for the crew. They were sure that there would be many more whales and that the summer would be successful and that they would return to New Bedford with a profitable voyage. With what they knew about world news, they had no idea that an enemy Confederate cruiser was heading their way and were not the slightest bit concerned about such a possibility.

313

On June 14, the *Milo* gammed with the *Euphrates* again. This was almost becoming a daily routine between these two whaling vessels from New Bedford. They were about fifty miles off the coast of Cape Thaddeus where the ice was getting more predominant as the ships were getting closer to the Siberian coastline. The weather was cold and damp, and the men continued to process and boil the whale blubber from the recent catch, and transfer the oil from the try-pots to barrels for storage in the ship's hold. On June 15, the ice continued to flow and the *Milo* gammed again with the *Euphrates* and also with the *J.D. Thompson* of New Bedford, as well as with the *Victoria*, out of Honolulu. Looking out on the horizon, Cape Thaddeus was visible and there were as many as ten sails in sight at any one time during the day. This was a busy place in spite of the cold and the ice and its distance from everywhere else on the earth. This was truly the best whaling spot in the world at this time of year.

By June 15, the *Shenandoah* was two days out from the Okhotsk Sea and was proceeding northward toward Cape Navarin on the coast of Siberia, under the direction of the newly acquired pilot, Thomas Manning, the disreputable defector from the prize, brig *Abigail*. The winds were favorable, but the weather was otherwise foggy, raw and cold. Although the course took them close to the east coast of Kamchatka, they lost sight of land, and this made navigation particularly hazardous. Sailing northward on this day, the *Shenandoah* found herself off the southern coast of Bering Island under continuing foggy conditions and nearly went aground on Copper Island, a sister island to Bering Island, but saw land just in time to avoid ramming the shore. Bering Island is the western end point of the Aleutian Islands, and is relatively close to the Siberian coastline. As soon as the *Shenandoah* sailed around Copper Island, it entered the Bering Sea. Bering and Copper Islands were somewhat celebrated for having fur bearing animals, both land and marine, that live there and in their vicinity. There were several varieties of seal which were occasionally hunted by whalers when there was a scarcity of whales, as the men had the means and ability to capture them. This was also true for foxes and bears that lived on the islands and whalers went after them when they had nothing better to do. Needless to say, the *Shenandoah* had no interest in these ventures.

While the *Shenandoah* was making her way into the Bering Sea, a draft letter from Captain Bulloch to Captain Waddell had been prepared and was proposed to be sent through British channels to be delivered to Captain Waddell should he arrive at one of the destination ports of the letter. In view of the fact that no one knew where the *Shenandoah* was, or where it was going, Bulloch chose three likely ports based upon his best judgment. The letter was quite detailed, but in summary, advised Waddell that the war was over, the Confederacy no longer existed, and essentially instructed Waddell to cease and desist any further acts of war and to surrender the *Shenandoah* to local authorities. The draft letter was sent initially to J. M. Mason, the Confederate diplomat in England, for his review and comments on any changes to the letter. Mason essentially approved the letter as written and forwarded the letter to Earl Russell, British secretary for Foreign Affairs, requesting that the letter be sent to British diplomats in Shanghai, Nagasaki, and Honolulu. After several exchanges of opinion, the letter was sent through diplomatic channels on June 29 to British consuls at the requested ports and to some other destinations as well. Unfortunately, it was a matter of too little, too late.[70]

17. The *Shenandoah* Meets the *Milo*

After several more days of sailing, the *Shenandoah* came in sight of Cape Thaddeus, off the coast of Siberia. It was then June 21. Cape Thaddeus is situated on the opposite meridian to Greenwich and was often used by Whalers for regulating their chronometers as well as a location for the best whaling in the world. A few days before the *Shenandoah* arrived, there were over thirty whalers in the vicinity and had her arrival taken place at that time, the destruction of property would have been almost incalculable.

In spite of missing this opportunity for destruction, for the next seven days, the most widespread assault on private shipping in the history of the world would take place in the Bering Sea by the CSS *Shenandoah*, and this would occur after the cessation of hostilities between the North and the South in the Civil War. Since Captain Waddell did not know the status of the war, he continued on his mission of destruction for the Confederate States of America. This would continue until he had proof that the war was over and that the Confederacy no longer existed. He did not know that all except one of the Confederate generals had surrendered by this time to their counterparts on the federal side, or that President Jefferson Davis was captured and imprisoned on May 10, in Georgia, and that the Confederacy had collapsed.

On June 22, the *Shenandoah*, while still sailing close to Cape Thaddeus, sighted two ships and steamed after the nearest, which was working on a captured whale. They knew it was trying out whale oil by the quantity of black smoke rising from the ship, even though the vessel was still at a considerable distance away. The *Shenandoah* soon came alongside of the New Bedford whaler, *William Thompson*, the largest ship in the fleet. Upon arrival, Waddell sent an officer and prize crew aboard the vessel to give notice to Captain Smith and crew that they were now prisoners of the *Shenandoah* and for them to pack up their personal belongings and to prepare the ship for destruction. Needless to say, the men aboard the whaler were reluctant to give up the ship, but there was not a thing they could do about it. The *Shenandoah* had the guns and the ammunition, the *William Thompson* had no armaments. It was easy taking for the *Shenandoah*. This was the fourteenth prize for the *Shenandoah* since being self-commissioned at sea. The Confederate officer and prize crew remained aboard the vessel while the *Shenandoah* steamed after the second vessel, and soon caught up while flying the English flag. The other ship hoisted the Stars and Stripes, and the *Shenandoah* immediately lowered the English flag and raised the Confederate Stars and Bars.

The second vessel was the *Euphrates* of New Bedford which had gammed many times with the *Milo* since leaving Honolulu several weeks before. In a very short time, Captain Hathaway and men of the *Euphrates* had packed their personal belongings and had used their own whale boats to transfer over to the *Shenandoah*. They were unhappy sailors but, there was nothing they could do about it. After confiscating all of the navigational instruments, the *Euphrates* was immediately put to fire and left helplessly burning in the sea. After that, the *Shenandoah* returned to the first ship, *William Thompson*, again confiscating the navigational instruments, and then set her on fire. Both ships were now burning with high flames and smoke that could be seen for miles around. Each vessel had a value of around $40,000 in 1865 dollars, so the destruction was costly for those who lost these valuable properties. Crews from the two ships were now all on board the *Shenandoah* as prisoners. One or two of the crew members signed over to the *Shenandoah*, which more or less showed that no one knew that the war had ended as those one or two were willing to go over to the side that appeared to be dominant. Furthermore, it showed that some crew members appeared to be less loyal to their country than to the ship they happen to be on at the time. In this case, the *Shenandoah* appeared to be the best choice to those one or two turncoats.

The lookout on the *Shenandoah* saw another sail on the horizon and at once, Captain Waddell steamed toward it, looking for another prize. Flying the English flag, they soon caught up with the vessel they were chasing, and this turned out to be the *Robert Towns*, an English whaler out of Sidney, Australia. By this time, it was about seven o'clock in the evening and this would be their last confrontation of the day. This turned out to be a more or less a social exchange as the *Shenandoah* had no enemies except the Americans. Waddell, however, did tell a white lie to the master of the *Robert Towns*. When asked the name of his ship, Waddell replied, "Our ship is the *Petropauluski*," and left it at that. According to Waddell, he was under the impression that this was the only English ship in the Bering Sea at that time. Of course, the *Robert Towns* was also a ship that gammed with the *Milo* on more than one occasion during the past several days. Furthermore, even though the vessel was from Australia, the captain was a native of

Nantucket and was well known by the American whalers. By this time of day, it was still light enough and the *William Thompson* and the *Euphrates* could be seen burning on the horizon. It was an eerie sight to behold. The weather was cold and damp, and there was ice all around almost to the point of being dangerous. The whaleships were built to withstand the ice in the Bering Sea, but the *Shenandoah* was not, and this was a concern for Captain Waddell and the other officers. It was something they had to take into consideration as they worked their way into more and more destruction of Yankee whalers under icy conditions. They were now at the end of their second day in the vicinity of Cape Thaddeus.

The next day, June 23, was the day that Brigadier General Stand Watie, the Cherokee Indian Chief, surrendered his battalion to the Union. At this point, there was no Confederacy at all. United States President Andrew Johnson had already issued a formal proclamation on the day Jefferson Davis was captured, May 10, stating that "the armed resistance to the authority of this Government may be regarded as virtually at an end." This proclamation was not known to many people outside of Washington, DC, and to only a very few people around the world.

On the day before, the *Milo* had discovered a "stinker," which is a dead whale found floating, and brought the dead whale alongside the ship for processing. On this morning of June 23, all hands were at work on the whale, and each man knew what his own responsibilities were. All the men were quite dirty on deck and completely unaware of anything else going on around them. They had been through this operation many, many times and had the tasks down to a science. Jessie and the children were inside the captain's quarters where they spent most of their time when a whale was being worked. Addie and Fred played games and read books that had been in the ship's library for this purpose. It was just too messy and slippery on deck during the trying-out process. All on board were glad to have this work to do, as they had only captured one whale since leaving Honolulu, and the hold was almost empty. This whale would be a welcome addition to the storeroom in the ship's hold.

However, after leaving Honolulu, there had been many gams with other ships and many social functions that were part of the gamming experience. Jessie was looking forward to another visit with one or more of the many whaleships in the vicinity, but that would happen after the current whale was completely processed and stored in the hold. This was a great time, and all hands were happy and content. It looked like a very good summer for everyone. Captain Hawes was thinking this would probably be the last summer on this voyage, as he was planning to return to New Bedford after the summer with a full hold of oil and bone and take a leave of the sea, maybe for good. Jessie was looking forward to a more normal life back home in New Bedford and getting the children settled. Yes, they had plans and everything looked good. This was the way things were on the morning of June 23, aboard the *Milo*.

It was a beautiful day and not a cloud could be seen on the horizon. Close by were two other whaleships, the *Jireh Swift* and the *Sophia Thornton*, both of New Bedford. To the eastward of the *Milo* was some scattering ice, and to the westward, Cape Thaddeus, on the Siberian coast. Cape Thaddeus was about twenty-five miles away. The *Sophia Thornton* had just arrived from Honolulu with fresh provisions and the latest news. This prompted Captain Hawes of the *Milo* and Captain Williams of the *Jireh Swift* to go on board the *Sophia Thornton* to partake in some of the fresh eatables and to talk about the latest news from Honolulu about the war and the country. Needless to say, they were enjoying the food as well as the news from home. It certainly appeared that the war was over with the latest newspaper accounts reporting that General Lee had surrendered to General Grant. This was something they could celebrate.

Suddenly, the lookout on the *Sophia Thornton* cried out, "Steamer on the horizon, heading for us from the south." This was a most unusual happening and the three captains suspected that something was wrong. Both Captains Hawes and Williams returned to their respective ships immediately. The *Sophia Thornton* then took a course to the eastward into the scattering ice in hopes of avoiding a confrontation with the unknown steamer. The *Jireh Swift* took the opposite direction and steered westward under full sail toward the Siberian coast. The *Milo*, on the other hand, was under a short sail as the men were busy working on the dead whale and the *Milo* was not in a position to go anywhere.

Shortly thereafter, the *Shenandoah* fired a shot over the bow of the *Milo* and approached very close. Lieutenant Whittle, an officer of the *Shenandoah*, yelled from the deck, "Who commands that ship?"

Captain Hawes answered, "Hawes."

Whittle responded, "Lower a boat and come on board."

Captain Hawes vacillated a moment and then asked, "What steamer is that?"

Whittle answered, "It makes no difference. Lower away your starboard boat and come on board with your papers."[71] It did not take long for Captain Hawes to realize that the steamer meant business and that he was in no position to debate the issue. A boat was lowered and Captain Hawes was transported to the *Shenandoah* promptly. As he crossed the *Shenandoah's* rail, he did so with the dignity of an admiral and stood tall and straight and was an impressive figure. He was then escorted by Whittle to a meeting with Captain Waddell and would then find out what this was all about. From that moment on, things would take a different turn and he would have to stand even taller.

Up until now, the lives of both Hawes and Waddell had been centered on the sea for many years. They had similar backgrounds, but yet different backgrounds. They were nearly the same age, Waddell was forty years old, his next birthday on July 13, and Hawes was thirty-nine, his last birthday having been on May 8. Both had undergone extensive education and training in preparation for leadership roles each had earned. Waddell spent several years as a midshipman and student at the United States Naval School and later as a junior officer in the United States Navy with many assignments that took him to the oceans of the world. Hawes spent several years as an apprentice in sail making followed by a step-by-step progression in the whaling business from greenhand seaman to master of the ship and was now on his third voyage as a ship's master. He also spent many years sailing the oceans of the world, particularly the Atlantic and Pacific Oceans. At this point, they were both masters in their own profession.

Captain Waddell represented Confederate President Jefferson Davis through the Confederate Navy Department, and his superior was the secretary of the Confederate Navy. He was a dedicated naval officer and always performed with outstanding skill and attention to duty. He could be counted on to get the job done, always. He was not in favor of the War between the States, but when it came to decision time, he felt his place was with his homeland, the South. In his role as a Confederate commander, he continued to perform with honor and skill and was seen by all as an outstanding leader. He was a military man and became accustomed to following orders from his superiors. He did what he was told to do without equivocation. His superiors had great confidence in him.

Captain James Iredell Waddell[72]

In contrast, Captain Hawes represented himself and the owners of the ship *Milo*. He, also, performed with outstanding leadership and skill. He became accustomed to making his own decisions, as he did not have a chain of command to issue orders that told him what to do. He was a self starter and was generally correct in the decisions he made. He was a tall man, six feet three inches, and commanded the respect of those about him, particularly his men. He was also an honest man, and a church leader in the Congregational Church, when home in New Bedford. He was a real man's man and worked as hard as any of his men during whale processing operations just to set the example. He was thrown overboard on a few occasions, but always managed to get back on the ship and take charge. To his men, he was their leader, and they considered him an admiral of the seas. Both captains were well prepared for the tasks at hand on that day in 1865. It seems that destiny had been at play all along, and that these two men, one from Massachusetts and one from North Carolina, were bound to meet one day, face-to-face, somewhere in the world. When they did meet, there was mutual respect between them, and this made a difference to the outcome.

For one thing, Waddell had a major problem. His mission was to destroy property, not lives, and he was very careful to carry out his mission without loss of life. Throughout the entire voyage of the *Shenandoah*, he had been able to live up to that commitment. No life had been lost in the performance of his mission to date. On this morning, he had about ninety prisoners on board the *Shenandoah*, and

Captain Jonathan C. Hawes[73]

this was restricting his ability to pursue Yankee shipping. He needed the means to rid himself of the prisoners as soon as he could. The *Milo* offered this opportunity, it was now available and, more importantly, Waddell had been informed that there was a wife and two children aboard the *Milo*. In spite of his military bearing, Waddell was a compassionate person and would do his best to treat all people fairly, whatever the circumstances. He did not want to make life too difficult for a wife or children, if he could avoid it. If the *Milo* would take the prisoners, he would be in a position to continue his assigned mission of property destruction and the lady and the children would not be harmed. This was a priority to him, and this was the something he wanted to get settled right away.

On the other side of the coin, the *Milo* was in grave jeopardy of being scuttled and lost forever. Captain Hawes did not know this as he crossed the *Shenandoah*'s rail, but he would soon find out. Upon being escorted into Waddell's cabin by Lieutenant Whittle, Waddell motioned Hawes to sit down. Captain Hawes held his six-foot-three frame stiff as a ramrod. No codfish aristocrat was he, but a distinguished member of New Bedford's whaling fleet. He took his unavoidable capture and certain loss of his ship with a dignity and honor that quickly won Waddell's respect.

"Here is one Yankee I won't have to take down a peg or two," he thought.

Upon taking a seat, the following conversation between Waddell and Hawes ensued.

"Captain, I have to inform you that you are on board the Confederate man-of-war, *Shenandoah*. Before proceeding any further, I propose to lay you under the solemn oath to tell the truth."

An oath to truly answer such questions as might be asked, or offered for discussion or consideration, was then administered. Waddell then asked for news. Hawes replied that the war was over. Waddell then asked for documentary evidence. Hawes had no evidence, but "believed the war to be over." Waddell then said this was unsatisfactory but that if Hawes could produce any reliable evidence, he would be glad to receive it. Hawes said again, that he could not, and that he had taken the steamer to be a telegraph vessel laying cable between Siberia and Alaska. After these introductory issues, Waddell went on with the questioning.

But first, Waddell informed Captain Hawes that he was willing to ransom the *Milo* if Hawes accepted the conditions. Captain Hawes was leery, but he knew that he had no choice but to listen and respond.

Waddell: "What is the value of your ship?"

Hawes: "Forty-six thousand dollars."

Waddell: "What quantity of oil and bone do you have on board?"

Hawes: "One hundred and fifty barrels of oil and three thousand pounds of bone."

Waddell: "How many pounds sterling is your oil worth?"

Hawes: "I am not accustomed to reckon sterling money. It is worth one dollar per gallon."

Waddell: "And your bone?"

Hawes: "Two dollars per pound."

Waddell: "That makes fifty-five thousand dollars in all."

Hawes: "No; taking into consideration the wear and tear of the vessel, it is not worth over forty-six thousand dollars in all."

Waddell then drew up a bond for forty-six thousand dollars, payable upon the acknowledgement of the independence of the Confederate States of America. He then compelled Captain Hawes to sign the agreement, or otherwise have his ship ransacked and burned on the spot. Captain Hawes signed the agreement without much hesitation and returned the paper to the Confederate captain. At this point, Captain Hawes became "a ransomed Yankee."

"Now," said Waddell, "I shall put on board your ship ninety paroled prisoners of war to be transported to San Francisco."

Captain Hawes countered that he did not have enough provisions or water to take on so large a number.

Captain Waddell replied that he did not care. "You had better send your boats for the prisoners as quick as you can, and I shall detain your clearance until it is done."

"Come, come," said Waddell impatiently, "bare a hand about it, I have other work to do." [74]

Captain Hawes knew that Waddell had the cards stacked in his favor and that he was helpless and could do nothing about it, and began complying with Waddell's instructions. He returned to the *Milo*, announced what had happened and ordered the work on the dead whale to be stopped and the decks to be washed and cleaned thoroughly in preparation for the paroled prisoners of war. He also ordered whale boats to be lowered to take the prisoners from the *Shenandoah* to the *Milo*. This operation depleted the *Milo* of the necessary men to make an escape even if they had this intention.

As soon as the *Milo* boat crews arrived alongside the *Shenandoah* and the prisoners had been placed aboard for transportation back to the *Milo*, Waddell steamed to the northeast in pursuit of the other two vessels and caught up with the *Sophia Thornton* first. The *Thornton* had tried to make an escape in the scattered ice to the east. After firing two shots over her bow, the *Thornton* came about, and a prize crew from the *Shenandoah* under Lieutenant Scales was sent to board her and take charge. The *Thornton* then sailed out of the scattered ice and toward water clear of ice, and awaited her fate. As soon as she reached clear water, her masts were cut so she could not sail away, and she was left as a wreck in mid ocean. Her master, Captain Tucker, and mates were received on board the *Shenandoah* while Lieutenant Scales was put in charge of the prize and directed to communicate with the *Milo* and make sure that Captain Hawes kept company with the *Thornton* while it followed the *Shenandoah*, and to send over boats to transport the new prisoners from the *Thornton* to the *Milo*.

Waddell directed the prisoners to take whatever they needed for the voyage back to San Francisco, and then to burn the ship when they had finished. This was difficult for the men to do, as they had become accustomed to the ship as their home, and the last thing anyone wanted to do was burn his home. The *Milo* could not escape because she was without a full crew and her ship's register, and she had given bond for $46,000, so there was no incentive to do so. Captain Waddell had planned well and had things going his way.

In the meantime, Jessie Hawes was frantic. She did not understand what was going on. From the first warning shot over the bow of the *Milo*, she was petrified and was afraid not only for herself, but also for Addie and Fred. When Captain Hawes returned to the *Milo*, she was greatly relieved, particularly to learn that they would be returning to San Francisco with a large number of men from the ships that were being destroyed. Both Addie and young Fred were upset and fearful of the events taking place and could not understand why these things were happening. They could see the burning ships and they were both alarmed by the number of people arriving on their ship. This was the first time anyone had ever taken control of the *Milo* away from their father, and they were not prepared to take this easily.

The *Milo* crew finished the job of cleaning the decks and getting things in shape for the new "passengers" coming on board. Jessie did not realize nor did anyone else realize that the *Milo* was ransomed primarily for two reasons. First, Waddell had too many prisoners on his ship and needed to remove them and second, the *Milo* had a wife and two children on board. Captain Waddell did not want to make war with women or children and this was part of his character. This was a stroke of luck for the *Milo*.

Once the men and whale boats of the *Sophia Thornton* had been brought over to the *Milo*, the *Milo* crews again boarded the *Thornton* and loaded up with all the provisions they could gather from the ship's stores to help provide for all the passengers going to San Francisco. At that time, it was not known how many passengers there would be as the day was still young and there was time for more destruction. As soon as Waddell had the *Thornton* under control, the *Shenandoah* took a course under steam and sail in pursuit of the *Jireh Swift* of New Bedford, which had hurried to the westward toward the Siberian coast. At a speed of eleven knots per hour, the *Shenandoah* quickly closed in on the fleeing whaleship. It did not take long before the *Jireh Swift* was within gun range and a shot from the thirty-two pound Whitworth rifle was fired over her bow. Captain Williams, the *Swift*'s master, realized the situation was hopeless, and he brought the ship about to face the consequences. In short order, the officers and men were taken from the doomed ship, sent over to the *Milo* using their own boats, and the *Jireh Swift* was set on fire. Waddell then set out to pursue another whaleship, but this ship escaped into the ice field as the *Shenandoah* was unable to follow any farther. In fact, there were several whaleships in the ice, and they all escaped capture. Waddell remarked that they were the lucky ones, in that he did not have the capability to follow them into the ice as the *Shenandoah* was not built for such an environment. Instead, the *Shenandoah* returned to the vicinity of the *Milo* and saw that the *Sophia Thornton* was on fire nearby and this confirmed that the men had done their duty correctly. Waddell was in total command of the situation notwithstanding the fact that he was the one with all the firepower. Although the Civil War was over, no one in the Bering Sea had any way to prove it, and thus the tragic destruction of American whaleships continued.

About fifty years after this event, Joseph Francis, a seaman of the *Milo* during its epic voyage, wrote a letter from Vila das Lages, Ilha do Pico, Azores, to Frank Vera, in the United States, describing in his own words the details of that day, as he remembered them. Joseph Francis was a member of the whaleboat crew that brought Captain Hawes from the *Milo* to the *Shenandoah* on that fateful day. Frank Vera was a whaling master who had immigrated to the United States from the Azores in 1864, and was an old friend of Joseph Francis. Captain Vera was also a well known and respected whaling master of the New Bedford community. A copy of the letter, unedited, is shown in appendix A[75], at the end of the book. It provides an eyewitness and true account of the event.

18. The Bering Strait

Captain Ebenezer Nye, who had recently arrived on board the *Milo* from the *Shenandoah* where he had been a prisoner since the capture of the *Abigail* in the Okhotsk Sea, saw a chance to become a hero and also get revenge. This was after his second loss of a ship to the Confederates, first to the *Alabama*, and just recently to the *Shenandoah*, and now he would do anything to get even. Nye was a colorful and witty old sea captain and gained the friendship of the *Shenandoah* officers and men with his feistiness and storytelling. They considered him a conniver and a rascal, but he was more of that than they thought. Now that he had been released from captivity on board the *Shenandoah*, he was in a position to show his daring and character. He had a plan and he put it into action.

Nye and his mate from the *Abigail*, who had also been released, took possession of two whaleboats from the *Sophia Thornton* that had been used to bring prisoners and provisions to the *Milo*. These boats had a sail and the capability of traveling great distances if supplied with water and provisions. This was what Nye and his mate did. They loaded the boats with all the necessities they needed and waited until the *Shenandoah* was out of sight and below the horizon while it was chasing the *Jireh Swift*. As soon as the *Shenandoah* disappeared, Nye and his mate lowered the *Thornton*'s whale boats and set sail, along with several volunteers, to the north to warn any whaleships in that direction of an impending confrontation with a Confederate cruiser. They did not coordinate this plan with anyone, but Captain Hawes was aware of what they were up to and wished them well. He would have liked to have taken the initiative himself, but his hands were tied and he was unable to do so. This was a most unselfish plan, as they had both signed a parole and given their word that they would be transported to San Francisco and they would do nothing to take any action against the Confederate Navy. If they had been caught, they could have been in a very precarious situation, perhaps even a hanging. Regardless, they pressed on toward the Bering Strait to the north in search of any whaleship they might find. These two boats are shown in Russell's watercolor just behind the *Milo* with the men on board and ready to cast off.

On June 25, two hundred miles to the north, they did make contact with the whaleship, *Mercury*, chasing whales in a stiff gale off Cape Bering. Their log keeper reported that

Captain Nye had warned them of the nearness of the Confederate cruiser, *Shenandoah*, and that they should steer westward to avoid a confrontation. The *Mercury* immediately made contact with the whaleships *Florida*, *Corinthian*, and *Peru*, and they all steered westward, hoping to keep out of sight. All of these ships escaped the wrath of the *Shenandoah* and were saved from destruction, no doubt by the action of Captain Nye. Captain Nye was a brave man, did a good deed to say the least, was not caught, and somehow returned home and commanded another whaleship and found himself back on the Bering Sea a number of years later.

The day after the *Shenandoah* had captured the *Jireh Swift*, Captain Waddell took a northeastward course toward St. Lawrence Island. St. Lawrence Island is about 150 miles south of the Bering Strait which leads into the Arctic Ocean. The *Shenandoah* was on course ultimately for the Bering Strait because that was where the turncoat navigator and newly acquired "ship's pilot" Manning was taking her. He knew where the whaling activity was taking place and he was anxious to show off this knowledge to the Confederates. Suddenly, they came across the brig, *Susan Abigail*, a ship that had just sailed out of San Francisco on April 19, and had on board copies of the latest newspapers.

341

This ship carried a supply of guns, pistols, needles, calico, twine, and Yankee notions in general to use in trading with, among other Arctic Ports, the Esquimaux natives of St. Lawrence Island, with whom the captain intended to barter for furs. A shot was fired and the *Susan Abigail* came to a halt. In no time at all, a boarding party from the *Shenandoah* went on board the *Susan Abigail*, advised Captain Redfield, the ship's master, that he and his men were prisoners and that their ship would be set on fire. Soon thereafter, when Captain Redfield came on board the *Shenandoah*, he wore a magnificent fur coat which was a relic of his last voyage to these parts, and he begged very hard that his ship might not be burned. Waddell was having none of this and when all prisoners were on board the *Shenandoah*, the Yankee brig was set on fire, and three of the prisoners joined the Confederate cause.

Newspapers dated April 17 from the *Susan Abigail* reported the surrender of General Lee to General Grant and also an announcement of a proclamation issued by President Jefferson Davis at Danville, to the people of the South declaring that "the war would be carried on with renewed vigor." This announcement by Davis led Waddell to continue his quest for Yankee shipping with no let up at all. It was an unfortunate circumstance of the times when communications were slow and inaccurate. Even though the Civil War was actually over and the South had rejoined the Union, no one in this part of the world was certain of the status of the war, and this paved the way for continued destruction of American shipping when further destruction should have been avoided. It was June 24 and the *Shenandoah* was now manned at full strength for the first time since the voyage began at Madeira Island. Following the capture of the *Susan Abigail*, she continued on course for the Bering Strait after making a short detour over to the *Milo* to drop off the officers and men from the newly burned vessel for their passage back to San Francisco. While this was taking place, the *Sophia Thornton* could be seen in the distance still burning in the water. At this point, the *Milo* was free to begin the voyage back to San Francisco with a full set of prisoners from the sunken whaleships, including five ship captains. For a ship designed to carry a crew of about thirty men, the two hundred or so extra people on board proved to be a difficult challenge for not only Captain Hawes, but also for all of the people on board. It was a very crowded vessel. Captain Hawes was anxious to get this part of the journey on track and to rid his ship of the extra passengers, which he would do as soon as they arrived in San Francisco.

Late the next morning, June 24, the *Milo* began her journey to San Francisco. The fog was thick and visibility was poor, but all sails were set by early morning and anchors weighed. The *Milo* headed southeast and passed the still-burning ships, *William Thornton* and *Euphrates*, and also three empty boats from the *William Thornton* and one from the *Euphrates*. On board with Captain Hawes, Jessie, the children, and the *Milo* crew were the paroled prisoners from six burned vessels, *Abigail, William Thompson, Sophia Thornton, Euphrates, Jireh Swift, and Susan Abigail*, along with four whaling masters and one merchant master. Captain Nye, of course, was no longer on board. In total, there were nearly two hundred people on board the *Milo*, which was way over the number the ship was designed to carry. The ship's carpenter and volunteers were busy building additional bunks for the extra passengers. Otherwise all hands were busy cleaning up the ship for the journey to San Francisco. There were good feelings and bad feelings among those on board. Good feelings for being alive and heading for home; bad feelings for loosing their ship and the opportunity to bring home a profitable venture. Moreover, there were those who resented the fact that the *Milo* was spared and their ship was destroyed. These thoughts did not make for a completely pleasant voyage back to the United States for all of those aboard. However, no one would benefit from this venture into the Bering Sea; even the *Milo* would not have a successful catch this season. In spite of the situation, they were all thankful to varying degrees for the way things worked out, at least their lives were spared, and that was something that no one could have predicted. By the end of the day, the *Milo* had traveled only about thirty miles to the south and was still up north in the Bering Sea.[76]

Around this time of the month, June 24, the days became longer and longer, finally daylight occurred throughout the day as the sun reached a low point above the horizon on its lowest path. As the *Shenandoah* headed north, there was an eerie feeling for those who were not accustomed to this phenomenon, and it certainly had a negative affect on rest and sleeping. The weather became more foggy and wet, and the visibility became less and less. In fact, it was reported by the *Shenandoah*'s mate, Cornelius Hunt, that one could not see beyond the length of the ship and it was even more dangerous because ice was building up almost without warning and the ship was not built for that environment. Then the fog lifted almost as quickly as it started. The *Shenandoah* was heading northeast toward the Bering Strait in search of American whaleships, under the direction of the renegade pilot, Thomas Manning, late of the whaleship *Abigail*. By the end of the day, no new sails were seen by the lookout.

About ten o'clock in the morning of June 25, two sails became visible on the horizon and the *Shenandoah* steamed toward both vessels. The first to come into view was a vessel flying the Oahu colors, and upon closer inspection, she proved to be not American, and the chase was immediately abandoned. This vessel was probably the brig, *Victoria*. The second ship was approached around noon time but was flying the French ensign and upon closer inspection, she did not appear to be a Yankee vessel by any stretch, and likewise, this chase was also abandoned. The second vessel was probably the *Winslow* of Havre. It was later learned that both ships had been warning other American whalers of the presence of the Confederate cruiser in the vicinity, and a number of warned whalers had thereby moved out of harm's way and escaped destruction. One, however, was not so lucky, and she had not been seen or warned by anyone. This was the whaleship, *General Williams* of New London, flying the Stars and Stripes, seen by the *Shenandoah* in the afternoon after having passed by the Oahu and French vessels earlier in the day.

The *Shenandoah* was now just west of St. Lawrence Island, on her way to the Bering Strait. As she approached the stern of the *General Williams*, she came within hailing distance and ordered the captain to come on board with his papers. Upon boarding, the skipper took it very hard and protested loudly of being hunted "like a wild animal and having his property destroyed." The words were to no avail as the captain and men were taken prisoners and the money in their possession was taken as well. This amounted to about four hundred dollars, which was the most cash any ship had provided so far. As soon as all of the prisoners arrived on board the *Shenandoah*, the *General Williams* was put on fire and destroyed.

At this time the *Shenandoah* was just north of St. Lawrence Island, and while standing by the burning *General Williams*, she was met by more than twenty canoes full of Esquimaux natives, all attempting to barter for goods from the ship. Neither party understood the other, but apparently sign language prevailed and there was some limited communication and some limited bartering and trading. The men on board found it amusing, but otherwise were not impressed with the thought of dealing with these natives any further, and the *Shenandoah* steamed away northward toward the Bering Strait.

The next day, June 26, proved to be a very successful day for the *Shenandoah*, but another disaster for the American whalers. It began at one o'clock in the morning when the Shenandoah spotted three sails. The sun was above the horizon, and the visibility was good, so Waddell began the chase. Furthermore, there was very little wind, so the *Shenandoah*, under steam, had little trouble intercepting the whaleships that only had sails for propulsion. It did not take long to make the first capture, the *William C. Nye*. The next two, the *Nimrod* and the *Catherine*, were taken shortly thereafter. All three were from New Bedford. All aboard these ships were taken prisoner, and this included three captains. The captured ships were then set on fire and burned at sea. The *Shenandoah* now had about one hundred prisoners aboard, and space was again getting crowded on the ship. At this point, Waddell decided to put the last installment of prisoners in twelve whale boats that were in tow behind the *Shenandoah* in order to reduce the number of prisoners on board the cruiser. He did this to reduce the possibility of a prisoner uprising with so many prisoners aboard.

At this time there were still more sails on the horizon and Waddell went for them. Waddell knew he would need to ransom the next ship captured in order for it to take the prisoners from his ship. Waddell was also getting a little nervous, as he began to suspect that federal cruisers could be in the vicinity, and he would be no match for them. Even he could not believe that the federal navy would not be in hot pursuit of him after the damage he had already done. He began to take a closer look at the sails on the horizon to make sure that they were not armed warships. The view from the deck of the *Shenandoah* was most striking. The three recently captured whaleships were burning among gigantic ice floats to the rear, twelve whale boats were being towed by the *Shenandoah* containing the captured prisoners, large ice floats were all around, they dared not to exceed six knots speed due to the danger of the ice floats, and there were five sails seen ahead.

One of the ships on the horizon was reported by the prisoners as having small pox on board, so Waddell decided to avoid that one at all cost, and it was left alone. Suddenly the next capture came into view. It was the *General Pike* of New Bedford and soon thereafter was another prize. The captain came on board and in a very few moments agreed to ransom the ship for $30,000 and to take prisoners from the *Shenandoah* back home. Soon thereafter, the prisoners were en route to the *General Pike* and the *Shenandoah* again had relieved itself of all temporary visitors. The *General Pike* was the twenty-forth ship captured by the *Shenandoah* since it began its sea voyage. It was the second ship ransomed in the Bering Sea for the purpose of taking prisoners away from the *Shenandoah* and back home. The day was not over yet as there were two more Yankee whaleships to be captured before this day was to end.

Shenandoah with Prisoners in Tow"

As soon as the *Shenandoah* had been freed of prisoners, she began to bear down on her next victim, which turned out to be the whaleship, *Gypsy*, out of New Bedford. Cornelius Hunt was the officer off duty on the *Shenandoah* and, as such, was assigned to board the *Gypsy* and make arrangements with her captain for the consequences. The captain was in a state of shock and could hardly articulate a word, as he was certain he would be burned with the ship or at the very best, run up the yard arm. Officer Hunt took note and assured the captain that "no personal injury or indignity was intended for him." These words relieved the captain substantially. His cabin was furnished with fine appointments including a large library of over one hundred volumes, a beautiful writing desk and furniture in style and finish that would have done credit to any upscale living room. He also had several cases of choice wines and liquors. All of this was to be destroyed except for a bottle or two with which to treat the crew on their return to the *Shenandoah*. In short order, the officers and men were transferred over to the *General Pike* for their passage back home. After that, a few furs and trinkets were appropriated, a torch was lit and the ship was burned. That was the end of the *Gypsy*.

An hour later, the whaler *Isabella*, also out of New Bedford, was approached, boarded, and condemned using the same procedures as in all other captures. The officers and men were sent off to join their fellow prisoners on the *General Pike* for the voyage home. The *Shenandoah* then steamed alongside the *Isabella* to fill water from her casks over to the *Shenandoah*'s water tanks. As soon as they had received enough water, a fire was set, and the *Isabella* was burned, and the *Shenandoah* steamed away. As soon as the crew returned from the *Isabella*, Captain Waddell set a course for northward to take them into the Bering Strait for more destruction, and this ended the day for the *Shenandoah*.

Farther south, the *Milo* had made good time during this same day and had traveled about three hundred miles since being ransomed by Captain Waddell and was sailing under favorable winds on its return voyage to San Francisco. During the day, the *Milo* crew was employed in clearing up the decks, building bunks for the prisoners, and cleaning bone from the last whale captured before the confrontation with the *Shenandoah*. Of course, there was a lot of storytelling and social exchange among all of those aboard ship. Jessie, Addie and Fred did their best to welcome all the guests and to listen attentively to their stories. The stories went on and on endlessly, and they all had plenty to tell. This was certainly a different kind of voyage than ever before. Also, Captain Hawes and the other five captains had much to talk about including discussions on how they would present the happenings to the authorities and newspapers upon arrival in San Francisco. It would be another twenty-four days until they arrived there. For now, this was the end of the day on June 26 aboard the *Milo*.

The next day, June 27, was a relatively quiet day for all of the ships cruising in the Bering Sea. The word had been passed around of the presence of the Confederate cruiser and many of the whalers were trying to stay out of harm's way, one way or another. Of course, not every ship captain was aware of the dangers lurking in the Bering Sea waters, and more would soon meet their fate of destruction at sea, but not today. The *Shenandoah* let her fires go down, lowered her smokestack, and continued heading northward under sail with favorable winds. The weather was cold and foggy. Five sails came into sight from the deck of the *Shenandoah*, and as they were tacking about, they had no thought that a dangerous foe was in their midst. Captain Waddell pondered what to do. Since it was quite breezy, he felt that the rest would get away in the surrounding ice while he concentrated on one or two of them. Consequently, he decided to wait for calm when he could swoop down on all of them under steam without loosing any of them. The wind persisted all day long, so this precluded any contact with Yankee whalers for the rest of the day as the *Shenandoah* approached closer to the Bering Strait.

In the meantime, farther south, the *Milo* was still making good time on her journey to San Francisco during the day of June 27. By the end of the day, she had sailed over four hundred miles from where she had been ransomed and was now halfway between Cape Thaddeus and Unalaska Island in the Aleutian Island Chain, where she would leave the Bering Sea and enter the North Pacific Ocean. The crew and passengers were still busy cleaning up and entertaining each other with stories and songs. By now, they were all relieved that they were out of harm's way and heading home. Captain Hawes was doing his best to make the voyage as comfortable as possible for all aboard. He had to put up with five other captains on board as well as an overcrowded ship, and this did not make his life any easier during this time. Jessie was most charming as the captain's wife and tried to help anyone who was ill or distraught in any way she could. Addie and Fred found this to be an exciting time for them, as this was not a normal kind of voyage with so many relieved people on board and so much activity going on. In spite of the crowding, it was a good time for them and a time for all on board to anticipate a change for the better in the coming days ahead.

The morning of June 28 began with very little wind and clear skies in the Bering Strait. These conditions made it ideal for the *Shenandoah* to employ steam and swoop down on its Yankee victims that had to rely on wind for speed. As the *Shenandoah* came into view of the Diomede Islands about 6:30 in the morning, at least eight sails were seen from the deck, and land was observed on the port side. This was on the Siberian side of the Bering Strait. On the starboard side, quantities of ice were forming to the southward and eastward. At this point, the Diomede Islands were about twelve miles distant, and the *Shenandoah* was nearing the center of the Bering Strait. At eight o'clock, Waddell began to chase a sail seen to the southward under steam, and at ten o'clock they captured the *Waverly* out of New Bedford, with five hundred barrels of oil. In short order, her officers and men were sent on board the *Shenandoah* and the ship set on fire. Then Waddell steered westward until noon, and then took a course to the north. At half past one, they neared a fleet of at least ten ships at the entrance of the Bering Strait, and Waddell raised the American flag. At this time the winds were totally calm with no chance for the ships to escape. This turned out to be the *Shenandoah*'s last achievement and perhaps the most notorious and destructive day of the entire cruise, if not the entire war at sea.

The ship *Brunswick*, from New Bedford had been badly damaged by running into the ice and was nearly capsized and in great distress. When something like this occurs, it is the custom of all whaleships in the vicinity to gather together and try to repair her. If this becomes impossible, then an auction is improvised and the contents are sold to the highest bidder. The *Brunswick* was in this condition and was requesting assistance from those ships nearby. As the *Shenandoah* approached under steam with the American flag flying, one of the boats from the *Brunswick* approached to find out if they could lend them a carpenter or two and render any other assistance that may be required. The officer on deck of the *Shenandoah* responded that they would be attended to in due time. Then Waddell ordered boats to be lowered along with officers and men to board the whalers and return with their captains and mates. As soon as the boats were on their way, the American flag was hauled down, the Confederate flag was raised, and a blank cartridge was fired toward the center of the fleet. This threw everyone on all Yankee whalers into turmoil as they were sitting ducks with no way to escape. There were groups seen on all of the ships, gazing at the Confederate, looking up at the idle sails, and one could sense a feeling of helplessness and anxiety. There was no wind and there was

356

no way out of this dilemma. It was a scene that would go down in history as a complete victory for the Confederate cruiser. Interestingly enough, this would be the last day of the Confederate's destruction, but by early afternoon, there was still a lot of work to be done before the end of the day.

Then, the next ship was approached and the *Shenandoah*'s boarding party was ready to board. It was the *Favorite* of Fairhaven, but this ship, unlike all others, was up and ready for a fight. As soon as the crafty old captain realized that an enemy warship had sneaked into their midst, he gathered his men on deck, armed them with muskets, positioned a harpoon gun ready to fire, and made a stand to defend his ship with a cutlass in one hand and an old navy revolver in the other.

"Boat Ahoy!" he yelled to the approaching boat.

"Ahoy!" answered the officer in charge, somewhat surprised.

"Who are you and what do you want?" the captain yelled back.

"We have come to inform you that your vessel is a prize to the Confederate steamer, Shenandoah."

"I'll be damned if she is, at least just yet, and now keep off or I'll fire into you."

From the way he acted and they way his men handled their weapons, it appeared that he was actually ready to carry out his threat. The officer in charge then contacted Captain Waddell aboard the *Shenandoah* for further instructions. They were ordered back to the *Shenandoah* which then steered immediately toward the recalcitrant skipper, and came alongside. The old skipper continued to stand firm on deck along with his men and still appeared ready to fight it out.

"Haul down your flag," ordered the officer on deck as soon as they were within hearing distance.

"Haul it down yourself! God damn you!" was the fearless response, "if you think it will be good for your constitution."

"If you don't haul it down, we'll blow you out of the water in five minutes."

358

"Blow away, my buck, but may I be eternally blasted if I haul down that flag for any cussed Confederate pirate that ever floated," was the unbelievable response.

Captain Waddell was so amused by what was going on, and he did admire the old fellow's bravery, although not so much for his discretion, that he would not permit a shot to be fired into his ship. He did, however, dispatch an armed boat crew to bring him off and over to the *Shenandoah*. When the skipper arrived on board, it was plain to see that he had been seeking help from alcoholic spirits, and, in fact, was three sheets to the wind. In spite of this, he was the bravest and most resolute man ever captured by the Confederate cruiser during her voyage.[78]

By five o'clock in the afternoon, the *Shenandoah* had made prizes of the whole fleet, eleven sails in all. One of the ships, the *James Murry*, had been pointed out, when asked, by the mate from the *Brunswick* when he had earlier approached for assistance. Captain Waddell had heard about the *James Murry* and the recent death of its captain when they were at Ponape Island and that his widow and three children had remained on board. He wanted to make sure this vessel would be ransomed and used to take prisoners from the burned ships, if it were captured. He did not want to harm a ship with a widow and three children aboard. Consequently when a boarding party from the *Shenandoah* boarded the *James Murry*, the frightened widow approached the boarding officer with tears in her eyes and begged him not to destroy the ship that had been her husband's home for so long. The officer soothed her as gently as possible and told her that no harm would come to her or the ship by any action of the *Shenandoah*, and that the South did not make war on women and children. The *James Murry* was accordingly ransomed and her mate was directed to take the vessel to Honolulu with as many prisoners as could be accommodated.

One other ship was ransomed in order to accommodate the large number of prisoners from the captured vessels, nearly four hundred in all. This was the *Nile* of New London, selected for no apparent reason except for the need of another ship to transport prisoners to their homes. As soon as all of the passengers were aboard the two ransomed vessels, all of the other ships were set on fire. These were the *Hillman, Nassau, Isaac Howland, Brunswick, Martha 2d, Congress, Covington*, and *Waverly* of New Bedford and the *Favorite* of Fairhaven. As soon as all fires were set, the *Shenandoah* dropped anchor to watch this greatest of all sea holocausts ever to be witnessed by mankind, nine ships burning in the gray skies of the Arctic with surrounding ice reflecting the pyrotechnics in an astounding display of bright color and explosion from the many flammable sources on board the vessels. It was a spectacular sight seen from aboard the decks of the *Shenandoah* and the two ransomed vessels, *James Murry* and *Nile*. Aboard the *Shenandoah* there was a feeling of mission accomplished and joy at a job well done. Aboard the two ransomed vessels, there must have been many feelings of despair, loss, fear, wonder, disappointment, and anger among those who watched what would be all that was left of a gallant whaling fleet. It is interesting to note that during this period, Captain Hawes's two former commands, the *Eliza Adams* and the *Emma C. Jones* were cruising in the Bering Straits and steering north while the *Shenandoah* was in the vicinity. Fortunately for them, both vessels escaped the raider and later returned to New Bedford.

As the remains of the burning hulks went hissing and gurgling down to the treacherous bosom of the ocean, those watching had just seen the last act in the tragic drama of the American Civil War. The first act was seen at Sumter where the roar of the cannons set the opening act of the Civil War and the entire world looked on in amazement.

361

This final act amid the drifting ice in the Arctic Seas of the burning vessels formed a pyrotechnic display seldom seen and had only an audience of one grim and silent cruiser and two weather-beaten whalers filled with despondent prisoners. Most of the world would never learn about this great tragedy until much later. Too bad there was no one there who would be able to produce a painting reflecting the magnitude of the event, which was even greater than that shown in the Benjamin Russell watercolor. Consequently, there was no painting or watercolor made of . this tragic event for history or for anyone to see.

By June 30, during her around-the-world cruise, the *Shenandoah* had captured thirty-seven American ships, destroyed thirty-two, ransomed five of them, and otherwise left prisoners either at ports that were visited, or on other foreign ships that agreed to take prisoners. These numbers do not include the *Adelaide Pendergrast*, intercepted on November 15, 1864, as it was determined to have an official bill of sale to a foreign consignee.

One of the recently captured whalers had provided copies of newspapers from San Francisco dated the fifteenth of April with news about the assassination of President Lincoln, but there was no confirmation that the war was over. As far as those aboard the *Shenandoah* were concerned, the war was not over and the Southern armies were still fighting the North, although the feeling was that the South was having a difficult time. Further, since some of the prisoners of the past few days had actually joined up with the *Shenandoah*, it was obvious that they did not believe the war was over either. Consequently, the *Shenandoah* officers and crew felt quite comfortable in continuing their mission of destruction in the name of the Confederacy.

With this in mind, turncoat Thomas Manning, recently a member of the *Abigail* crew and now the new pilot for the *Shenandoah* had now been advanced to the position of acting master's mate. Further, he had learned from an anonymous informant that a fleet of some sixty whaleships had passed through the Bering Strait into the Arctic Ocean a short time earlier. With this intelligence, Captain Waddell decided to overtake this very large fleet of whalers and make its largest killing yet, if this were possible. Therefore, about eleven o'clock in the evening of June 28, the *Shenandoah* weighed anchor and proceeded to the Bering Strait under steam in hot pursuit. By ten o'clock the next morning, the Shenandoah had passed through the Bering Strait and was well within the Arctic Ocean and could view the extreme frontiers of Asia and North America. Also in view was one vast unbroken sea of ice as far as the eye could see ahead that, only a few days earlier, had been comparatively open water.

At this point, the *Shenandoah* was about 66° north latitude and at the most northern latitude of the entire voyage. In spite of the large number of Yankee whalers that were ahead of them and so coveted, Captain Waddell decided that he could go no farther north, and must turn south. If the ice overtook him, he would be icebound and would have no means to escape for possibly several months and could become a sitting duck for United States warships if he were trapped in the ice. Further, the *Shenandoah* was not built to withstand this kind of ice and this kind of environment. The risk was too great, so he turned south without hesitation. No one on board objected, as they all knew they had gone too far. Although no vote was needed or requested, the vote would have been unanimous to steer to the south immediately. About an hour later as the evening hours approached, they passed the still-burning hulks of the previous day's work and the two ransomed vessels with the four hundred prisoners aboard, also still there preparing for the voyage home.

As she continued south, the *Shenandoah* was not out of trouble as yet. Approaching St. Lawrence Island which was south of the Bering Strait, ice began forming all around the ship and began to impede the forward progress. Somehow, the ice was forming faster than the *Shenandoah* could move forward, and suddenly, the ship came to a sudden stop. Waddell ordered the men to stand on the ice and sink anchors into the surface in order to find leverage to pull the ship out of trouble. Steam was brought up to provide some forward force along with the lines sunk into the ice. After some time had elapsed, the ship slowly moved forward, almost inch by inch. After several hours of this procedure, the *Shenandoah* gradually moved toward clear water just south of St. Lawrence Island. It finally broke into clear water on the morning of June 30, much to the relief of the entire crew of Confederate sailors. The only damage sustained was that a small amount of copper that had been chipped off the forward hull by the ice, but nothing to be concerned about. The *Shenandoah* was now clear of ice and the waters ahead were clear and comfortable. As of the end of this day, there would be no more captures and no more ships destroyed during the rest of the cruise. This was also the day after the letter from Captain Bulloch to Captain Waddell had been dispatched through British channels to advise him that the war was over and to cease and desist any further acts of war. Of course, Waddell never saw this letter.

Captain Waddell began to be concerned about the ransomed ships arriving at port in the United States at any time now. He knew that as soon as the news broke about the destruction in the Bering Sea, the United States Navy would be seeking him out. He did not want to be confronted by a United States warship, because he knew it would not be a fight he could win. The United States would be the winner with a larger concentration of warships and greater firepower. Waddell rationalized that he had already performed his mission to destroy the Yankee whaling fleet in the North Pacific, and it was time to leave the scene. He continued to steer south and thought it would be more fitting to intercept merchant shipping on the routes from San Francisco to Asia. First, however, he had to depart the Bering Sea and consequently took a course back to the Amukta Island passage in the Aleutian Islands chain. Sailing through this passage would take him from the Bering Sea to the North Pacific Ocean and into warmer waters. Amukta Island would be several days away.

By this time, the *Milo* had already made it to the Unalaska Island passage and was sailing through to enter the North

Pacific Ocean. During the day, the *Milo* had made contact with the schooner *Tecoa* which had just started out on a trading voyage to the Arctic from San Francisco. Captain Hawes sent a boarding party to the schooner for news and copies of the latest newspapers from San Francisco. Needless to say, all of those aboard the *Milo* were anxious to read the latest news. The *Milo* was getting closer to San Francisco, but still about twenty-four hundred miles away. Covering close to 120 miles per day, she was about twenty days away from San Francisco. Captain Hawes became concerned about the water supply on board the *Milo* in view of the large number of passengers. After a thorough inspection, it was determined that the supply was sufficient for the rest of the voyage and all was well at that point. The *Shenandoah* would enter the Pacific Ocean about 330 miles west of the Unalaska passage where the *Milo* entered, but several days later.

On July 5, the *Shenandoah* sailed through the Amukta Island passage into the North Pacific Ocean and at that time was about nine hundred miles to the northwest of the *Milo*. After entering the North Pacific, the *Milo* steered southeasterly and the *Shenandoah* also headed southeasterly, but was a few days behind the *Milo*. Time was of the essence for both the *Shenandoah* and the *Milo*, but for different reasons. The *Shenandoah* was about to find itself in harm's way as soon as news of the destruction in the Bering Sea was delivered, and the *Milo* was about to deliver the news to San Francisco, and then the news would be delivered to the world. After that, the *Shenandoah* would have to rely on its own ability to stay one step ahead of the enemy, wherever she intended to go. This would not be an easy task.

19. San Francisco

As the *Shenandoah* headed south into the North Pacific Ocean on July 5, Captain Waddell took stock of the situation. Newspapers taken from the stricken ships in the Bering Sea contained intelligence about the disposition of American warships in the Pacific area and he was familiar with some of the commanding officers and of their sagacity. He learned that one of his old United States Navy shipmates, David McDougal, had command of an ironclad vessel protecting San Francisco harbor. He later wrote that McDougal was "fond of his ease," which meant that he would find the easy way to go about his business. Believing that McDougal would not put up a good fight, Waddell contemplated entering San Francisco harbor at night, colliding with the ironclad, opening the hatches, taking McDougal, officers, and men as prisoners, and firing volleys from both ships in to the city. That, he thought, would make a significant impact and statement to the world. However, before doing this, he thought it would be prudent to communicate with a vessel that had recently left San Francisco in order to gain more recent intelligence. He would have to wait until such a ship became available, but

he had not seen another ship since passing the two
ransomed ships, *James Murry* and *Nile*, on June 29, while
they were still in the Bering Strait, preparing to sail for
Honolulu and San Francisco. Aside from a possible attack
on San Francisco, Waddell's plan was to sail toward the
coast of California and coast of Mexico in hopes of
intercepting American ships en route from San Francisco to
the Orient, or steamships from San Francisco to Panama.
On July 7, back in Washington, DC, Mary Surratt, David
Herold, Lewis Powell, and George Atzerodt, the four
condemned conspirators in the assassination of President
Lincoln, went to the gallows at Washington's Old
Penitentiary and were executed. Mary Surratt, the owner of
the boardinghouse where the conspirators met, was
convicted on suspect testimony by a witness who was
granted immunity. "Mrs. Surratt is innocent," Lewis Powell
said on the scaffold. "She doesn't deserve to die with the
rest of us."[79]

In the meantime, the *Milo* was proceeding southeastward
and somewhat parallel to the coastline of North America on
its way to San Francisco. She was sailing at a cruising
speed of about one hundred miles per day. By July 12, she
had traveled over eleven hundred miles from the Unalaska
Island passage. The voyage to San Francisco had so far

been uneventful. Generally the days were mostly clear with rain on and off, but mostly clear weather. All aboard were anxious to get to the destination as conditions on the ship were crowded and somewhat lean, in terms of useful things to do. Jessie was more than happy that the *Milo* had not been destroyed and, further, would soon be able to discharge the extra passengers on board. Addie and young Fred were excited and intrigued with all of "guests" on board and the stories they told, when prompted. There was not a lot to do on this leg except be patient and let the winds do the work of getting the ship to her destination.

On July 12, the *Shenandoah* was about 410 miles to the west of the *Milo*, and cruising at a somewhat higher speed, about 132 miles per day. Actually, the *Shenandoah* was catching up to the *Milo*, but would never overtake her before the *Milo* arrived in San Francisco. In fact, just the opposite occurred between July 12 and July 16. During these four days, the *Milo* increased its distance from the *Shenandoah* from 410 miles to 533 miles, probably due to different winds at different places. However, neither captain knew the position of the other. Waddell was of the opinion that ransomed vessels were perhaps already at their destination and the word was out on the *Shenandoah*. This was not the case until July 20, on which day the *Milo* arrived in San Francisco harbor. On July 19, however, the *San Francisco Evening Bulletin* published an article provided by their Honolulu correspondent telling of the meeting between a local schooner and another ship believed to be the *Shenandoah* in March.[80] The article went on to caution its readers about the possibility of the *Shenandoah* heading up to the Arctic Ocean in search of American whalers. Of course, no one was certain if any of this was correct. The world would soon find out. At that time, the *Shenandoah* was about 450 miles to the northwest of San Francisco, and heading southerly, cruising parallel to the coastline. Captain Waddell had decided to delay any entry into San Francisco harbor until he had communicated with another ship which had recently departed from there. He had not seen another vessel since the Bering Strait, and he continued to search for one, friendly or otherwise.

As soon as the *Milo* arrived in San Francisco harbor, they were greeted by the harbor pilot who told Captain Hawes the news about the war.[81] It was over, Jeff Davis had been taken prisoner, and the Confederacy no longer existed! Soon all on board learned of the news, and all were happy and excited, this was what they had all been waiting for, and the outcome was what they had hoped. As soon as they dropped the anchor and collected themselves, Captain

Hawes and the other five captains made arrangements to go ashore and report on the activities of the *Shenandoah*. They wanted to make sure that no more time was lost before letting the world know about this pirate ship and the enormous destruction it had caused to the whalers. Furthermore, they wanted to see some immediate action by the United States Navy to seek out and destroy the pirate.

The first stop was the Mare Island Navy Yard where Captain Hawes and the other five captains went to brief the commandant, Captain David S. McDougal, on the recent destructive activities of the *Shenandoah* in the Bering Sea. Hawes, along with Captains Smith of the *William Thompson,* Tucker of the *Sophia Thornton*, Hathaway of the *Euphrates,* Williams of the *Jireh Swift,* and Redfield of the *Susan Abigail*, spelled out in detail their experiences with the *Shenandoah* up to June 23. Captain McDougal was shocked, to say the least, to learn about the destruction caused by the *Shenandoah* and immediately went into action. He fired off a telegram to Secretary of the Navy Welles and also sent a message to the commander of the United States Navy Pacific Squadron, Rear Admiral George F. Pearson, of the new intelligence on the Confederate cruiser *Shenandoah*. Until the *Milo* brought this news out in the open, no one knew the whereabouts of the *Shenandoah*, since it was last known to be in Melbourne, Australia. However, give some credit to the U.S. Navy, as there were standing orders delivered to the fleet from late 1864 to seek and destroy this rebel vessel.

In the meantime, Captain Hawes and the *Milo* made front page news in both San Francisco newspapers, the *Evening Bulletin* and the *Daily Alta California*, on July 20 and July 21 respectively. They all got together for a meeting with reporters and newspaper executives to tell their stories of the destruction in the Bering Sea. All five of the ship captains told individual stories about their confrontation with the *Shenandoah*, and all of this was published in both newspapers in great detail. Following are edited excerpts of the title and paragraphs of the article published in the *Daily Alta California*, on July 21, 1865:[82]

THE PIRATE SHENANDOAH IN THE ARCTIC OCEAN

Raid on the Whaling Fleet

DESTRUCTION OF SHIPS

What the Shenandoah *Is— The Intentions of Her*
Officers

Disbelief in the End of the Rebellion

Belief in the Assassination of Lincoln

Full Particulars of the Condition of the Whaling Fleet, etc.

Intense excitement was created in this port yesterday morning by the arrival of the whaleship Milo, *from the whaling ground in the North Pacific, having on board, in addition to her crew, about one hundred and ninety officers and men of the Pacific whaling fleet, from vessels which had been captured and burned by the rebel pirate* Shenandoah.

The article went on to say that it had been long suspected that this pirate would turn up in some safe water in the Pacific to prey on American commerce, as the last anyone had heard of her she had been anchored at Melbourne, and was apparently preparing for a cruise of devilish destruction on our merchantmen. Then, the article went on to say,

Like a sneak in the night, she crawls about in fear and trembling of meeting a vessel which might have a gun or

375

two on board, but as soon as satisfied that there is no danger—only a whaleman—she hoists the flag of a friendly nation, (in the Pacific Ocean, the Russian flag), runs boldly down on the unarmed foe, lowers the friendly ensign, runs up the rebel flag, and like a footpad with an unarmed traveler, raises the demand of "your money or your life," and to "bring your ship to," seizes the officers and crew while the pirate's cannon are trained upon them, steals whatever is valuable, applies the match and destroys the ship.

Not knowing of any further ship destruction except that reported by the *Milo*, the article continued to say that

This has been the fate of at least 10 American whalemen while braving the dangers of the Arctic seas in pursuit of their arduous calling.

With inputs from all of the captains of the captured ships, the article went on to tell the various stories from each.

The rebel pirate appeared in June in the Okhotsk Sea, where she sneaked up to the barque Abigail *of New Bedford, commanded by Captain Nye, captured her, stole what was valuable, fired the vessel, and steered for the Bering Sea. On June 22nd she fell in with the* William Thompson *of New Bedford commanded by Captain Smith, with 240 barrels of oil on board. After ransacking the ship, as with the* Abigail, *she was fired and destroyed, the officers and crews being taken on board the pirate and confined in a compartment below decks. From thence, she continued to cruise the Bering Sea, where she captured and burned several more New Bedford vessels. The next morning, she had captured and burned the following vessels putting their officers and crew on board the ship* Milo, *which was bonded:*

Ship Euphrates, *Captain Hathaway of New Bedford*
Ship William Thompson, *Captain Smith of New Bedford*
Ship Sophia Thornton, *Captain Tucker of New Bedford*
Barque Jireh Swift, *Captain Williams of New Bedford*

It continued with coverage of the destruction at Ponape Island.

On April 1ˢᵗ, at Ascension Island (Ponape Island) she had captured and burned the following:

Ship Pearl, *Captain Thompson of New London*
Ship Hector, *Captain Chase of New Bedford*
Ship Edward Cary, *Captain Enos of San Francisco*
Barque Harvest, *Captain Eldridge of Honolulu*

The latter vessel belonged to Honolulu and had the Hawaiian flag and clearance papers, but the excuse given for burning her was that she did not have the transfer papers on board.

377

The newspaper article also told of the methods used by the pirate to take property from the members of the victims' ships.

> *After plundering the captured vessels of all valuable ships'*
> *property, the pirates would rob everyone on board, and if*
> *anyone was unfortunate enough to have over $25 in*
> *money, the whole of it was stolen, but if less than $25 they*
> *would let the owner retain the money.*

Also told was how the pirate treated the crew members after capture.

> *When the first vessels were captured, all the officers and*
> *men were confined together, white and black, below decks,*
> *but when the* Milo *was captured, a number of men were*
> *put on board as a crew and Captain Hawes was ordered to*
> *follow in the wake of the pirate; failing in that she would*
> *be fired into and destroyed. Under this pleasant threat, the*
> Milo *kept her company.*

And then, how the French ship, *Gustave*, was contacted by the *Shenandoah* and the communication between the *Gustave* and Captain Hawes of the *Milo*.

> *While with the Shenandoah they fell in with the French ship,*
> Gustave, *the former exchanging signals with the latter, but*

did not speak her. But Captain Hawes of the Milo *hailed the* Gustave *and on running under her stern informed her Captain of the condition of affairs, requesting him to sail in search of the American fleet and warn them of the danger. This was heeded and before she got out of sight that night was seen to speak to other whalers, which from their actions had evidently taken the alarm making all sail and standing off.*

The article went on further to provide more details from each of the captains covering the main points of each capture. This news caused much excitement among the citizens of San Francisco, particularly the mercantile community, as well as concern about the possibility of an attack on the city by the Confederate pirate, which we now know was contemplated by Captain Waddell.

On July 22, a poetic article appeared in the San Francisco Evening Bulletin and was written by C. H. Webb and reflects the excitement and great interest in the event by the media at that time. The title of the poem is "The Cruise of the *Milo* as told by the Captain," and is interesting but also humorous to read and is printed complete and unedited in appendix B.[83]

Capt. Smith, Capt. Tucker, Capt. Hawes, Capt. Hathaway, and Capt. Williams

Captains of the Whaleships[84]

In the meantime, new intelligence was being processed by officials in the diplomatic service regarding the *Shenandoah*. On June 24, James McBride, U.S. Minister Resident in Honolulu sent a report with local newspaper clippings to the Collector of Customs, Charles James, at the Port of San Francisco, regarding the suspected whereabouts of the Confederate cruiser *Shenandoah*. This was based on intelligence gathered from the Oahu schooner, *Pftel*, which had arrived back in Honolulu on June 22 from a cruise in the western Pacific Ocean, and reported of being

380

intercepted by a vessel purported to be the CSS *Shenandoah* on March 30. Since the *Pftel* was not an American vessel, she was allowed to proceed by the intercepting vessel, which gave her name as the *Miami* from England. The *Pftel* was questioned as to intelligence on the whereabouts of American whalers, and particularly of any at Ascension (Ponape) Island, which was about four hundred miles away from their present position. Captain Hammond of the *Pftel* went on to say that he had visited Ascension Island about twenty days before and the there were three whalers there at the time, but all getting ready to leave the island. They were the *Charles W. Morgan*, *Helen Snow* and the bark, *Mercury*. However, he was quite suspicious about this vessel, and thought it might be the Confederate cruiser *Shenandoah*.

This was the first time anyone had reported anything about the *Shenandoah* since it had sailed out of Melbourne. U.S. Minister McBride went on to say the there was not any pretense of defense in this part of the Pacific and has not been for four years. He warned that unless something was done to beef up the defense situation, this would remain an open invitation for a pirate to destroy property in and around Honolulu, as well as other whaling areas in the Pacific. His only surprise was that it had not happened already. Of course, we now know that it had already happened!

This letter was received by Charles James on or about July 18, and the contents forwarded on that date to the Secretary of the Treasury, Hugh McCulloch, who received it on August 10. McCulloch immediately transmitted all of this intelligence on the day it was received to the Secretary of the Navy, Gideon Welles. By the time this was received by Secretary Welles, the *Shenandoah* had already completed her acts of destruction and, in fact, on August 2 had been informed by the English ship *Barracuda* that the war was over and furthermore, Captain Waddell had already removed all armaments from the deck of the *Shenandoah* and was proceeding on a course back to England.

In the meantime, Admiral Pearson received the message from Capt. McDougal relating to the activities of the *Shenandoah* by the packet steamer *America* on July 29, a few days after his arrival on the U.S. Flagship *Lancaster* at Acapulco, Mexico, on July 25. He immediately took charge and then sent a message to Secretary Welles detailing his actions in response to communications from both the collector of customs in San Francisco reporting on news from the Oahu schooner *Pftel* and from Capt. McDougal reporting on the news from the whaleship *Milo*. He had not heard from Secretary Welles as yet on this matter. He reported that the USS *Saranac* was in port on his arrival and that he immediately dissolved a court-martial on board and ordered the USS *Saranac* with Captain Scott in command to proceed in search of the *Shenandoah*. The USS *Saranac* left on that duty the next morning, July 30, and coincidently the USS *Suwanee* had just arrived from the United States on that same day with Captain Paul Shirley in command. He then ordered Captain Shirley to leave with all practical dispatch in search of the *Shenandoah*. He also wrote that he had ordered the USS *Saginaw* to proceed to Acapulco without delay in order to have a United States vessel there in case the French retook Acapulco which was confidently expected. He certainly had a lot of bases to cover and was not finding it an easy task in view of the number of available federal warships.

Admiral Pearson was obviously short of at least one vessel to protect American property along the west coast of Mexico and Central America in view of all that was going on. He wanted to send a second vessel to Acapulco as soon as he could find a spare one, but that would take some time. Both the USS *Saranac* and the USS *Suwanee* headed first for Mare Island in San Francisco for additional provisions and ammunition in order to search for and intercept the *Shenandoah*.

On July 30, there is little doubt that no one knew where the *Shenandoah* was, but it was actually about six hundred miles off the coast of Baja California directly west of Acapulco and heading south. On that day, Captain Waddell did not know with certainty that the Civil War was over. He would find out four days later on August 2. Both the *Saranac* and the *Suwanee* were well within six hundred miles of the coast on their way to San Francisco. The *Saranac* sailed from San Francisco on August 14, and the *Suwanee* sailed from San Francisco on August 20. Both vessels were headed for the North Pacific in search of the *Shenandoah*.

USS *Saranac*[85]

On July 31, Rear Admiral Goldsborough, commander of the European Squadron, sent a detailed message to Captain A.P. Harrell, commander of the USS *Kearsage*, to be on the lookout for Confederate cruisers, particularly the *Rappahannock* and the *Tallahassee*, which were currently being held by British authorities in Liverpool, England, and that both were under arrest by the English Court of Admiralty at the suit of the United States. However, Goldsborough warned that either of these vessels "may be released and put to sea." He went on to reaffirm that only in neutral waters could any Confederate vessel be taken by the *Kearsage*, and this included the *Shenandoah*. On August 31, Captain J.P. Bankhead, commander of the USS *Wyoming* sent a message to Secretary Welles advising of his arrival on August 30 at the island of Mauritius in the Indian Ocean. He went on to say that he had heard nothing of the *Shenandoah* since it was reported in April that the British frigate, HMS *Ruryalus*, had seen what was thought to be the *Shenandoah* in the Bass Strait sometime after departing Melbourne. These incidents confirmed that the United States was global in its pursuit of Confederate vessels at that time.

About ten days after the *Milo* arrived, both ransomed whaleships, *General Pike* and the *Nile*, arrived in San Francisco on August 1 and 2 respectively, causing another round of excitement among the citizens of this port city. On August 3, the *Evening Bulletin* published the complete story of both ships arriving and of the destruction of so many more whaleships than had been reported earlier. It also published the names of all twenty-four ships burned between April 1 and June 28, and of the four ships bonded, the *Milo*, *General Pike*, *Nile*, and *James Murry*. Furthermore, the article went on to say that no one had any idea of where the *Shenandoah* was or where it was going. One merchant ship, the *Milan*, reported seeing a steamer that appeared to be the *Shenandoah* after departing Puget Sound on July 23, but this was later confirmed to be the British ship-of-war, *Chameleon*, which was cruising off the west coast at that time, according to the British Consul. We now know for certain that the *Shenandoah* was no where near the Puget Sound at that time.[86]

Following the arrival of the *General Pike* and the *Nile* in San Francisco, the *James Maury* arrived in Honolulu on August 11, with 150 men on board after a passage of forty-four days from the time of capture by the *Shenandoah*. About the same time, another whaleship, the *Richmond*, also arrived with fifty-two survivors of the devastation in the Bering Sea. These were survivors taken from the *General Pike* at the request of several masters of the destroyed ships who were on board the *Pike* and who pleaded with Captain Weeks, skipper of the *Richmond*, to relieve the *Pike* of some of the prisoners as they simply had too many men on board, over two hundred, to make the voyage to San Francisco safely. Captain Weeks was sympathetic, took fifty-two men on board the *Richmond* as a humanitarian matter, gave up his search for oil this time, and sailed back to Honolulu, arriving about the same time as the *James Maury*. Needless to say, Captain Weeks was considered a great humanitarian and unselfish hero for providing this service to these men.

While this was going on, Captain Hawes was busy during the rest of July and into early August getting the ship ready for another voyage. Jessie and the children were glad to be out of the cold Bering Sea and close to shopping and entertainment, which they found in abundance in San Francisco. The children needed some new clothes for another voyage, and they also wanted some new books and games for those quiet times at sea. The *Milo* crew was busy getting the ship cleaned up, painted, and repaired after the ordeal they had gone through in the Bering Sea.

Some of the crew members decided they were through with whaling after the experience with the *Shenandoah*, and left the *Milo* in San Francisco for different ways to make a living. New crew members were recruited by Captain Hawes and soon the ship had a full contingent for the work ahead. Since the past year's effort had been derailed by the *Shenandoah*, Captain Hawes decided to extend the voyage for at least another year to make up for the losses incurred. Jessie and the children were happy to go on living at sea for the next year or so. By now, they had gotten used to life at sea and thought nothing of it. The children were still young enough, so they would not suffer from the isolation of being by themselves most of the time. Addie was now seven years old, and Fred was two. They did have friends on other whaleships and saw them from time to time. However, both Jessie and Captain Hawes knew that sooner or later they must establish a home for the children back in New Bedford. They had time for that, but first, Captain Hawes wanted to make this voyage profitable for his family and for the other *Milo* owners. He was in a position to make that happen, but it would take more time in lieu of the one-year setback caused by the *Shenandoah*.

Two days after the USS *Suwanee* left Acapulco and sailed north, en route to San Francisco to begin her search for the *Shenandoah,* the *Shenandoah* came in contact with the English bark, *Barracuda,* en route from San Francisco to the Orient with a full cargo load. This was on August 2, and the meeting took place about one thousand miles southwest of Acapulco, out in the Pacific Ocean. This was the first vessel that had come into contact with the *Shenandoah* since leaving the Bering Strait on June 30. Captain Waddell's intention was to continue destroying American vessels and particularly those sailing from California to the Orient, or to Panama. He did not know if this vessel was a prize, although she was flying the English ensign. Waddell ordered the English ensign flown on his own ship and then chased the *Barracuda* until they were within hearing distance. He sent a prize crew to board the *Barracuda* to find out what she was and to get the latest news on world developments, which they had not had since leaving the Bering Strait.

In the course of half an hour, the boat returned bringing news that no one on board wanted to hear. The Southern cause was lost and the war ended. All the rebel generals had surrendered. All Southern states had been overrun and occupied by the United States and the Confederacy had ceased to exist. Furthermore, and most importantly, Jeff Davis had been captured and was behind bars in a federal fortress and charged with being an accessory to the murder of Abraham Lincoln. This news was overwhelming and unexpected and caught everyone by complete surprise. They realized that now they were on their own with no one to help or guide them. They were told by the *Barracuda* that several United States cruisers and one English man-of-war had been ordered to search and intercept them. They also knew that if they were caught before reaching an English port, their days would be numbered.

The men on the *Barracuda* sympathized with their plight, but could do nothing else to help. Captain Waddell and the men on the *Shenandoah* were in a pickle. They took leave of the *Barracuda* and headed in a direction away from the North Pacific where Waddell expected the federal cruisers to be searching. Captain Waddell would soon order that all armaments be removed from the deck of the *Shenandoah* and stored below. This would change the vessel from a warship to a merchant vessel from outward appearance. He also decided that the best course of action was to avoid capture and return to wherever they had the best chance of a fair adjudication. He had now put himself in the position of saving his men from harm. The trick was to cover the distance to wherever they decided to surrender the ship without first being noticed and intercepted by enemy warships from the United States, England, or other nations. He gathered the officers and men on deck and laid out his plan. At this point, the *Shenandoah* was heading south toward Cape Horn. This all took place on August 2, 1865.

On August 9, the *Milo* was again ready to go to sea. Anchors were weighed and a harbor pilot came on board early in the morning to guide the ship out of the misty San Francisco harbor. As soon as they were clear of the harbor, the pilot was discharged and returned to shore while the *Milo* proceeded on her own with full sails. The men were employed in storing anchors and getting the ship ready for catching whales as soon as the opportunity presented itself. By August 20, the *Milo* had traveled nearly fourteen hundred miles along the coast of California and Mexico to a location about seven hundred miles northwest of Acapulco, Mexico, that promised good whaling. Captain Hawes had decided to sail south and begin the new whaling voyage by spending the next several months off the coast of Mexico where whaling was best during the winter months.

In the meantime, The USS *Saranac* departed San Francisco on August 14 in pursuit of the *Shenandoah*, and arrived at the Esquimalt Navy Yard, Vancouver Island, Canada, on August 20, and sailed away on August 23. The USS *Suwanee* departed San Francisco on August 20, and arrived at Puget Sound on August 24. They were both far away from the *Shenandoah* at this time, as the *Shenandoah* was approximately nineteen hundred miles west of Chile on August 23, and heading south. This was the same day Admiral Pearson arrived at Mare Island Navy Base in San Francisco. Upon his arrival, Mare Island Commandant McDougal sent a telegram to Secretary Welles advising that Admiral Pearson had received the earlier telegram from the secretary directing a search for the *Shenandoah*, and that the *Saranac* and *Suwanee* were both in pursuit of the rebel ship on that date.[87] The problem was that they were not even close to the Confederate; they had no idea where the Confederate was or where she was going, and further, there was no technology available to help them find the answers. At that time, the *Milo* was closer to the *Shenandoah* than the federal warships. But of course, the *Milo* was not in pursuit, as we know she was fishing for whales and had no idea where the *Shenandoah* was located at that time. More importantly, Captain Hawes and all those on board the *Milo* would have been happy to never again come into view of the *Shenandoah*.

During this same time period, a message was sent by the assistant secretary of the Treasury to the secretary of the navy containing copies of telegrams received by the Treasury from the collector of Customs in San Francisco informing that the men left stranded on Ponape Island by the *Shenandoah* had been left on the island for about two months. In other words they had been rescued by another vessel, and the men were returning to their homes during this time. The overall situation was getting better.

20. *Shenandoah* on the Final Run

Soon after Captain Waddell briefed his crewmembers on news from the *Barracuda* and the condition of the Confederacy, the crew got together, wrote up and signed a petition for the *Shenandoah* to go to Sydney, Australia, as a destination and place to surrender. The majority of men aboard felt this was the most favorable destination as it was the shortest distance to go to a port that may offer freedom. The longer they remained on the high seas, the better the chances of being intercepted by a federal or other foreign man-of-war, and the possibility of the worst of all outcomes. As a whole, the men were frightened and paranoid about being alone on the ocean without a country or friend to support them. They felt like criminals on the run without a secure place to go. They were devastated, but they still had what they thought was a rational plan. Five of the crew did not sign the petition, as they chose to side with whatever Waddell decided. The signers presented the petition to Waddell. Waddell read the petition, but remained silent.

Waddell had other plans. His plan was to take the *Shenandoah* south, around Cape Horn and then sail up the Atlantic Ocean, and head back to Liverpool where everything began. He felt a great responsibility for protecting the 130 or so crew members on board, and he was convinced that the British would be the best government to deal with on conditions of surrender. This would be a voyage of seventeen thousand miles over rough seas around Cape Horn with the possibility of being intercepted by federal or foreign cruisers and not having a chance of victory in a fight with any one of these. He felt he could at least outrun any enemy warships as he had a fast vessel, and that would be his advantage. He did not feel compelled to tell anyone about this, and let it go at that.

In very short order, the conversion from Confederate cruiser to a merchant ship began. Waddell wanted to make sure that the ship did not appear in any way to be a ship of war to any other vessel they would come into contact during the voyage back to England. The same tackles used to transfer the armaments from the *Laurel* to the *Sea King* were again placed from positions aloft to assist in dismounting the heavy guns and placing them below the deck, beyond reach of prying eyes. Port holes were closed up and the smoke stack was whitewashed so that the vessel now appeared to be a quiet merchantman, peacefully on course without any intent on threatening any other ship on the high seas. The attitude of the crew was now subdued and quiet as opposed to the high spirits and hilarity prior to the news from the *Barracuda*. Lookouts still mounted aloft, not to scan the ocean for ships that might be captured, but instead to maintain a watchful eye on any suspicious sail that may show itself on the horizon.

Between the time of the meeting with the *Barracuda* and rounding Cape Horn in mid-September, there were a number of sails seen on the horizon, mostly merchant vessels heading west on known shipping routes. None of these caused any concern for the *Shenandoah*, but Waddell wanted to avoid contact with any ship at all. On the other hand, none of the sails observed showed any interest in the *Shenandoah* either and that was Waddell's plan and strategy.

One day, the lookout reported a vessel on the horizon with full sails, heading on nearly the same course as the *Shenandoah*. Closer inspection revealed that the other ship was English and a merchant ship, not a man-of-war. Moreover, it appeared to be much of the same design as the *Shenandoah* itself. Waddell decided to gain speed and find out more about this ship, and so ordered all sails up. The other ship was also observing the *Shenandoah* and quickly realized that a race was taking place. It began to slowly leave the *Shenandoah* behind and became the very first ship that had greater speed than the *Shenandoah*. Upon further signaling between these two ships, it was discovered that the other ship was a sister ship to the *Shenandoah* and was built by the same shipyard. The difference in speed was attributed to the fact that the *Shenandoah* had received damage on its hull cruising . through heavy ice in the Arctic Ocean. If this had not been the case, the two ships would probably have been equal in speed. The *Shenandoah* actually rounded Cape Horn on September 16 and entered the South Atlantic Ocean after that.

Also on September 16, Rear Admiral Goldsborough, commander of the European Squadron sent a message to Commander A.D. Harrell, commander of the USS *Kearsage*, with instructions to intercept either former Confederate cruisers, *CSS Rappahannock* or CSS *Tallahassee*, both currently anchored in Liverpool, should he learn from reliable sources that one or both were about to leave Liverpool and return to sea. If that actually occurred, and one or both vessels were captured, the

Kearsage was instructed to take the captured vessels to Boston for adjudication.[88] At that time, the British government considered itself a neutral nation with regards to the Civil War belligerents, United States and Confederate States of America. As such, International Maritime laws applied that spelled out how a neutral nation could handle transactions with vessels from the belligerent nations within its territorial ports. Basically, the laws attempted to be fair to both parties and were quite restrictive on what the neutral nation was able to provide to either belligerent, certainly not furnish weapons of war or supplies. Among the many other details of the rules, there was a time limit on how long a belligerent vessel could remain in port; usually twenty-four hours which was considered sufficient time to purchase enough supplies to get to a port friendly to the belligerent vessel. Further, the neutral nation could not favor one party over the other, but had to treat both equally. The neutral nation was charged with the responsibility with upholding the law within its own territory. If vessels from both belligerents were in a port or territorial waters at the same time, for example, neither belligerent vessel could take any action against the other belligerent vessel while in port or territorial waters. Further, the rule was that if one vessel left the port, the opposing belligerent vessel must delay its departure at least twenty-four hours before it could leave port. This would give the first departure sufficient time to get out of harm's way.

Since England declared itself a neutral nation at the outset of the Civil War, United States naval vessels were restricted from entering British ports as per the laws of neutral nations, and this restricted the actions of the United States Navy significantly. In this case, the USS *Kearsage* simply had to wait at sea for any news that either the CSS *Rappahannock* or the CSS *Tallahassee* had left port. However, it was unlikely that either would leave Liverpool as both had essentially surrendered to the British. These laws were in effect in most countries around the world during the Civil War, including the United Kingdom, Australia, France, Spain, Netherlands, Brazil, Chile, Peru, and so on. Needless to say, the rules were not always followed by the neutral nations, particularly England during this time, and local authorities tended to look the other way more often than not.

Although no one knew the whereabouts of the *Shenandoah*, there was a global effort in process by the United States to find her. Among many other messages during October 1865, two reports from different parts of the world were received by Secretary Welles regarding the *Shenandoah*, but both were negative. On October 5, the USS *Wyoming* reported on her arrival at Singapore on September 25, twenty-two days from the island of Mauritius, and having made port calls at Galle in Ceylon (now Sri Lanka) and Penang in Malaysia. The only information reported on the *Shenandoah* was that there was nothing on the English newspapers delivered by the steamer from Hong Kong which arrived this day. In fact, the local news on the *Shenandoah* was that she "has not been heard from" in this part of the world since the reports from the *Milo* in San Francisco on July 20.

A second report was sent on October 27 by Commander F.K. Murry, commander of the USS *Wateree* from Callao, Peru. Murry had been in contact with an American citizen living in Lima, who told him of meeting with Peruvian authorities who believed the *Shenandoah* was cruising along the coast of the Chincha Islands and was being offered for sale to revolutionary forces. This was a strong possibility, as Spain was planning a major effort to retake the independent countries of Peru and Chile by military force, and the Spanish Navy was operating near the Chincha Islands. This belief soon spread to the citizens of Chincha and everyone was alarmed and "on edge" about the *Shenandoah*. Commander Murry took his vessel to the Chincha Islands and investigated the notion. Upon arriving, he was informed that the vessel was probably a Spanish war vessel and that there was no evidence that the *Shenandoah* had ever been there. His message to Secretary Welles was to squelch any idea that the *Shenandoah* had been there if such had been reported. The fact is that no one at this time knew the whereabouts of the *Shenandoah* and, just as strange, Captain Waddell had no guarantee that the *Shenandoah* was invisible to the world either. In this regard, Waddell proceeded onward with extreme caution.

Some very good news for the United States was announced by the British government on October 14, and relayed from Ambassador Adams in England to Secretary Seward and then to Secretary Welles on October 30. The dispatch from Mr. Adams referred to a note from Lord Russell of the British government regarding restrictions placed on United States national vessels which were lately maintained by Her Majesty's government in British ports and waters. The dispatch stated that all the objectionable restraints referred to have now been entirely removed, and that "it is the desire of Her Majesty's Government that unrestricted hospitality and friendship shall be shown to vessels of war of the United States in all Her Majesty's ports, whether at home or abroad."[89] This meant that for all intents and purposes, the rules applying to neutrality and international law had been suspended by the United Kingdom and her possessions, and now the twenty-four hour rules no longer apply.

Also, of equal importance, the note from Lord Russell referred to instructions given to Fleet Admiral Denman of the British Navy to detain the CSS *Shenandoah* if she came into any British port and to capture her if she was found on the high seas. This meant that now the British Navy and the U.S. Navy were both in search of the *Shenandoah*. This was a gigantic turn of events. Following this dispatch, Secretary Welles sent out instructions to all U.S. Navy commanders advising them of the new open-door policy at British ports and waters, and directing them to provide customary hospitality and courtesy between friendly nations to the British Navy. In the meantime, no one anywhere in the world had a clue as to the whereabouts of the *Shenandoah*.

The *Shenandoah* crossed the equator near the thirtieth Meridian on October 11, heading north. At that time, another lengthy and rational petition was delivered to Waddell by a majority of the crew to take the *Shenandoah*

402

to Cape Town, but again, Waddell declined and instead maintained a steady course toward Liverpool. For the rest of the voyage, the *Shenandoah* came into contact with a great many sails, but was able to maintain a polite distance from them. On October 25, about 375 miles west of Madeira Island and heading directly for Liverpool, the masthead lookout cried, "Sail Ho!" Glasses swept the northern horizon in search of the sail, but she was only visible from aloft. The lookout got the attention of all aboard, and their anxious glasses reflected their state of mind, for if a federal cruiser were to be found anywhere, she would be in this part of the ocean. Waddell sent a quartermaster aloft with orders to communicate all that he could ascertain from the appearance of the sail.

Soon the quartermaster made a survey and reported the stranger under short sail and that she looked like a steamer. The *Shenandoah* was moving too fast and the distance between the two ships was closing; soon the other vessel could be seen from the deck. Waddell then ordered the propeller down to provide some drag and slow the speed somewhat; he did not want to get any closer to the other vessel. The propeller helped, but not enough, so Waddell wanted to add more drag to slow down the *Shenandoah* even more without showing his hand. To do this, they brought out two hawsers on the aft deck and tied a bite to the end of the hawsers. This did the trick and the ship slowed down enough so that the *Shenandoah* did not gain on the other ship. Waddell did not want to get any closer and he hoped to maintain the separation at least until nightfall.

Nightfall came so slowly that Waddell thought it was the slowest he had ever experienced. Then, when darkness came, sails were brought down; steam was brought up for the first time since leaving the Bering Sea, a distance of about thirteen thousand miles. Waddell then changed the heading to easterly for about fifteen miles and after feeling more secure, Waddell made a course correction and the *Shenandoah* again took a northerly heading for Liverpool. The *Shenandoah* had escaped into the night. By the next morning, the other vessel was nowhere in sight, and the *Shenandoah* found herself alone again on the high seas and about nine hundred miles from Liverpool. During the days, steam was shut down to avoid suspicion and sails were brought up so she would appear like any other peaceful sail on the ocean. So far, she had escaped a possible capture by a federal warship. All of the men on board were relieved, but one officer put it this way,

Things went from bad to worse and when our government collapsed, it left our ship a veritable Ishmael of the Sea, with none to claim or recognize her for other than a lawless freebooter. Such was the culmination of misfortunes as none of us had counted on.[90]

The men were disappointed, but, at the same time, relieved to remain free men. Later on, Waddell wrote that he had been told that the steamer was probably the USS *Saranac* with Captain Walke on board. Waddell was given some erroneous information, as the USS *Saranac* was still in the North Pacific at that time under the command of Captain Scott.

On October 26, Captain Waddell continued on course for St. Georges Channel which would lead them to Liverpool. Then a strong southwest gale pushed them along to within seven hundred miles of Liverpool. Suddenly, the winds ceased, and they found themselves in calm, clear weather and in sight eleven sails on the horizon, but all of them fortunately not close enough to cause any concern. The *Shenandoah* continued under sail during the daylight, because if she had employed steam, she would have been observed. Each ship under sail was ignorant of the character of the other, and had no reason to look further.

However, any sailing ship would have directed attention to a steamer, and one of the other sailing ships could have been a federal cruiser. Waddell was wise and perceptive about these concerns, and he was able to stay out of harm's way, up until then. When nightfall came, steam was applied and the *Shenandoah* moved swiftly through the water, unseen and safe. The weather continued calm and beautiful and the *Shenandoah* spotted the Tuskar Lighthouse upon entering St. George's Channel on November 5, just 122 days from the Aleutian Islands. Much credit was given to the young navigator on board, Irvine S. Bulloch, James Dunwoody Bulloch's half brother, who was right on target after being at sea, with no land in sight, for such a long period.

A short time after midnight, the *Shenandoah* took on a Liverpool pilot who confirmed all the news they had heard from the *Barracuda* on August 2. Waddell then directed the pilot to take the *Shenandoah* to Liverpool in order to communicate with the British government. On the morning of November 6, the proud ship, *Shenandoah*, steamed up the Mercy River in a thick fog with the Confederate flag at her peak and was anchored close to Her Majesty's ship-of-the-line, HMS *Donegal*, with Captain Paynter, RN, commanding. Shortly after dropping anchor, a lieutenant from the *Donegal* arrived on board the *Shenandoah* and asked the name of the vessel, and then provided current intelligence on the termination of the American Civil War. Then, the only remaining official Confederate flag was taken down for the last time. For all intents and purposes, this was the last official act of the American Civil War. Following this, Captain Waddell provided a letter to the lieutenant to be delivered through Captain Paynter of the *Donegal* to Lord Earl Russell that effectively surrendered the *Shenandoah* to British authorities for appropriate disposition. He also gave a brief but accurate summary, as well as defense, of the entire voyage from his point of view. At that point, the *Shenandoah* was placed under custody of British authorities and the British gunboat *Goshawk* was lashed alongside to guard the vessel.

The next day, November 7, United States Minister Charles Adams addressed a letter to the Earl of Clarendon, secretary of state for Foreign Affairs, requesting that appropriate steps be taken to take possession of the *Shenandoah* and secure the property on board with the view of her delivery to the United States. Adam's letter and that of Captain Waddell along with other related documents were referred to the law officers of the Crown later in the day on November 7, which resulted in the following advice by the following persons who signed the document, Sir Roundell Palmer, Sir R.P. Collier, and Sir Robert Phillmore:

> We think it would be proper for her Majesty's government, in compliance with Mr. Adam's request, to deliver to him, in behalf of the government of the United States, the ship in question, with her tackle, apparel, etc., and all captured chronometers or other property capable of being identified as prize of war, which may be found on board of her....With respect to the officers and crew...if the facts stated by Captain Waddell are true, there is clearly no case for any persecution on the ground of piracy in the courts of this country, and we presume that her Majesty's government is not in possession of any evidence which could be produced before any court or magistrate for the purpose of contravening the statement or showing that the crime of piracy has, in fact, been committed...With respect to any persons on the Shenandoah who cannot immediately be proceeded against and detained under legal warrant upon any criminal charge, we are not aware of any ground upon which they can properly be prevented from going on shore and disposing of themselves as they think, and we cannot advise her Majesty's government to assume or exercise the power of keeping them under any kind of restraint.[91]

With the above guidance from the law officers of the Crown, instructions were sent to Captain Paynter of the *Donegal* to release all officers and men who were not found to be British subjects. Captain Paynter reported on November 8, that upon receiving the instructions, he went on board the *Shenandoah* and was satisfied that there were no British subjects among the crew on board, or at least none of whom he could prove to be British subjects. Consequently, he permitted all hands to go ashore with their private property. With this move, the infamous and destructive voyage of the *Shenandoah* was ended, and her crew was scattered to the four winds, so to speak. Most of the crew would never see one another again.

21. The *Milo* Sails Home

In the meantime, back in the Pacific, the *Milo* was doing very well with a large number of whales caught off the coast of Mexico. Almost every day the whale boats were out on the water chasing whales and taking many back to the side of the ship for processing. This was a busy time for the crew and there was little let up in the work. Jessie and the young ones stayed mainly in the captain's quarters and occasionally ventured out on deck to watch the hard work being done. The ship's hold was getting filled with barrels of whale oil and bone. This was a very successful time for the *Milo* in the late fall of 1865, particularly after the last summer's tragedy in the Bering Sea. It was a nice turn of events for Captain Hawes and had a great impact on the profitability of the overall voyage.

Captain Hawes had no fear of the *Shenandoah* during this busy time, and only when things got quiet did he let his thoughts drift to that subject. The *Milo* was making up for lost time, and this was a joy for all aboard. Captain Hawes wanted to fill the hold with all he could gather, and then make a run for Honolulu to sell the oil and bone on the open market. He hoped that would take place during the next spring. In the meantime, the *Milo* was enjoying the peaceful and productive cruise, usually within one hundred miles off the coast of Mexico, and making plans for next summer's cruise back into the Bering Sea. From time to time, the *Milo* would lay anchor in one of the many bays along the coast of Baja California, and enjoy the rest and quiet.

November 1865 was a significant turnaround period for both the *Milo* and the *Shenandoah*. For the *Milo*, the cruise along the Mexican coast was most productive and she filled her hold with the products from the sea. On the other hand, for the *Shenandoah*, when she finally dropped anchor at Liverpool and surrendered to the British authorities, all the glory was gone and the officers and crew were considered to be outlaws in their own country, without much hope for the future. The *Shenandoah* was the last Confederate military unit in the Civil War to surrender. Some of the officers and men would never return to the United States after that. So it was at the end of the year in 1865.

Following the release of all officers and crew of the *Shenandoah*, the British government made arrangements to turn over the *Shenandoah* to the United States, in response to United States Minister Charles Adam's request. The United States Navy appointed Captain Freeman the task of returning the *Shenandoah* from Liverpool to New York. Shortly after departing Liverpool, the vessel ran into a violent storm at sea and lost some of its rigging, causing the captain to return to Liverpool. After that, it was not tried again. The ship was finally sold by the United States to the Sultan of Zanzibar for His Majesty's pleasure as his personal yacht. This arrangement did not work out very well for him, and the ship was converted into a merchant ship. She was finally lost on a coral reef in the Indian Ocean in 1879, fourteen years after the last Confederate flag was hauled down.

The three years following the summer of 1865 saw much of the same for the *Milo*. She would winter off the Mexican coast and summer in the Bering Sea. This turned out to be a highly profitable three years for the *Milo* as she caught a large number of whales during this period and filled her hold with oil and bone. In between the seasons of winter and summer, she would anchor in Honolulu and sell off the harvest, adding to the profits of the whaling voyage.

Addie and Fred circa 1866[92]

Honolulu

During these stopovers in Honolulu, Captain Hawes was busy doing business with local ship brokers. Jessie and the children again enjoyed the change from sea to land and the opportunities to explore the island, shop, and have new pictures taken. In 1866, Addie was eight years old and Fred, three. Jessie was beginning to wish for the whaling voyage to end so she and the family could set up a permanent home in the New Bedford area and become normal people again with a house, yard and friends to visit. She and Jonathan had talked about this often and both were now willing and ready to settle down back home.

Furthermore, Jonathan had been corresponding with his older brother Simeon Hawes and together they invested as partners in a sawmill business in 1867, along with substantial landholdings. Jonathan had acquired enough personal wealth to afford this kind of business, and he felt that he was nearing the time to retire from the sea and begin a new life on shore. By the spring of 1868, both Jonathan and Jessie agreed to return to New Bedford in the spring of 1869, regardless of the additional profits from more whaling. However, profits from whaling were enticing enough for them to continue the whaling voyage until then.

The *Milo* sailed from Honolulu on March 19, 1868, on her final journey to the Bering Sea. This time, Captain Hawes decided to venture all the way north to the Anadyr Sea which is close to the Siberian coastline and northwest of the Bering Sea. This was a perfect location for whaling during that period of time in 1868. His decision proved to be the best choice in terms of the large amount of oil and bone ending up in the ship's hold at the end of the summer. By the end of July, following the summer's successful whaling, the *Milo* set course on a return run to Honolulu to sell off the proceeds stored in the ship's hold. There was no room for another barrel of oil in the *Milo*'s hold.

Captain Hawes wanted to first unload the summer's harvest in Honolulu and then make a run for San Francisco to load up on provisions for the journey back to New Bedford. This was to be the final run to Honolulu for this lengthy whaling cruise. After all, the *Milo* had now been away from New Bedford for nearly five years, long enough for anyone! Jonathan and Jessie were talking more and more about what they would do in the new business after their return to New Bedford, as there were other options open as well. What would Jonathan really do to make the new business a success? Where would they have their new home? What would the children do for friends and school? All of these and more questions came up as they spent hours trying to get their plans in order. Captain Hawes went by the principal of "plan your work, and then work your plan." He knew that things change as time goes on, and certainly there would be changes made to any plan they had. Of course, it was very exciting to wonder about the future, and it appeared likely to both of them that they would have a successful and rewarding life on shore.

The return cruise to Honolulu was going quite smoothly with reasonably good weather and comfortable temperatures during this time of year. After business in Honolulu, they would sail eastward to San Francisco and then set out for the long journey around Cape Horn in the winter months for the return voyage to New Bedford. The winter months offer the best weather around the southern tip of South America. It would be several months before the *Milo* would arrive back in New Bedford, but Jonathan planned that this would his final voyage as a whaling master and Jessie's final sea voyage as well.

By late July, the *Milo* was about nineteen hundred miles north of Honolulu, and on a direct course to arrive there in a few weeks. Things appeared to be going very well; Jessie and the children were keeping busy with lessons, games and looking for sails on the horizon. They hoped to meet up with friendly whalers from New Bedford and spend some time on a gam, and it would even be better for Addie and Fred if some of their young friends were on board. As it turned out, there were few sails in sight during this journey to Honolulu, and they were not able to get together with another ship at all.

In the meantime, Jessie was beginning to feel rather weak, and was troubled by something that seemed like the flue or just a bad cold. With no doctor on board, no one was able to diagnose what the problem was, and why she was feeling so weak and tired. By early August, things went from bad to worse. Jessie became terribly distraught and could hardly get out of bed. Up until her illness, Jessie had been the glue that kept the family together and content. Addie, now ten years old, took charge of the woman's side of things, and was very helpful to her mother during this time. She was able to take full charge of young Fred who was now five years old, but he was now old enough to be somewhat on his own. Then, on August 7, Jessie simply died and the whole world changed for the Hawes family.

Jessie was forty-two years old when she died, and the *Milo* was located at 33° degrees, 12′ north latitude and 165° west longitude, which put it about fifteen hundred miles west of San Francisco. Notice of her death was published in October 1868 in the marine journal, the *Friend*, Port of Honolulu, Sandwich Islands.[93] Jonathan was devastated and could not believe what had happened. Jessie had been like a right arm to him, and she was his precious advocate and beloved friend. Now, he would have to reevaluate his plans and what he would do in the future. For now, he was quick to direct the shipwright to fashion a suitable casket for the lady. He did this in spite of the fact that sailors are a superstitious lot, and normally will refuse to sail with a corpse, as it portends bad luck. The coffin was placed among the barrels of oil in the ship's hold. It would be dispatched back to New Bedford by land after the *Milo* arrived in San Francisco.

In the meantime, the *Milo* continued her course to Honolulu, arriving there on September 16. Captain Hawes was now determined to set course for San Francisco after quickly doing all the business he could in Honolulu. He did not want to take any more time than necessary for the stay in Honolulu and was ready to weigh anchor after a short few days there. He now planned to return to New Bedford, but he had to make that one port call in San Francisco in order to dispatch Jessie's coffin overland to New Bedford, and to procure provisions for the long voyage around Cape Horn on the homeward journey.

Jonathan had plenty of time to get his plans in order during this last voyage home. He did not know how he would get along without Jessie, but that was something out of his control now. His life would change, but he was not certain how. He was relieved that Addie and Fred were able to get along without their mother, as Addie had grown up quickly in the past few months. She was quite capable of keeping family things in order during the voyage home. Jonathan was sad, but at the same time happy to be going home, and getting ready for the next phase of his life.

418

After a rather uneventful cruise around Cape Horn and up the Atlantic, the *Milo* arrived in New Bedford on May 7, 1869. This was the final cruise for Captain Hawes and his last voyage on the *Milo* as master of the ship. The *Milo* was quickly sold to new owners and continued to sail under a new master. Shortly after his arrival in New Bedford, Captain Hawes met with the pastor of the Congregational Church. He declined the pastor's invitation for one last view of Jessie's remains prior to internment; because he knew full well that the crew had jettisoned the body under the cover of first dark, weighing the box with stones from the hold. When asked by the pastor, Captain Hawes said, "No, no, just leave it alone." The deed had been done, but no one was ever officially notified that this had happened. So it was in May of 1869.

22. Epilogue

In retrospect, the six-year cruise of the *Milo* proved to be an epic and successful voyage, but also a sad journey with the loss of Jessie. Captain Hawes began the voyage in search of whale oil to meet the world's demand. He was not alone as there were literally hundreds of whaling ships out on the oceans of the world, all seeking their own fortunes. Most were successful, but most of those who had been unfortunate enough to meet up with the *Shenandoah*, did not make the journey home. The *Milo* was lucky to be ransomed and to be able to continue in whaling after the summer of 1865. The decision to ransom the *Milo* was really based on having a wife and two children on board, too many prisoners on the *Shenandoah*, and a compassionate captain of the Confederate raider. His war was not with women and children, and he made that clear on several occasions. He furthermore did not take any lives, but on the contrary, took prisoners and then put them on ransomed vessels or ports of call when he had too many. No lives were lost due to the actions of the Confederates, only property, and the only reason that some of the whaleships were ransomed was to provide for the return of prisoners to a home port. Most likely, if a captured ship had women and children on board, Captain Waddell would ransom the vessel. However, anytime he had more prisoners than he could handle efficiently, he was determined to ransom the next Yankee ship regardless of who was on board if he needed to find space to transport excess prisoners off his ship.

Captain Waddell was a naval officer who could be counted on to finish the job. He always followed orders, and consequently was a sought-after subordinate by leaders in both the United States Navy and later in the Confederate Navy. Throughout his career, he was the one to "stay the course," regardless of the obstacles that got in the way. He was focused on completing any mission ordered by his superiors in the chain of command, regardless of changing conditions. His battle cry must have been like the old saying, "Yours is not to reason why; yours is but to do or die." He lived by this rule.

Too bad he was so focused. He could not accept the facts that as things change, so must those involved in dealing with change. He was sent on a mission that would put him out of contact with his headquarters and with complete power to make decisions on his own with no link to current intelligence or changing conditions. He relied only on intelligence from contacts he made at sea. On several occasions before the large-scale destruction that occurred in the Bering Sea, he was informed that the war was over and that the Confederates had surrendered. He had even seen newspaper articles related to these events, but he chose not to believe these stories. He was paranoid and yet determined to finish the job. He was simply not courageous or open-minded enough to accept the changing conditions as they were relayed to him, and he continued on his mission of destruction. Certainly, most reasonable men would want to listen to the voices of others and at least give them some credit. Not so Waddell. If he had listened to the voices telling him that the war was over and exercised some rational judgment, he would have terminated his mission before all the destruction took place in the Bering Sea. This alone would have saved the country from all of the property loss that occurred. From this consequence, it appears that the old saying of "Yours is not to reason why…" should be barred from the thinking of anyone who is ever put in command of a major undertaking.

The *Milo* happened to be the first ransomed ship to return to an American port and announce the news of the destruction of whaleships in the Bering Sea by the

Confederate ship *Shenandoah*. Up until that time, no one knew the whereabouts of the *Shenandoah*, but many suspected that she would show up and cause a major impact somewhere. By the time that the *Milo* arrived in San Francisco, the Civil War was over, and everyone in the world knew it except those on board the *Shenandoah*. However, once the news was released, it did not take long for the word to get out and for Captain Waddell to find out, and realize to his satisfaction, that the war was over. This occurred within a few weeks after the arrival of the *Milo* in San Francisco. The news was delivered to Waddell several hundred miles off the coast of California by the English bark, *Barracuda*, on August 2, 1865. This important meeting between the two ships at sea ended the Confederate's mission of destruction once and for all, and she immediately converted back to a merchant vessel and set a new course for England where she would surrender.

Interestingly enough, the mission of the *Shenandoah* was the brainchild of Confederate Secretary of the Navy Stephen R. Mallory. He knew that whale oil was a very profitable business for the Yankees and had a positive economic impact in the North. He wanted to hit the North where it hurt financially, and he knew the impact would be felt. He even thought it could help the South win the war along with other successes. As it turned out, the main thrust of the *Shenandoah*'s greatest destruction took place after the end of the Civil War and therefore it had no impact at all on the outcome. But it did have a great impact on the whaling cities in New England, particularly New Bedford. Too bad that Mallory's counterpart in the North, Navy Secretary Welles did not have the same appreciation for whaling's contribution to the Yankee economy as did the Confederate. If so, he would have protected the fleet in the Bering Sea by positioning at least one warship there and perhaps intercepting the Confederate raider's destruction.

The year 1865 was also the beginning of the end of the whaling industry, but this was not actually caused by the acts of the Confederate, it was simply the fact that another source of oil had been discovered in the ground and soon would be cheaper to produce than whale oil. This new source of oil would ultimately have more markets and more uses than whale oil ever did. Crude oil was discovered in Pennsylvania around the mid-1800s and it would soon spread around the world as methods were discovered to process crude oil more cheaply. Today, we are beholden to the massive oil-producing industry in places around the world, and this is the cause of discontent to those who do not participate in the rewards. As with the whaling industry, we will discover new sources of energy in the future that will put the crude-oil giants out of business. This is the way of the world and we can certainly count on discoveries of energy sources in the future that will benefit all of us in terms of cost, convenience and utility.

The Civil War began not long after the country had achieved its goal of "Manifest Destiny" by acquiring practically all the land between the Atlantic and Pacific Oceans, i.e. "from sea to shining sea." Most of this occurred during the first half of the nineteenth century. To be sure, not all of the current states had been admitted by the time that the war started; in fact fifteen additional states have joined the Union since the end of the Civil War. But all of the land between the oceans was available to the Union before Fort Sumter was fired upon by the South.

Starting in 1803, the Louisiana Purchase took place, and the country acquired almost a third of the entire land in the country with that purchase from France. However, this did not make the land acquired free and clear, as the American Indians had no part in the agreement with France. The army had to physically take over the land from the Indian Tribes before it became safe for American citizens. In fact, the famous Battle of Big Horn with General Custer in command was fought in 1876, many years after the Civil War ended. The Oregon Territory was settled with England in 1846, providing for the forty-ninth parallel to be the dividing line between the United States and Canada. The only deviation to this line was that it dropped down to allow the Island of Vancouver to remain with the Canadians.

Texas became independent from Mexico in 1836, a few weeks after the famous defeat at the Alamo. This time it was on the battlefield near Houston by defeating General Santa Ana in a brilliant tactical maneuver. Later on, Texas officially became a state of the Union in 1845. Following this addition to the nation, almost a quarter of the country's landholdings were acquired from Mexico with the Treaty of Guadalupe in 1848, and finalized with the Gadsden Purchase in 1853. This included California, Nevada, Utah, Arizona, New Mexico, and parts of Colorado and Wyoming. But all of the land was not readily available to the country as the American Indian Tribes fought fiercely to hold on to the land they called their own. The country was stretched thin for settling with the many tribes prior to the Civil War and many deadly battles were fought. This was enough of a challenge to the country, not to mention any thought of fighting a long and drawn-out rebellion between the states.

Prior to the Civil War, the country had a relatively small army and a small navy. The cost of maintaining a larger military force was prohibitive at that time. Our military efforts were primarily offensive in terms of dealing with both the Mexicans and the Indian Tribes, but we found it very difficult to win the victories and secure a peaceful solution. After the outbreak of the Civil War, President Lincoln began the effort to build a larger army and navy, but this took too much time. Consequently the war began to drag on without an end in sight. In terms of military strategy, defense is a costly option, but offense is a more costly option. The Union came very close to not having the resources to launch a successful offense against the South. One can take the philosophy about military strategy one step further by adding that no defense is perhaps the most costly option. This was exactly what happened in the Bering Sea in the summer of 1865. The Union simply had no naval defense at all positioned in the Bering Sea where there was significant activity by the American whaling fleet. The outcome that was brought about by the Confederate raider in the Bering Sea was a disaster that could have been avoided with the presence of one single federal warship. The United States Navy was simply too small and had no warship available for the task.

Another ambiguity during the Civil War centered on the meaning of the word, "neutrality." England and France, among other nations, had chosen to remain neutral nations in their relationship with the United States during the war. However, the term neutrality proved to have different meanings among different countries. The British appeared to look the other way when ships were built and launched and then turned over to the Confederate Navy in violation of the laws of neutral nations. France was somewhat more subtle about adhering to the laws but still managed to supply arms and military equipment to the South. Even the United States violated the laws of neutrality when the USS *Wachusett* captured the CSS *Florida* in 1864 at Bahia, Brazil. Brazil was a neutral nation at that time.

The supply of Confederate cruisers and other military equipment by the neutral British played a significant part in the length of the Civil War. The most notorious cruisers supplied by England were the *Alabama*, *Florida*, *Georgia*, *Rappahannock*, *Shenandoah*, and *Tallahassee*. In all, they collectively destroyed over three hundred American merchant ships and whaleships. In a matter of time, the destruction caused by these cruisers became the basis of adjudication, called the "Alabama Claims," by an International Court of Justice. Some said that the British actions contributed two additional years to the war. This could be translated into over four billion dollars in loss, not to mention the additional loss of lives on the battlefields. The United States government wanted appropriate compensation and some advocates even demanded the transfer of all Canadian territory to the United States as a fair price for all the damage done. Needless to say, this was never taken seriously by the majority of the negotiation commissioners.

However, the British supply of ships and arms to the South did not go without a legal remedy being sought by the Americans. After several years of heated discourse between English and American diplomats, disagreement between President Grant's administration and the Senate, and even some unethical diplomatic initiatives, England and the United States finally came together in Washington, DC, in May 1871. This resulted in the Treaty of Washington. During this conference, both sides found themselves in agreement about settlements between the two countries which included the Alabama Claims. These claims were finalized in Geneva by an arbitration commission in

September 1872 with the award of $15.5 million dollars, payable by Great Britain to the United States. These funds were finally allocated by the federal government to the owners of the vessels lost by the Confederate cruisers. In this regard, the owners of the *Milo* were granted some twenty-five thousand dollars. The British apologized for the destruction caused by the British-built cruisers, while admitting no guilt.

Perhaps more importantly, the Treaty of Washington had a more positive outcome as Great Britain and the United States formed an alliance at that time that has never been broken. This was the beginning of a peaceful and friendly relationship between both countries, now including Canada that has lasted to this day.

The real visionary of the Civil War was President Abraham Lincoln. He was thrust into the hot seat shortly after his inauguration when the South's General Beauregard ordered the assault on Fort Sumter on April 12, 1861. Lincoln had hardly had time to get used to being president when the war began on that day. As commander in chief, when the war started, he had a small army and a small navy, but was able to increase both in time to defend the North, and then to attack the South. He put together a very capable cabinet of distinguished men although they were all very independent and did not get along well together. Many had been political competitors prior to his election, and some had been presidential contenders. Dealing with these men was not easy, but Lincoln was always in charge and never backed down unless he thought it would be wise to do so.

He worked most closely with secretaries of navy and state in matters of naval and international importance. These were Gideon Welles and William M. Seward respectively. He also worked closely with Secretary of War Simon Cameron, who was soon replaced by Edwin M. Stanton in January 1862. However, Lincoln also chose to work directly with his top generals on military issues, and he tended to do this with face-to-face meetings frequently.

His meeting with Generals Grant and Sherman on the James River at City Point in late March of 1865 set the stage for his vision of the country and for its Reconstruction after the war. In short, it was to forgive and unite as one indivisible nation. He had already expressed his vision during his Second Inaugural Address on March 4, 1865. General Grant used this vision in his terms with General Lee to surrender. General Lee was more than pleased with the terms and agreed to surrender. General Sherman used this vision in his terms with General Johnson who not only also agreed to surrender but also disobeyed direct orders from Confederate President Davis to continue the fight. The surrender of these two top generals set the stage for ending the war. General Lee later supported Lincoln's vision publicly and this greatly influenced all others to lay down their arms. All of this saved the country from likely insurgent actions by rebel forces and for all intents and purposes, brought peace to the entire land in a relatively short time. Lincoln's vision was further enhanced by the fact that the top generals of both the North and the South graduated from the same military academy at West Point. Out of 583 generals, 228 on the Union side attended the academy. Out of 425 generals, 176 on the Confederate side attended the academy. All of these academy graduates were members of "The Long Gray Line", where the life and experience at the academy bonds the graduates in a special way. Very few members of this fraternity would ever be inclined to harm any other member, regardless of the situation, as they are each a single member of the "Long Gray Line." Furthermore, Jefferson Davis and General Grant were also West Point graduates and both held the highest positions in government. Jeff Davis was elected president of the Confederacy in 1861, and General Grant was elected president of the United States in 1868. West Point graduates had a great influence on the outcome of the war and its Reconstruction, and Lincoln's vision helped them to help each other. In this way, they were an instrument to carry out Lincoln's vision. Although he did not live to see the outcome, this was what Lincoln wanted and it worked.

Lincoln's vision of forgiveness also influenced the lives of three significant leaders who had joined with the Confederates during the war. It is what happened to them after the war that tells the story. Jefferson Davis became essentially a free man after two years in confinement. This happened after his inclusion in a general amnesty in 1868. Following his release, he became president of an insurance company in Memphis, Tennessee. He was never brought to trial, although there were many men of influence that wanted him tried and punished. Later, in 1879, he resided in a home on an estate in Beauvoir, Mississippi, that was bequeathed to him by a sympathetic lady of the South. He remained there and spent his time in literary pursuits and became the darling of Southern admirers for the rest of his life.

Captain James Dunwoody Bulloch chose to remain in England and became a British subject. He knew that with the enormity of his effort during the Civil War for the South, he would be an easy target for any number of disgruntled Americans should he return. After all, his efforts extended the war for two additional years with related costs of nearly four billion dollars, according to some. More importantly, as a secret Confederate agent, James Bulloch was not included in the general amnesty that came on the heels of the Civil War. Therefore, in spite of his close relationship with the Roosevelt family, he decided to stay in Liverpool, where he became a cotton importer and broker, and became quite successful along with his half brother, Irvine. Bulloch never returned to the United States after the war. He died in England in 1901. Both James and Irvine were buried in Liverpool, England.

Following the surrender of the CSS *Shenandoah* to the British in November 1865, many of her officers fled to South America fearing prosecution by the United States government, but James Iredell Waddell and some others remained in Europe after their release. Finally, Waddell did return safely to the United States in 1875, when he became captain of the commercial steamer, *City of San Francisco*, which sailed between San Francisco and Yokohama. He later chose to return to his favorite place, Annapolis, Maryland. There, he took charge of the Maryland's oyster regulatory force. During this time, he wrote his memoirs and defended his activities. Waddell died in Annapolis, Maryland, in 1886. Over the years after his death, James Waddell has been the focus of a sympathetic Southern movement and his feats are well known by those who have studied the Civil War and the Confederate Navy.

All three of these men as well as everyone else benefited from the vision of Abraham Lincoln. Lincoln was truly one of our greatest presidents. His legacy was realized by bringing the country together and avoiding a long-lasting insurgency that could have destroyed the country. He simply offered forgiveness, amnesty, and fairness to all, and it worked.

Lincoln's successor, Andrew Johnson, had a different point of view on how to bring the country together. His way was initially opposite that of Lincoln in that he pursued harsh treatment and punishment for those who had rebelled against the United States. Specifically, he disapproved the surrender between General Joe Johnston and General Sherman, and actually caused the war to drag on by ordering Sherman to continue the fight. However, as time went on, Johnson actually began to exercise an authority in violation of the Constitution that many congressional leaders did not accept to the extent that in 1868, he was impeached for these actions as president. At the impeachment trial, the Senate finally came to a vote and Johnson was acquitted by one vote falling short of the two thirds majority needed. He continued as president until being succeeded by Ulysses S. Grant after the election in 1868.

In sharp contract to the high-profile lives of the celebrities of both the North and South, Jonathan Hawes quietly returned to New Bedford in 1869, and began a low-profile, but productive career in the sawmill business. He had acquired substantial wealth and became a prominent member of New Bedford society. Without Jessie, there was no desire to go back to sea, and furthermore, he had long planned to retire from the sea and begin a new business. In 1869, Jonathan was forty-three years old, young enough for a new career ahead of him. More importantly, Addie and Fred needed a normal life on shore. When the *Milo* returned to New Bedford after her long sea voyage, Addie was eleven years old and Fred, six.

J.C. Hawes Estate, Acushnet, circa 1880

Jonathan handled his life as best he could. With family help in the New Bedford and Acushnet communities, he was sure he could get along the way things were. Jonathan was a self starter who had made it to the top in the whaling profession, now it was time to start again and make it to the top in the business world. He now owned a new business and property that was purchased from the Lund family by Simeon and Jonathan Hawes as a partnership in 1867, while Jonathan was still at sea. The sawmill continued in the business of supplying wood products to the shipbuilding, fishing and cranberry industries which had been ongoing for nearly fifty years, but now under the new name of Hawes Saw Mill. There was enough land in the business to supply the mill with lumber from trees on the land. In time, the business grew and expanded in both business and in landholdings. Addie and Fred attended New Bedford public schools. Addie completed her formal education at Wheaton Seminary in Norton, Massachusetts, while Fred completed his education at New Bedford High School.

In the meantime, three years after Jessie died, Jonathan married the youthful Sylvia Tucker Leonard in 1872. She was the widow of Captain John Wood Leonard who at twenty-seven years old had already retired from the sea and was seeking his fortune in Salina, Kansas. Sylvia had three sons from this marriage, Will, Joe, and John Wood Leonard II. After her husband's death, Sylvia traveled back to Dartmouth, Massachusetts, with her three boys. Sadly for Jonathan Hawes, Sylvia died unexpectedly four years after their marriage in 1876, but Sylvia had already delivered one child to him, Alice Tucker Hawes.

Then, on April 10, 1877, at fifty-one years of age, Jonathan was married for the third time to Mary Wardell Davis of Fall River, Massachusetts. He had three more children in this marriage, Jonathan C. Jr., Mary Alice, and Grace Winifred. In the same year, Addie Hawes married her stepbrother, John Wood Leonard II. Regrettably, Addie died of scarlet fever in 1879, but had already given birth to her only child, John Leonard Jr., who became the first grandson of Captain Hawes. Further tragedy struck in 1879, when year-old Jonathan Jr. died of croup and young Alice Tucker died of diphtheria. These untimely deaths were a severe blow to Captain Hawes. A year later, Mary Alice was born to Jonathan and Mary Davis, and was named after her mother and departed half sister. Fortunately, the three surviving children, Frederic, Mary Alice, and Grace lived long lives and were always a comfort to their father for the rest of his life. Frederic married Caroline Gifford in 1897 and they had one son, Richard born in 1906 and one daughter, Alice, born in 1909. On December 17, 1900, Mary Alice was married to Frank E. Sisson, in New Bedford, Massachusetts. The newly married couple sent invitations out to friends and family to visit their home in Acushnet on Fridays in February.

The sawmill business was incorporated in 1907, and named Acushnet Sawmills Corporation with officers Jonathan C. Hawes, president, N. Hervey Wilber, treasurer, and son Frederic B. Hawes, clerk. Simeon Hawes had sold his interest in the company to Jonathan. Frederic had joined the firm in 1886 and rose through the ranks from a sawyer's assistant at the beginning to managing the company later.

Over the years, additional land was acquired and at one point, the company had holdings of over several thousand acres of land in New England. There were five separate mills and over one hundred employees supplying products for a growing market in the fishing, housing, shipbuilding, and cranberry industries. During this period, several fires destroyed property at several mills, but all were rebuilt and continued to operate well into the late 1900s.

Jonathan Hawes was as good a businessman as he was a ship's master. He was also a highly respected community leader and served on several corporate boards and also as a deacon of his church. The sawmill business flourished and continued to grow during his time at the helm. However, on September 3, 1908, Jonathan Hawes died at age eighty-two, and five days later, Frederic B. Hawes was named president of the corporation. Frederic continued to act as the principle administrative officer until his death in 1946 at age eighty-three. Frederic's leadership had steered the company into even more success and growth by the time of his death. When Frederic first entered the company's business in 1886, it was cutting up to five hundred thousand feet of lumber annually. When he died in 1946, the company was cutting over seven million feet of lumber annually. Years before, Frederic gave his daughter Alice a parcel of land in southeastern Massachusetts for cranberry bogs and he built her a home nearby. Prior to that gift, Alice had married Kenneth Garside, who held positions of responsibility with the National Cranberry Association, and later on, she later became famous internationally for her work in reading disability and dyslexia. Following Frederic's death, the company growth slowed for a period of time but continued under the leadership of son, Richard, who was also left with the Acushnet Sawmills stock. Then, Jonathan's daughter Grace died in 1954, and this left Mary Alice Hawes Sisson as the only surviving child of Captain Hawes.

As time went on, Richard developed health problems. He died in 1965. However, the company continued to operate under Ralph E. Saltus, president, along with the Old Colony Trust Company of Boston as executors, under the will of Richard G. Hawes. There was no family member prepared to take over the firm at that time. Later on, some small parcels of land were sold for commercial and industrial use, but this was a tiny fraction of all of the land owned by the company. These sales helped the company pay the bills over some harder times.

More recently, the legacy of Captain Hawes has begun to be realized, thanks to the generosity and foresight of the

Hawes family descendants in recent times. Over the years, there were numerous proposals from outside business interests to purchase land from the Acushnet Sawmills Corporation for various business purposes, including industrial use, land for a casino, and other commercial ventures. The remaining members of the Richard Hawes family, however, wanted the land to be used to benefit the people of the State of Massachusetts and to be enjoyed by everyone. In the late 1990s, the Hawes family agreed to sell a parcel of land to the state for the Southeastern Massachusetts Biosphere which was just getting planning under way. This was the beginning of turning over thousands of acres of land for this use to Massachusetts.

In 2007, landholdings of over thirteen thousand acres had been purchased by state and local governments for the Biosphere development; this represented less than half the landholdings of the Acushnet Saw Mills at its peak. The Biosphere was the result of a civic initiative to provide a large recreational land area for nature viewing, camping and hiking for all and also for a protected area to restore and enhance the biological and ecological integrity of a large scale ecosystem representative of the region. A major share of the land was made available by the Acushnet

Sawmills Corporation in accordance with the Hawes family wishes.

For the Hawes family to be able to do this, it must be remembered that Jonathan C. Hawes was the primary procuring source for the landholdings which he was able to acquire through compensation for his work as a whaling master during his time at sea. In retrospect, this has become his legacy and his final payback to the community. I am reminded of all the trials and tribulations that he must have gone through during those summer days in 1865, as I view the scene of destruction in the watercolor painted by Benjamin Russell. It is quite clear that the Hawes name has not been publicized widely as a major contributor to the Biosphere project. But this is perhaps by design and through the vision of Jonathan Hawes, as he did not want to be in the spotlight. As a consequence, the Hawes family always maintained a quiet and low-profile life, without a lot of public fanfare.

Mary Alice Hawes was the last surviving progeny of Captain Hawes, following the death of sons Jonathan Jr. and Frederic, and daughters Alice and Grace. Mary Alice died in 1980, at age one hundred, survived by a daughter and six grandchildren. Prior to her death, Mary Alice received a letter from President Jimmy Carter on her hundredth birthday, January 18, 1980, with congratulations and wishing her a happy year ahead. In her early days, she was a beautiful and very proper lady and always lived a quiet and reserved life. Throughout her life, she abstained from tobacco, alcohol, and any kind of medication, preferring to let nature do the healing. Even if she were upset, she would never speak harshly or raise her voice, and always maintained a level head. Further, she was representative of those who strive to live above the common level of life.

Mary Alice Hawes Sisson

Mary Alice was always thankful that her father's ship had been ransomed, but was also aware that others may have resented his good fortune, particularly those who did lose their ships to the Confederates. Some of these thoughts were passed on to her by her father, as he had the same feelings. She taught others to be kind to their neighbors, to maintain a quiet profile, and to treat everyone with utmost respect. After her death, an unknown author wrote the following about Mary Alice:

Tribute to a Real Person

People are of two kinds and she was the kind of person I'd like to be. Some preach their virtues and a few express their lives by what they do. That sort was she. No flowery phrase of gifty spoken words. She was not shallow, but her course ran deep. Not many in life you find whose deeds outrun their words.[94]

These words were right on target. I resided with her for a number of years after my father died, and therefore knew her very well. I learned about her perceived feelings of perhaps being resented by other families whose ships were not ransomed during the destruction in the Bering Sea as was the *Milo*. She learned how to forgive those who she believed held those feelings, and faced the world courageously in spite of them.

The End

Bibliography

Books:

Bockstoce, John R. *Whales, Ice and Men*. Seattle and London: University of Washington Press, 1986.

Busch, Briton Cooper. *Whaling Will Never Do For Me*. Lexington, KY: The University Press of Kentucky, 1994.

Chaffin, Tom. *Sea of Gray*. New York: Hill and Wang, a division of Farrar, Straus and Giroux, 2006.

Druett, Joan. *Petticoat Whalers*. Hanover, NH: University Press of New England, 2001.

Druett, Joan. *In the Wake of Madness, The Murderous Voyage or the Whaleship* Sharon. Chapel Hill, NC: Algonquin Books of Chapel Hill, 2003.

Hall, Elton W. *Sperm Whaling from New Bedford*. New Bedford, MA: Old Dartmouth Historical Society, 1982.

Horan, James D. *C.S.S.* Shenandoah, *the Memoirs of Lieutenant Commanding James I. Waddell*. New York: Crown Publishers, 1960.

Hunt, Cornelius. *The* Shenandoah *or the Last Confederate Cruiser*. New York: G.W. Carleton & Co. Publishers, 1867.

Mawer, Granville Allen. *Ahab's Trade, the Saga of South Seas Whaling*. New York: St. Martin's Press, 1999.

Melville, Herman. *Moby-Dick, or The Whale*. Los Angeles: the Arion Press and The University of California Press, 1979.

Pinsker, Matthew. *Lincoln's Sanctuary*. New York: Oxford University Press, 2003.

Philbrick, Nathaniel. *In the Heart of the Sea, the Tragedy of the Whaleship* Essex. New York: The Penguin Group, 2001.

Schooler, Lynn. *The Last Shot.* New York: HarperCollins Publishers, 2005.

Watters, Gerry. *Privateers, Pirates and Beyond.* South Dennis, MA: Dennis Historical Society, 2003.

Whitman, Nicholas. *A Window Back.* New Bedford, MA: Spinner Publications, 1994.

Winik, Jay. *April 1865.* New York: HarperCollins Publishers, 2002.

Manuscripts and Papers:

Hawes, Jessie C. *Journal of the Whale Ship* Emma C. Jones, *1858, 1859, 1860, South Atlantic Ocean.*

Logbook of the Milo, *1863–1869,* Dartmouth Historical Society, New Bedford Whaling Museum, New Bedford, MA.

New Bedford & Old Dartmouth, "A Portrait of a Regions Past," Old Dartmouth Historical Society, New Bedford Whaling Museum, New Bedford, MA, 1976.

Art Sources:

Whaleship Milo Arthur Moniz Gallery, Arthur & Cheryl Moniz, 22 William Street, New Bedford, MA, 02740.

The Burning Ship, by Albert Bierstadt 1830–1902. Courtesy of Shelburne Museum, Shelburne, VT.

Maps of Interest, by Kay Brand, Bradley Paper "All Things Paper," Wichita, KS.

Civil War Maps by courtesy of Stephen G. Brown and Ray Summers, Interstate Image, Salt Lake City, UT.

The Shenandoah towing prisoners from three burning whaling vessels in the Bering Sea, June 25, 1865 by courtesy of Alaska State Library, Juneau, AK.

Newspapers:

The Friend, Marine Journal, Port of Honolulu, Sandwich Islands, October 1868.

"The Pirate Shenandoah." *The San Francisco Evening Bulletin,* July 19, 1865.

"The Shenandoah and her Doings." *The San Francisco Evening Bulletin,* July 20, 1865.

"The Pirate Shenandoah in the Arctic Ocean." *The San Francisco Daily Alta California,* July 21, 1865.

Webb, C.H. "The Cruise of the *Milo,* As Told by the Captain." *The San Francisco Evening Bulletin,* July 22, 1865.

"Address to Captain Waddell." *The San Francisco Evening Bulletin,* July 24, 1865.

"The Shenandoah Again." *The San Francisco Evening Bulletin,* August 3, 1865.

Government Documents and Publications:

Civil War Naval Chronology, 1861–1865. Washington, DC: U.S. Government Printing Office, Naval Historical Division, 1971.

CD ROM:

Naval Records of the War of the Rebellion. Historic Print & Map Company: <www.ushistoricalarchive.com>, 2004.

Burns, Ken. *The Civil War.* Five Disks for years 1861, 1862, 1863, 1864 and 1865. Produced by PBS.

Humpbacks of Hawaii. Honolulu: Video Rights Corporation, 2004. <www.hawaiimedia.com.>

Internet:

The Ten Costliest Battles of the Civil War. <http://www.civilwarhome.com/Battles.htm>, 2003.

Samuel Barron. Wikipedia, The Free Encyclopedia, 2007. Wikimedia Foundation, Inc. <http://en.wikipedia.org/w/index.php?title=Samuel_Barron&old id=176999927>.

John S. Mosby. Wikipedia, The Free Encyclopedia, 2007. <http://en.wikipedia.org/wiki/John_S._Mosby>.

Fisher, Ted. *Bits of Blue and Gray, James Dunwoody Bulloch, Covert Confederate.* <http://www.bitsofblueandgray.com/june2002.htm>.

Chincha Islands War. Wikipedia, The Free Encyclopedia, 2008. Wikimedia Foundation, Inc. <http://en.wikipedia.org/wiki/Chincha_Islands_War>

USS Saranac. *Wikipedia, The Free Encyclopedia,* 2008. Wikimedia Foundation, Inc. <http://en.wikipedia.org/wiki/USS_Saranac_(1848)>.

USS Suwanee. *Wikipedia, The Free Encyclopedia,* 2008. Wikimedia Foundation, Inc. <http://en.wikipedia.org/wiki/USS_Suwanee_(1864).>

Letter of Marque. Wikipedia, The Free Encyclopedia, 2008. Wikimedia Foundation, Inc. <http://en.wikipedia.org/wiki/Letter_of_marque.>

French Intervention in Mexico. Wikipedia, The Free Encyclopedia, 2008. Wikimedia Foundation, Inc. <http://en.wikipedia.org/wiki/French_intervention_in_Mexico#1 864:_Arrival_of_Maximilian.>

Hunt, Aurora. *The Pacific Squadron of 1861–1866.* <http://www.militarymuseum.org/Pac%20Sqdn.html.>

The Oregon Territory.
   <http://www.state.gov/r/pa/ho/time/dwe/16335.htm.>

The Treaty of Washington, 1871. Wikipedia, The Free Encyclopedia,
   2008. Wikimedia Foundation, Inc.
   <http://en.wikipedia.org/wiki/Treaty_of_Washington_(1871).>

The Alabama Claims, 1862–1872.
   http://www.state.gov/r/pa/ho/time/cw/17610.htm.

The Treaty of Guadalupe Hidalgo. Wikipedia, The Free Encyclopedia,
   2008. Wikimedia Foundation, Inc.
   <http://en.wikipedia.org/wiki/Treaty_of_Guadalupe_Hidalgo.>

Louisiana Purchase. Wikipedia, The Free Encyclopedia, 2008.
   Wikimedia Foundation, Inc.
   <http://en.wikipedia.org/wiki/Louisiana_Purchase#Treaty_signi
   ng .>

Gadsden Purchase. Wikipedia, The Free Encyclopedia, 2008.
   Wikimedia Foundation, Inc.
   <http://en.wikipedia.org/wiki/Gadsden_Purchase.>

Glossary

Anti Fouling	Coating for ship hulls to avoid animal growth
Bark	A three masted ship. First 2 square, 3d fore & aft
Berth Deck	Deck for sleeping quarters on board ship
Blubber	Whale substance
Boatsteerer	Crew position on whale boats
Boatswain	A petty officer in charge of hull maintenance
Brig	A two masted square rig vessel
Bulwark	Ship's railing
Cutlass	Knife
CSS	Confederate States Ship
Flensing	A strip of whale blubber
Full Rigged Ship	Vessel with three masts, all square rigged
Fore & Aft Rig	Sails lie along same path as ship fore & aft line
Forecastle	Crew's quarters in the forward part of a ship
Gam	Social meeting between ships at sea
Greenhand	Apprentice seaman
Hawser	A large rope for towing a ship
Hove To	Turn ship into wind and stop her motion
Humpbacks	Type of whale
IJN	Imperial Japanese Navy
Ironclad Ram	An armored naval vessel, nineteenth century
Latitude	Distance, North or South of the Earth's Equator
Lay	Share of profit on board a whaleship

Longitude	Distance east and west of the zero meridian
Lookout	Position on top of main mast to view horizon
Main Yard	A sail support on a square-rigged ship
Mate	Officer
Mizzenmast	Aft mast on a sailing vessel, fore and aft sails
Parallel	Imaginary circle parallel to the Earth's Equator
Petty Officer	Junior Officer
Pincer Movement	Tactical military movement
Poop Deck	Flat roof on aft ship's cabin. Good for viewing location
Port	Looking forward, left side
Quartermaster	A petty officer who tends to the ship's signals
Right Whale	Type of whale
Sandwich Islands	Hawaiian Islands
Schooner	Vessel with two or more masts, fore & aft sails
Scrimshaw	Carved or engraved images on whale ivory
Scuppers	An opening in the ship's bulwarks
Short Sail	Most sails down
Side Bunkers	Compartment used for coal storage
Sloop	Vessel with one mast, fore and aft sails
Spermaceti	A waxy solid obtained from sperm whales
Sperm Whale	Type of whale
Square Rig	Sails are rigged across ships fore & aft line
Starboard	Looking forward, right side
Steerage	A section of inferior accommodations in a ship
Top Gallant Forecastle	Forward part of ship's deck
Trying Out	Boiling whale blubber into whale oil
USS	United States Ship

Ward Room   Quarters for officers aboard ship

Acknowledgements

I would like to begin by giving thanks to my wife, Anne, for putting up with me during the lengthy time period of writing this story and for her advice and counsel on how to organize and execute the effort.

There are many people who have contributed to this history story, both directly and indirectly, and it is hard to find the words to express gratitude to everyone. First, without the records of most of the Hawes family members written or told by my grandmother, Mary Alice Hawes Sisson, it would have been difficult to put the story into perspective. She must have suspected that someday her family "book" would be put to use, and now it has been. Others who have provided valuable photos, suggestions, contributions and material are Clealand Baker, Charles E. Beckman, Lucy Beckman, Kay Brand, Lucy Brown, Stephen G. Brown, Anne Cann, Frederic Cann, Paul Cyr, Sarah Field Culver, Lavinia Gerould, Jo Goeselt, Peter Hawes, Mary Alice Huidekoper, Sandra Johnston, Michael Lapides, Mary Ellen Hawes Lees, Beth Luey, Leonard J. Matteson, William B. Matteson, Arthur Moniz, Laura Periera,

Benjamin H. Sisson, Elliott H. Sisson Jr., Frank E. Sisson III, William M. Sisson, Julie Sopher, Lucy Sisson Wilhelm and Ric Wolford

I would also like to thank all of those authors who have written about this subject and have provided me with the knowledge to write a true story about the history of this country. Among them are John Bockstoce, Tom Chaffin, Joan Druett, Elton Hall, James Horan, Cornelius Hunt, Granville Mawer, Herman Melville, Mathew Pinkster, Nathaniel Philbrick, Lynn Schooner, Gerry Watters, Nicholas Whitman, and Jay Winik. Their book titles are listed in the bibliography section.

I would further like to give thanks to the several museums and sources of material that have been used in this book. These are: New Bedford Whaling Museum, Arthur Moniz Gallery, Shelburne Museum, Alaska State Library, San Francisco Public Library, New Bedford Free Public Library, United States Naval Historical Center, National Archives and Records Administration, and the Library of Congress.

Without the contributions from all of the above people and organizations, this book would not have been possible. I am grateful to all of them.

Finally, since this is a story about Jonathan C. Hawes, and his place in the history of America, I would like to acknowledge those descendants down to the forth generation, for they have all been influenced in some way by the accomplishments and work ethic of Jonathan to this day. The list of descendants will go on and on, but after the forth generation, the list becomes too large to list herein. Subsequent generations can use this as a beginning source for adding names in future generations.

This is a story about the lives of Jonathan and Jessie Hawes and their two children, Addie and Frederic, before, during and after the epic voyage of the whaleship *Milo* from 1863 to 1869. However, Jonathan would marry three times due to the untimely death of his first two wives.

Jonathan's first wife Jessie died at sea from unknown health causes in 1868, while sailing en route from the Bering Sea to Honolulu. Jessie, of course, had given birth to daughter Addie Hawes and sons Elsworth Levi and Frederic Blake Hawes. There are no further records on

Elsworth and no known descendants. Silvia Tucker Leonard, widow of a twenty-seven-year-old whaling captain, John Wood Leonard, became Jonathan's second wife in 1874, several years after returning from the *Milo* voyage. At that time, Sylvia had three sons by her first marriage, Will, Joe, and John Wood Leonard II. Sylvia died unexpectedly in 1876 of diphtheria but had already given birth to daughter, Alice Tucker Hawes. Unfortunately, Alice Tucker died soon after birth of scarlet fever. So, there are no descendants of Jonathan from the Sylvia Leonard marriage.

Sometime after Jonathan and Sylvia were married, Jonathan's daughter Addie married Sylvia's son, John Wood Leonard II. Addie then gave birth to a son, John Leonard Jr. John Leonard became Jonathan's first grandson. Then, another tragedy occurred when Addie died of diphtheria at a time when medical knowledge was quite limited, leaving her only son John as a survivor. John Leonard Jr. never married and produced no descendants.

Then in 1877, Jonathan married his third wife, Mary Wardell Davis, who gave birth to son, Jonathan Jr. in 1879, and daughters, Mary Alice born in 1880 and Grace Winifred born in 1882. Jonathan Jr. died shortly after birth of croup, but Mary Alice and Grace lived long lives and were always a comfort to their father, Jonathan. Then in 1908, Jonathan C. Hawes died at age eighty-two, leaving son Frederic Blake Hawes, daughters Mary Alice Hawes Sisson and Grace Winifred Sturgis, and grandson John Leonard Jr. as survivors.[95]

Frederic B. Hawes married Caroline Gifford in 1897. This marriage produced one son, Richard Gifford Hawes born in 1906, and one daughter, Alice Blake born in 1909. Richard married Ellen Veronica Coggin, and they had one son, Peter Hawes born in 1947, and two daughters whose married names are Mary Ellen Hawes Lees born in 1949 and Cynthia Hawes Ritter born in 1951. Richard died in 1965 leaving his wife Helen Coggin Hawes and the three children, Peter, Mary Ellen and Cynthia as survivors.

On December 17, 1900, Mary Alice Hawes married Frank Elliott Sisson of New Bedford, Massachusetts. Mary Alice gave birth to one son, Elliott Hawes Sisson, born in 1901, and two daughters, Lucy Livingston Sisson born in 1903, and Natalie born in 1907. Natalie died a little over a year after birth.

Grace Winifred Hawes married Leroy Sturgis and they had one son, Malcom (Mac) Capen born in 1908, and one daughter, Mary born in 1912, who went by the nickname Mollie. Mollie had no children. Malcom married Ethel Ekholm and they had two sons, Bruce Capen Sturgis born in 1949, and Barry Ekholm Sturgis born in 1951.

Lucy Livingston Sisson married Carl Beckman in 1924, and subsequently gave birth to one daughter who became Mary Alice Huidekoper born in 1925, and one son Charles Elliott Beckman born in 1928. Elliott Hawes Sisson married Lila Hazel Goslin Smith in 1925, and this marriage produced four children who in time became Nancy Sisson Field Stork born in 1926, Frank Elliott Sisson II born in 1927, Elliott Hawes Sisson Jr., born in 1934, and Lucy Livingston Sisson Brown born in 1935.

Alice Blake Hawes married Kenneth Greenwood Garside, an engineer and Cranberry Association Executive, in 1930. The marriage produced three daughters who became Anne Garside Cann born in 1932, Elizabeth Garside (Jo) Goeselt born 1934, and Caroline Garside born in 1939.

Index

462

463

464

465

Appendix A

Unedited Eyewitness Letter by Joseph F. Francis
50 Years Afterward

What I am going to relate will go to History of the United States of America.

In the summer of 1865 fifty years ago, I was on board the old Ship Milo *of New Bedford Mass. Capt. Jonathan C. Hawes of Acushnet on a whaling voyage and at this time cruising in the Behring Sea.*

To the eastward of us was some scattering ice and to the westward, the Siberian coast was about 25 miles off.

It was a beautiful day not a cloud could be seen in the horizon. Near our ship was two other vessels the Jerry Swift and the Sophia Thornton the latter had just come out from home loaded with fresh provisions and the latest news from Honolulu therefore our Capt. Hawes and Capt. Williams of the bark Jerry Swift went on board the bark Sophia Thornton to regale themselves with some fresh eatables and the latest news, they were not at it long.

When the men at the masthead cried out a Steamer in the horizon coming for us from the southward it was the steamer Shanandoha Capt. Wardell but no one knew her. Although the Captains mistrusted something was wrong and they left in haste the Sophia Thornton and went on board their respective ships; the Sophia Thornton went to the eastward in to the scattering ice hoping to escape destruction by the Privateer Shanandoha; and the Bark Jerry Swift she steered under all sail to the westward to the Siberian coast.

As for us in the ship Milo we were under short sail trying out a stinker (a dead whale found floating) and we were very dirty on deck and very far from knowing that so very soon we would have to wash and clean up everything in good shape to receive Prisoners of war.

The Privateer came right up to us and when she got up within a hearing distance a voice asked whom commands that ship? Hawes, answered our Capt.

A voice from the Privateer said lower a boat and come on board, then Capt. Hawes vacillated a moment and then asked what Steamer is that? The answer was it makes no difference lower away your starboard boat and come on board and bear a hand about it! Of course Capt. Hawes went on board the Privateer but when he went up the side and crossed the Privateer's rail he did so with the dignity of an Admiral. (I was in that boat that took Capt. Hawes alongside the Privateer)

As soon as we got alongside the Privateer she steamed up to the ice, sent a prize crew through the scattering ice to the Sophia Thornton and shot several shot at her and as she saw that they could not get away they wore a round for clear water and as soon as she got in clear water her masts were cut away and she was left a wreck in mid Ocean.

Meantime our Capt. came on board and told the mate what arrangements he had made with Capt. Wardell of the Privateer. Capt. Hawes said that the Milo was bonded for

45 thousand dollars that he had signed a deed to that effect and that we had to take the crews of the Sophia Thornton and the Jerry Swift and also several crews of other vessels he had on board from ships he had burned before he came in the Behring Sea, that Capt. Wardell also gave him permission to take all the provisions he could from on board the Sophia Thornton to help to provide for these men until we got to San Francisco therefore we all turned to with a will turned the blubber overboard cleared and washed the decks in very short time; we lowered our boats also with the Sophia Thornton's boats to bring provisions from on board the Sophia Thornton to the Ship Milo.

Meanwhile the Privateer started at full speed for the Jerry Swift and she caught up with her in short time. (I was told the following by an ocular witness from on board the Jerry Swift) that as soon as the Privateer was within a hearing distance and as Capt. Williams was not in his best mood he turned to the Privateer and said in a lo there you are a coward why don't you do down south and fight our men of war instead of coming up here and take a defenseless whaler or come on my quarterdeck and fight me if you thrash me burn my vessel but if I thrash you let me go in peace but not a word was said from the Privateer she sent her prize crew on board to cut away the mast and then set fire to her and in short time the Bark Jerry Swift was all in a blaze. Then the Privateer turned to us and called our attention not to take any more provisions from the Sophia Thornton and to come alongside of her to take all the crews he had on board to the Milo, we did as commanded meantime she sent a crew on board the Sophia Thornton and set fire to her and then she went off for other preys and we started for San Francisco under full sail loaded with prisoners of war.

When we arrived off San Francisco and the Pilot came on board he told us the joyful news of the End of the greatest calamity that ever befell the United States of America.

Joseph F. Francis to Frank Vera
Vila das Lages. Ilha do Pico, Azores. [96]

Appendix B

SAN FRANCISCO EVENING BULLETIN
July 22, 1865

The Cruise of the *Milo*
As Told by the Captain[97]

"Mariners! Mariners! What might ye be,

And what is the news ye bring from the sea?"

The chief of the group made a sudden halt,

And the words that he uttered were very salt:

"We might be now— had our mothers been fish—

Just the prettiest mackerel heart could wish."

"As it is, we're but seamen—isn't it queer?

Rated as 'ables,' to hand, reef and steer."

"But what the devil, O lubber to thee

Is the traverse you're working, what we might be?"

"Gently, my mariner, pickled in brine,

You should know the ropes if you've crossed the

line;

"Tell me the news from the northern fleet,

And we'll shake it out in a flowing sheet."

"Well stranger, if so, and you're anxious to learn,

Relay your jaw tackle and real in the yarn;

"My name it is Hawes; I'm the Captain bold

Of the *Milo*—crew, thirty men, all told."

470

"It was off Cape Thaddeus, June twenty-second,

By the deadliest reckoning ever was reckon'd,

"We were cruising about under shortened sail,

Expecting no blow but the blow of a whale,

When the man at the masthead hailed the deck:

'Sail ho'—so far off it looked a mere speck."

"But instead of a sail bearing down on our beam,

Came a damned iron kettle that went by steam!"

"A new-fangled notion—scaring the fish—

Not at all the craft a whaleman would wish.

"We were 'cutting in' and 'cutting it fat,'

When the stranger hailed: 'What ship is that?'

"I answered him back: 'The good ship *Milo*,

Owned in New Bedford, last from Hilo!"

"Any more questions, if not, good-by,

For you see we have other fish to fry."

"He spoke through his trumpet: 'Skipper, avast!

Lay your mizzen topsail close to the mast:

"Send a boat aboard; by the beard of Noah,

You're a prize to the cruiser *Shenandoah*!"

"It was hard to decide, or I am a lubber,

Whether he wanted our blood or our blubber."

"For it scarcely seemed so many a mile

He'd have sailed for the sake of 'striking ile.'

"We bore a hand, for his long thirty-twos

Would have slapped a stop on the *Milo*'s cruise."

"You may think we were shy cocks—just as well;

None of us shipped to pick up shell!"

"We lowered a boat, and bent the oars double—

Haste makes waste, but it sometimes saves trouble."

"There on his decks, let me tell you true,

Never saw I such a Cockney crew."

'Hall' 'ands a 'oy!' the boatswain said;

It was 'eave on the' 'slyards' and 'ow does she ead?'

They called me, 'Awes,' though I said, "If you

please,

Don't be spilling the H in these Arctic Seas!"

"English the craft by the cut of her sails—

Was she sent in revenge by the Prince of Whales?

"He is 'Lord of the Iles' and perhaps didn't like

So many prospectors bound on a strike.

"They asked me what luck we had on the trip,

And what was the value set on the ship."

"They could not have talked of our oil and bone

With more concern had it been their own."

"But cut the yarn short— it runs off the wheel

Like a log-line marking ten knots by the reel."

"A bond I put first to— it promised to pay

A great many dollars at no definite day."

"And I smiled in my soul— that bright June morn,

To think how that bond would be paid in a horn."

"Our purses, our watches, they took without fuss—

We never tried whales as those rascals tried us."

"Sea sedges will sigh through the long summer
noons,
'Captain Waddell, alas! has a weakness for spoons!"
"When they'd taken all they let us make sail
And I said, while their faces looked over the rail,
"To borrow your phrase, "blast me bloody nibs,"
If I much like the cut of your Cockney jibe!"
"But here we all are— if you'd know any more,
You must look up the log of the *Shenandoah*!"
"O, mariner, hither come share my grog,
"But, don't cut me adrift on that pirate's log!"

San Francisco, July 22, 1865. C. H. Webb

473

Appendix C

Endnotes

[1] Courtesy of Peter Hawes and the Arthur Moniz Gallery.
[2] Courtesy of New Bedford Whaling Museum.
[3] *U.S. Navy, Civil War Naval Chronology*, part VI, p. 302.
[4] Courtesy of Peter Hawes and the Arthur Moniz Gallery.
[5] Milo Log Book, November 26, 1863.
[6] New Bedford Port Society Seaman's Register, 1863.
[7] Milo Log Book, December 2, 1863
[8] Courtesy of New Bedford Whaling Museum.
[9] *Petticoat Whalers*, Joan Druett, pp. 6–11
[10] *CSS* Shenandoah, James I. Waddell, p. 54.
[11] *CSS* Shenandoah, James I. Waddell, p. 55.
[12] *CSS* Shenandoah, James I. Waddell, p. 56.
[13] Passed exams and eligible for promotion to lieutenant.
[14] *CSS* Shenandoah, James I. Waddell, p. 58.
[15] *CSS* Shenandoah, James I. Waddell, p. 60.
[16] Courtesy of New Bedford Whaling Museum.
[17] Journal of the Whale Ship E. C. Jones, Mrs. Jessie C. Hawes.
[18] *Petticoat Whalers*, Joan Druett, p. 53.
[19] *CSS* Shenandoah, James I. Waddell, p. 63.
[20] *CSS* Shenandoah, James I. Waddell, p. 65.
[21] *CSS* Shenandoah, James I. Waddell, p. 71.
[22] *CSS* Shenandoah, James I. Waddell, p. 71.
[23] *CSS* Shenandoah, James I. Waddell, p. 73.
[24] *CSS* Shenandoah, James I. Waddell, p. 75
[25] Privateers, Pirates and Beyond, Gerry G. B. Watters, pp. 3–7.
[26] Courtesy of Alice Hawes Garside Photo Archives
[27] Courtesy National Archives and Records Administration.
[28] Courtesy of U.S. Naval Historical Center
[29] Courtesy of U.S. Naval Historical Center.
[30] *The Shenandoah*, Cornelius E. Hunt, pp. 26–27
[31] *The Shenandoah*, Cornelius E. Hunt, p. 31.
[32] *CSS* Shenandoah, James I. Waddell, p. 106
[33] *CSS* Shenandoah, James I. Waddell, p. 106
[34] Courtesy of Alice Hawes Garside Photo Archives.
[35] *The Shenandoah*, Cornelius E. Hunt, pp. 59–60.
[36] *CSS* Shenandoah, James I. Waddell, p. 118.

[37] *CSS* Shenandoah, James I. Waddell, p. 120.
[38] *The* Shenandoah, Cornelius E. Hunt, pp. 86–87.
[39] *CSS* Shenandoah, James I. Waddell, p. 123.
[40] Courtesy of U.S. Naval Historical Center.
[41] Courtesy of Library of Congress
[42] Courtesy of the Shelburne Museum, Shelburne, VT
[43] April 1865, Jay Winik, p. 118
[44] April 1865, Jay Winik, pp. 134–137.
[45] April 1865, Jay Winik, p. 138.
[46] The Surrender at Appomattox Court House, Horace Porter, BG USA.
[47] The Surrender at Appomattox Court House, Horace Porter, BG USA.
[48] The Surrender at Appomattox Court House, Horace Porter, BG USA.
[49] The Surrender at Appomattox Court House, Horace Porter, BG USA.
[50] The Surrender at Appomattox Court House, Horace Porter, BG USA.
[51] *CSS* Shenandoah, James I. Waddell, p. 156.
[52] *Lincoln's Sanctuary*, Matthew Pinsker, p. 203.
[53] *April 1865*, Jay Winik, pp. 221–224.
[54] *April 1865*, Jay Winik, pp. 224–226.
[55] *April 1865*, Jay Winik, p. 257.
[56] Milo Log Book, April 17, 1865.
[57] *April 1865*, Jay Winik, pp. 265–268.
[58] Milo Log Book, April 26, 1865.
[59] *April 1865*, Jay Winik, p. 290.
[60] *April 1865*, Jay Winik, p. 291.
[61] *April 1865*, Jay Winik, p. 316.
[62] *April 1865*, Jay Winik, p. 335.
[63] Authority to attack enemy merchant ships during time of war.
[64] Aurora Hunt. *The Pacific Squadron* 1861–1866.
[65] *The Cruise of the Shenandoah*, Captain W. C. Whittle, pp. 235–258.
[66] *The* Shenandoah, Cornelius E. Hunt, pp. 152–153.
[67] *The* Shenandoah, Cornelius E. Hunt, pp. 154–156.
[68] Milo Log Book, June 1865.
[69] Milo Log Book, June 12, 1865.
[70] Official Records of Union and Confederate Navies, 1894.
[71] Milo Log Book, June 23, 1865.
[72] Courtesy of U.S. Naval Historical Center.
[73] Courtesy of New Bedford Whaling Museum.
[74] *The San Francisco Evening Bulletin*, July 21, 1865.
[75] Letter from Joseph E. Francis, Azores Is, to Frank Vera.
[76] Milo Log Book, June 24, 1865.
[77] Courtesy of Alaska State Library.
[78] *The* Shenandoah, Cornelius E. Hunt, pp. 199–202.
[79] Eyewitness to the Civil War, *National Geographic Society*, 2006.

[80] *The San Francisco Daily Evening Bulletin*, July 19, 1865.
[81] Milo Log Book, July 20, 1865.
[82] *San Francisco Daily Alta California*, July 21, 1865.
[83] Webb, C.H., *San Francisco Evening Bulletin*, July 22, 1865.
[84] Courtesy of New Bedford Whaling Museum.
[85] Courtesy of U.S. Naval Historical Center.
[86] *The San Francisco Evening Bulletin*, August 3, 1865.
[87] Official Records of Union and Confederate Navies, 1894.
[88] Official Records of Union and Confederate Navies, 1894.
[89] Official Records of Union and Confederate Navies, 1894.
[90] *The* Shenandoah, Cornelius E. Hunt, p. 239.
[91] *The Cruise of the* Shenandoah, Captain W. C. Whittle, pp. 235–258.
[92] Courtesy of Alice Hawes Garside Photo Archives.
[93] *The Friend*, Marine Journal, Honolulu, October 1868.
[94] Anonymous.
[95] Mary Alice Hawes Sisson Personal Diary
[96] Letter from Joseph E. Francis, Azores, to Frank Vera, New Bedford.
[97] Webb, C.H., *San Francisco Evening Bulletin*, July 22, 1865.

Printed in the United States
205287BV00003B/1-60/P